MODERN GREEK IDIOM AND PHRASE BOOK

CONSTANTINE N. TSIRPANLIS

Former Instructor in Modern Greek Language and Literature
at New York University and New School for Social Research

Former Consultant for the Program in Modern Greek Studies
at Hunter College (CUNY)

Professor of Church History and Greek Studies at
Unification Theological Seminary

BARRON'S EDUCATIONAL SERIES, INC.

All inquiries should be addressed to:
Barron's Educational Series, Inc.
250 Wireless Boulevard
Hauppauge, New York 11788

Library of Congress Catalog Card No. 75-11952

International Standard Book No. 0-8120-0476-0

Library of Congress Cataloguing in Publication Data
Tsirpanlis, Constantine N
Modern Greek idiom and phrase book.
1. Greek language, Modern—Conversation and phrase books. I. Title.
PA1059.T73 489'.3'83421 75-11952
ISBN 0-8120-0476-0 pbk.

PRINTED IN THE UNITED STATES OF AMERICA

456 510 987

CONTENTS

INTRODUCTION

Modern Greek Idiom and Phrase Book is the result of 12 years' experience teaching the modern Greek language to Americans at New York University, the New School for Social Research, and various Greek-American schools. It is intended as a practical guide for English-speaking people who find themselves in Greece or among Greeks and who would like to acquire a working knowledge of standard, spoken modern Greek phrases and idioms. Moreover, it is valuable to those who want to study the modern Greek language more seriously. With these aims in mind, the basic organization of this book evolved to include the sections: "Everyday Conversation," "Idioms," "Outline of Modern Greek Grammar," and "Greek-English Vocabulary."

1. ORGANIZATION OF THE BOOK

The main sections of this book are the "Everyday Conversation" (in 25 units) and the more than 1000 "Idioms." In the section for "Everyday Conversation" you will find a large and useful selection of the words and phrases of everyday life which you need in order to make yourself understood. Each sentence is accompanied by a phonetic transcription and a translation to help you learn the pronunciation of the words and phrases and use them easily and without embarrassment. Here, also, you will find the sentence patterns which are needed in general conversation. With these basic patterns you can build sentences to suit your own particular needs.

All the idioms in the "Idioms" section are presented in the alphabetical order of the key word, often the verb in the idiomatic phrase. Only the idioms which are used in daily conversation and generally throughout Greece are included. A number of them, however, are used also in written language, journals, novels, stories, correspondence, and so forth. These words are marked with an asterisk. The references to similar idioms are made by italic printing of the key word. Each idiom is accompanied with transliteration and translation as well as one or more examples of its use. For certain idioms, however, more illustrations and exercises are included, which make understanding and retention easier.

The "Outline of Modern Greek Grammar" is indispensable for correct conversation and will provide a rapid understanding of the grammatical structure of modern Greek. A new method of treating modern Greek verbs, both regular and irregular, has been used. This method, tested intensively, has been found to be the best way of learning the Greek verbs without forgetting or confusing them.

The book concludes with a "Greek-English Vocabulary" arranged in alphabetical order, which includes all the words used in the "Everyday Conversation" and "Idioms" sections. Thus, the "Vocabulary" forms a compact and extremely useful tool for anyone learning the language.

2. THE GREEK ALPHABET

Capitals	Small letters	Name		Phonetic Pronunciation	as in
Α	α	ἄλφα	álpha	a	father
Β	β	βῆτα	víta	v	very
Γ	γ	γάμμα	ghámma	y or gh	yes (or ghost when followed by a, o, ou)
Δ	δ	δέλτα	δélta	δ	the, then
Ε	ε	ἔψιλον	épsilon	e	net
Ζ	ζ	ζῆτα	zíta	z	zone
Η	η	ἦτα	íta	i	milieu
Θ	ϑ	ϑῆτα	thíta	th	death
Ι	ι	ἰῶτα	yota	i[1]	orient
Κ	ϰ	ϰάππα	káppa	k	king
Λ	λ	λάμβδα	lámδa	l	lion
Μ	μ	μὶ	mi	m	month
Ν	ν	νὶ	ni	n	north
Ξ	ξ	ξὶ	xi	x	exodus
Ο	ο	ὄμιϰρον	ómicron	o	role
Π	π	πὶ	pi	p	pronounce (but softer)
Ρ	ϱ	ϱὸ	ro	r	roar (but trilled, as Italian rosa)
Σ	σ (ς)[2]	σίγμα	sígma	s	sound
Τ	τ	ταὺ	taf	t	but, tea (but softer)
Υ	υ	ὔψιλον	ípsilon	ee	meet
Φ	φ	φὶ	phi	ph, f	phoenix, father
Χ	χ	χὶ	chi	ch, h	Germanich, he
Ψ	ψ	ψὶ	psi	ps	hips, lips
Ω	ω	ὠμέγα	oméga	o	ocean

Note that the modern Greek alphabet (shown above) has retained the 24 letters of the classical Greek alphabet. (The classical alphabet does not represent all the sounds of present pronunciation.)

Footnotes to Table:

1. Often the i (η, υ, οι, ει,) before another vowel or a diphthong ου, αι, ει, οι, is pronounced as one syllable, i.e. πoιὲς (pyes), ποιοὶ (pyeè), ἀλή-θεια (alíthya), αὐτιὰ (aftyà). Also the i is pronounced as y when it is after the voiced μπ, ντ, β, δ, ζ, ρ, i.e. βιαστικὸς (vyastikós), μαγαζιὰ (maghazyá), καρδιὰ (karδyá), βαθιὰ (vaϑyá), καινούργιος (kenoù-ryos, γαλάζιος (ghalázyos), δόντια (δóndya).

2. Sigma at the end of a word is written ς, elsewhere σ, e. g., σεισμός (earthquake). It is prononced like z in front of β, γ, δ, λ, μ, ν, ρ, i.e. koz-mos (world), κόσμος.

3. DIPHTHONGS

	Phonetic	
	Pronunciation	as in
αι	e	net
ει, οι, υι	ee	meet
ου	oo	food
αυ	av	avarice
ευ	ev	every
ηυ	iv	privilege

The last three diphthongs when followed by the consonants ϑ, κ, ξ, π, σ, τ, φ, χ, ψ, are pronounced -af,-ef,-if, respectively, as af-tós (this), αὐτός; éf-ko-los (easy), εὔκολος; and if-xí-thi (increased), ηὐξήθη.

The above diphthongs are technically classical diphthongs. The modern diphthongs are ai as in toaí (tsai) and oi as in pojói (roloi).

4. LETTER COMBINATIONS

γγ ng Ang-lía, Ἀγγλία; áng-e-los, ἄγγελος; feng-á-ri, φεγγάρι
γκ g when initial: ga-míla, γκαμήλα; ng when medial: ángi-ra, ἄγκυρα

γξ nks fά-lanks, φάλαγξ
γχ nch me-la-ncholίa, μελαγχολία
μπ b when initial: beé-ra, μπύρα
mb when medial: O-leem-bos, Ὄλυμπος
ντ d when initial: do-mά-ta, ντομάτα; nd when medial: kéndro, κέντρο
τσ ts as in Tsar, *ts*é-pi (τσέπη)
τζ dz dzά-ki, τζάκι; dzά-mi, τζάμι

5. PRONUNCIATION

Throughout this work:
αι is to be pronounced e as in *net*;
η, ι, υ, ει, οι, υι, are to be pronounced i as in *meet*;
ο-ω are to be pronounced o as in *long, thought*.

If the second vowel of a diphthong has a diaeresis (¨), then the vowels are pronounced separately as in καϋμὸς (ka-y-mós).

Greek pronunciation is very simple. Every letter is pronounced. The sound for each letter must be heard from a native speaker.

PUNCTUATION marks are the same as in English, except for the semicolon (;) which is (·) and the interrogation mark (?) which is (;).

ACCENTS

There are three kinds of accents but only two are in use (except in printing): a) acute (΄) oxeéa, ὀξεῖα; b) grave (`)vareéa, βαρεῖα; c) circumflex (῀)perispoméni, περισπωμένη.

These accents indicate that the syllable which is accented must be stressed. Words beginning with a vowel take the aspiration marks (᾿) psilί (ψιλὴ) or (῾) δaseéa (δασεῖα). In the case of a diphthong the aspiration is placed on the second letter, i.e. αὐτός, εὐγενής, εὔκολος. The grave is used on the last syllable. When words, written in isolation, take the acute, this acute becomes grave when these words are written in a sentence context and are not followed by a punctuation mark or an enclitic, e.g. ὁ ἀδελφὸς (the brother); ὁ ἀδελφὸς τοῦ Παύλου (Paul's brother); ὁ ἀδελφός του (his brother). Most Greeks do not observe the distinction between acute and grave, and use the acute for both.

6. TABLE OF CONSONANTS

GREEK		BI-LABIAL	LABIO-DENTAL	INTER-DENTAL	ALVEOLAR	PALATAL	VELAR	GLOTTAL
STOPS	Voiceless	Π P			τ t	τσ ts	k k	
	Voiced	μbπ/μπτ			ντ d	τζ dz	γk = f	
NASALS	Voiced	μ m	χψ—=ηbz		ν n		ng=γγ γk	
FRICA-TIVES	Voiceless	μβ = νβ	φ f	Θ th	σ s		χα, χο, χου	χ h
	Voiced		β ν	δ f	ζ z		γ=gh γ=y	γχ = νχ
LATERAL	Voiced				λ β ρ τ			

		FRONT	CENTRAL	BACK
SEMIVOWELS		γει γα = ye	p	γ = gh,y
VOWELS	high	ι, n, U		ou
	high-mid mid	I ε	 α	OU o
	lower-mid	ε	α	ω
	low	ια = yo	ιο = yα	

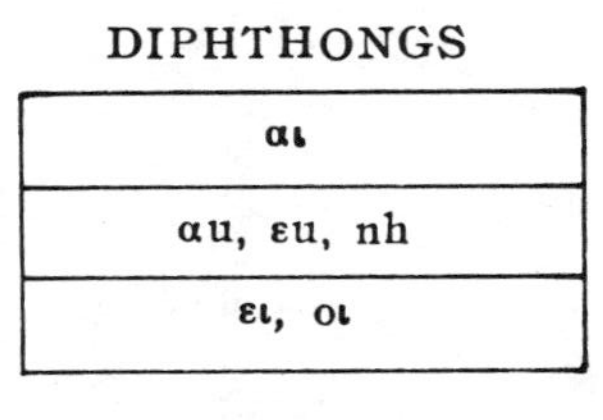

DIPHTHONGS
αι
αu, εu, nh
ει, οι

7. BASIC SENTENCE PATTERNS

'Ο πατέρας εἶναι καλός.
O patéras eéne kalós.
The father is good.

Τὸ βιβλίο εἶναι καλό.
To vivlío eéne kaló.
The book is good.

Αὐτὴ ἡ κόρη εἶναι πολὺ καλή.
Aftí i kóri eéne polí kalí.
This (daughter) girl is very good.

'Εκεῖνος ὁ πατέρας δὲν εἶναι καλός.
Ekeénos o patéras δen eéne kalós.
That father is not good.

'Εκεῖνο τὸ δωμάτιο εἶναι μεγάλο.
Ekeéno to δomátio eéne meghálo.
That room is large.

Εἶναι μιὰ πολὺ καλὴ μητέρα.
Eéne mía polí kalí mitéra.
She is a very good mother.

Ἕνα ποτήρι νερὸ* (κρασί, μπύρα), παρακαλῶ.
Éna potíri neró (krasí, beera), parakaló.
A glass of water (wine, beer), please.

Τὸ πρωϊνὸ (γεῦμα, δεῖπνο) εἶναι ἕτοιμο.
To proinó (yévma, δeépno) eéne étimo.
Breakfast (lunch, dinner) is ready.

Αὔριο θὰ εἶμαι στὴν Εὐρώπη.
Àvrio ϑa eéme stin Evrópi.
Tomorrow I will be in Europe.

Χθὲς ἤμουνα στὴν Καλιφόρνια.
Chϑés ímouna stin Kalifórnia.
Yesterday I was in California.

'Η μητέρα εἶναι καλή.
I mitéra eéne kalí.
The mother is good.

Αὐτὸς ὁ πατέρας εἶναι πολὺ καλός.
Aftós o patéras eéne polí kalós.
This father is very good.

Αὐτὸ τὸ παιδὶ εἶναι πολὺ καλό.
Aftó to peδí eéne polí kaló.
This child (boy) is very good.

'Εκείνη ἡ κοπέλλα εἶναι ὄμορφη.
Ekeéni i kopélla eéne ómorfi.
That girl is beautiful.

Εἶναι ἕνας καλὸς ἄνθρωπος.
Eéne énas kalós ánthropos.
He is a good man.

Εἶναι ἕνα ὡραῖο κορίτσι.
Eéne éna oréo korítsi.
She is a beautiful girl.

Τὸ μεσημέρι (βράδυ) ἦταν ζεστό.
To mesiméri (vráδee) ítan zestó.
It was hot at noon (in the evening).

Τὸ ἀπόγευμα θὰ ἔχω παρέα.
To apóyevma ϑá écho paréa.
In the afternoon I will have company.

Τὸ δωμάτιό μου εἶναι κρύο.
To δomátió mou eéne krío.
My room is cold.

Τὸ δικό μου καπέλο εἶναι μικρό.
To δikó mou kapélo eéne mikró.
My hat is small.

Ὁ δικός μου πατέρας εἶναι ἄρρωστος.
O δikós mou patéras eéne árostos.
My father is ill.

Ὁ πατέρας μου εἶναι πλούσιος.
O patéras mou eéne ploùsios
My father is wealthy.

Ἡ ἀδελφή μου εἶναι ἐδῶ (ἐκεῖ, μέσα, ἔξω).
I aδelphí mou eéne eδó (ekí, mésa, éxo).
My sister is here (there, inside, outside).

Ἡ δική μου ἀδελφὴ δὲν εἶναι ἐδῶ.
I δikí mou aδelphí δén eéne eδó.
My sister is not here.

Ποῦ εἶναι;
Pou eéne?
Where is she?

Δὲν ξέρω.
δén xéro.
I do not know.

Ὁρῖστε.
Oríste.
Help yourself; come in.

Εὐχαριστῶ. Τίποτε (παρακαλῶ).
Efcharistó. Típote (parakaló).
Thank you. You're welcome;
(don't mention it.)

Καλημέρα σας.
Kaliméra sas.
Good morning.

Τί γίνεστε;
Tí yíneste?
How are you?

Πολὺ καλὰ εὐχαριστῶ ἐσεῖς;
Polí kalá, efcharistó, eseés?
Very well, thank you, and you?

Ὄχι καλὰ (ἔτσι κι' ἔτσι).
Ochi kalà (étsi ki' étsi).
Not well (so so).

Τὰ ἴδια.
Ta íδia.
The same.

Πῶς πάει ἡ δουλειά;
Pós páee i δouliá?
How is work going?

Ἡσυχία.
Iseehía.
Quiet.

EVERYDAY CONVERSATION

8. BASIC GREETINGS AND EXPRESSIONS

VASIKEE CHAIRETIZMEE KAI EKPHRASEIS
ΒΑΣΙΚΟΙ ΧΑΙΡΕΤΙΣΜΟΙ ΚΑΙ ΕΚΦΡΑΣΕΙΣ

Καλημέρα σας, Κυρία. Kaliméra sas, Keería. Good morning, Madam.	Καλησπέρα σας, Κύριε. Kalispéra sas, Keeérie. Good evening, Sir.	Χαίρετε. Chérete. Good-by.
'Αντίο Δεσποινίς. Andío δespinís. Good-by, Miss.	Καληνύχτα σας. Kalineéhta sas. Good night.	Πῶς εἶστε; Pós eéste? How are you?
Τί κάνετε; Tí kánete? How do you do?	Εἶμαι πολὺ καλά, εὐχαριστῶ. Καὶ σεῖς; Eéme polí kalá, efcharistó. Ke seeés? I am very well, thank you. And you?	Γειά σου. Yásou. Hello.
Πῶς εἶστε; Pós eéste? How are you?	Εἶμαι θαυμάσια. Eéme θavmásia. I feel wonderful.	
Μὲ συγχωρεῖτε. Me seenghoreéte. Excuse me.	Μιλᾶτε σιγὰ καὶ πιὸ δυνατά, παρακαλῶ. Miláte sighá ké pyó δeenatá, parakaló. Speak slowly and more loudly, please.	Συγγνώμη. Seeghnómi. Excuse me.
Τί συμβαίνει; Tí seemvénee? What is going on?	Τί ἔχετε; Tí éhete? What is the matter with you?	Τί εἶναι; Tí eéne? What is it?

Μιλᾶτε 'Αγγλικά ('Ελληνικά); Miláte Angliká (Elliniká)? Do you speak English (Greek)?	Μιλῶ πολὺ καλὰ 'Αγγλικά, ἀλλὰ (μὰ) ὄχι 'Ελληνικά. Miló polí kalá Angliká, allá (má) óchi Elliniká. I speak English very well, but not Greek.
Διαβάζω 'Ελληνικά. δyavázo Elliniká. I read Greek.	Καταλαβαίνω λίγο (λιγάκι) 'Ελληνικά. Katalavéno ligho (lighaki) Elliniká. I understand a little Greek.

Καθῆστε, παρακαλῶ. Kaϑíste, parakaló. Sit down, please.	Εὐχαριστῶ. Efcharistó. Thank you.	Παρακαλῶ. Parakaló. You are welcome	Τίποτε. Típote. Don't mention it.
Λυπᾶμαι (πολύ). Leepáme (poli). I am (very) sorry.	Μάλιστα. Ναί. Málista. Né. Yes. Yes.	Ὄχι. Γιατί; Ôchi. Yatí? No. Why?	Τί εἴπατε; Tí eépate? What did you say?
Πότε; Ποῦ; Póte? Poù? When? Where?	Πῶς; Pós? How?	Πόσο; Póso? How much?	Μοῦ ἀρέσει αὐτό. Mou arésee aftó. I like this.
Δὲν μοῦ ἀρέσει αὐτό. δén mou arésee aftó. I don't like this.	Μοῦ ἀρέσει ἐκεῖνο. Θέλω. Mou arésee ekeíno. Θélo. I like that. I want.		Δός μου. δóz mou. Give me.
Δῶστε μου. δóste mou. Give me.	Ἔχετε δίκαιο. Éhete δíkeo. You are right.	Ἔχετε ἄδικο. Éhete áδiko. You are wrong.	Εἶναι λάθος. Eéne laϑos. It is wrong.
Πῶς σᾶς λένε; Pós sás léne? What is your name?	Πῶς σὲ λένε; Pós sé léne? What is your name?	Τ' ὄνομά σου; Tónomá sou? Your name?	Μὲ λένε Κώστα. Me léne Cósta. My name is Costas.
Ὀνομάζομαι Κώστας. Onomázome Kóstas. My name is Costas.	Τί κρῖμα. Tí kríma! What a pity!		

9. MOST COMMON WISHES

EE PYO SEENIΘIZMÉNES EFCHÈS
ΟΙ ΠΙΟ ΣΥΝΗΘΙΣΜΕΝΕΣ ΕΥΧΕΣ

Συγχαρητήρια. Χρόνια πολλά.
Seenharitíria. Chrónia pollá.
Congratulations. Many happy returns (birthday or feast day). Happy New Year (also said at Easter and Christmas).

Γειὰ χαρά. Yá chará. So long; good-by.	Στὴν ὑγειά σου (σας). Stin eeyá sou (sas). To your health (when drinking or eating refreshments).

Συλλυπητήρια (Ζωὴ σὲ σᾶς).
Seellipitíria (Zoi se sas).
My sympathy (in death, funeral occasions).

Καλὴ ὄρεξη.
Kali órexi.
Bon appetit (Eat heartily).

Καλὴ τύχη.
Kalí teéchi.
Good luck!

Καλὰ Χριστούγεννα.
Kalá Christoùyenna
Merry Christmas!

Καλὴ Χρονιὰ (Εὐτυχὲς τὸ Νέον Ἔτος).
Kalí Chroniá (Efteechès to Néon Étos).
Happy New Year!

Καλὸ Πάσχα.
Kaló Páscha.
Happy Easter!

Καὶ εἰς ἀνώτερα.
Ke ees anótera.
I wish you continued success (on graduation, promotion, etc.).

Καὶ τοῦ χρόνου.
Ke tou chrónou.
And (again) next year. (Referring to a happy Christmas, Easter, birthday, any annual event.)

Καὶ στὰ δικά σου.
Ke sta δiká sou.
And to your (engagement).

Στὶς χαρές σου.
Stis charés sou.
To your marriage!

Νὰ σᾶς ζήση.
Na sas zísi.
May he (she) live long for you (at birth, christening, nameday).

Νὰ σᾶς ζήσουν.
Na sas zísoun.
May they live long for you (at wedding or engagement to parents or family; also at baptism of twins to same).

Καλὸ ταξίδι.
Kaló taxiδi.
Have a nice trip.

Καλὴ ἐπάνοδο.
Kalí epánoδo.
Return safely.

Καλὴ ἀντάμωση.
Kalí andámosi.
Au revoir.

Καλὰ στέφανα.
Kalá stéphana.
Happy marriage (to couple at engagement).

Νὰ ζήσης.
Na zísis.
May you have a long life (at person's birthday or nameday).

Περαστικά.
Perastiká.
Get well soon.

Περαστικὰ σου (σας, του, της, τους).
Perastiká sou (sas, tou, tis, tous).
May you (you, he, she, they) get well soon.

Καλὴ ἀρχή.
Kalí archí.
A good beginning (of school, job, project, etc.).

Γειά στὰ χέρια σου.
Yá sta chéria sou.
Congratulations (for something well done).

Καλὴ δύναμη.
Kalí δeénami.
More power to you (on a tough job).

Καλὴ λευτεριά.
Kalí lefteryá.
Good luck (to an expectant mother).

Καλορίζικο (Γούρικο).
Kaloríziko (Ghoùriko).
Good luck with it (for a new house, car, etc.).

Μὲ γειά.
Me yá.
In health. (May you wear it, e.g. new dress, in health.)

Ἄ, στὸ καλό.
À sto kaló.
Darn it. Oh gosh!

Στὸ καλό.
Sto kaló.
So long; take it easy.

SOME OF THE MOST COMMON EXCLAMATORY PHRASES

Εἴθε!	Μακάρι!	Ἀλλοίμονο!	Κακομοίρη (μου)!	Πούφ!
Eethe!	Makari!	Allemono!	Kakomeeree (mou)!	Poùf!
I wish!	I wish!	Alas!	(My) poor man!	Pouf!
Εὖγε!	Φτού!	Σούτ!	Τὸν καημένο!	Οὔφ!
Evye!	Phtou!	Sout!	Tongaeeméno!	Ouf!
Bravo!	Ugh!	Sh! (hush)	The poor man!	Oh!
Μπράβο!	Θεέ μου!	(Τί) Κρῖμα!	Χριστὸς καὶ Παναγιά!	Ὤχ!
Bravo!	Theé mou!	(Tí) Kríma!	Christós ke Panayiá!	Oh!
Bravo!	My God!	What a pity!	Christ and Virgin help us!	Oh!
Μπά!	Ζήτω!	Ἔλα (δα)!	Ὁρίστε!	Ὤ!
Baa!	Zeéto!	Ela (tha)!	Oriste!	Oh!
What!	Long life!	Come on!	Here it is! (Help yourself!)	Oh!

'Εμπρός! Embros! Forward! Come in; hello.	Ἔξω! Exo! Out!	Περαστικά! Perastika! Speedy recovery!	Τί ὄμορφη! Tí ómorphee! How beautiful!
Σὲ καλό σου! Sekalósou! How could you!	Μάτια μου! Mátyiamou! My dearest!	Γρήγορα! Ghreéghora! Hurry up!	Σιγά - σιγά! Sighá-sighá! Take it easy!
Προσοχή! Prosocheé! Attention! (Careful!)	Καρδιά! Karthyá! Courage!	Λοιπόν! Leepón! So! (then)	'Εν τάξει! Endáxee! Okay!

10. MEETING PEOPLE

GHNORÍZONTAS XÉNOUS
ΓΝΩΡΙΖΟΝΤΑΣ ΞΕΝΟΥΣ

'Από ποῦ εἶστε; Εἶμαι ἀπὸ τὴν 'Αμερικὴ ('Ελλάδα, 'Αγγλία).
Apo poù eéste? Eéme apó tín Amerikí (Ellaδa, Anglía).
Where do you come from? I come from America (Greece, England).

'Η κυρία μου (σύζυγος), ὁ πατέρας μου, ἡ κόρη μου, ὁ γυιός μου.
Ee keería mou (seézeeghos), o patéras mou, i kóri mou, o yóz mou,
Here are my wife, my father, my daughter, my son,

ἡ πεθερά μου, ὁ πεθερός μου, ὁ ἀδελφός μου, ὁ φίλος μου, ἡ φίλη μου.
i peθerá mou, o peθeróz mou, o aδelphóz mou, o phíloz mou, i phíli mou.
my mother-in-law, my father-in-law, my brother, my friend, my girl friend.

Ποῦ μένετε στὶς 'Ηνωμένες Πολιτεῖες;
Poù ménete stís Inoménes Politeées?
Where do you live in the U.S.A.?

Μένω στὴ Νέα 'Υόρκη (Βοστώνη κλπ.).
Méno sti Néa Eeórki (Vostóni, etc.).
I live in New York (Boston, etc.).

Τί δουλειὰ κάνετε;
Ti δoulyá kánete?
What kind of work do you do?

Εἶμαι γραμματεύς, (σερβιτόρος, τεχνίτης, ράφτης, μηχανικός, κομμωτής,
Eéme ghrammatéfs, (servitóros, techn ítis, ráphtis, mihanikós, kommotís,
I am a secretary, (waiter, craftsman, tailor, engineer, hair dresser,

ἐργολάβος, δικηγόρος, γιατρός, τυπογράφος, δημοσιογράφος, δάσκαλος, μαθητής).
ergolávos, δikighóros, yatrós teepoghráfos, δimosioghráfos, δáskagos, maϑitís).
contractor, lawyer, doctor, printer, journalist, teacher, student).

Ἔχετε ἀδέλφια; Πόσες ἀδελφές; Ἀδελφούς;
Échete aδélphia? Póses aδelphès? Aδelphoùs?
Do you have brothers and sisters? How many sisters? Brothers?

Ἔχω μίαν ἀδελφὴ καὶ τρεῖς ἀδελφούς.
Écho mían aδelphí ke trees aδelphoùs.
I have one sister and three brothers.

Θὰ ἤθελα αὔριο νὰ φᾶμε μαζί στὸ ξενοδοχεῖο.
Θά íϑela ávrio na pháme mazí sto xenoδocheéo.
Tomorrow I would like for us to eat together at the hotel.

Ποῦ θέλετε νὰ συναντηθοῦμε; Στὸ λιμάνι (στὴν Τράπεζα, στὸ θέατρο,
Poù ϑélete na seenandiϑoùme? Sto limáni (stin Trápeza, sto ϑéatro,
Where do you want us to meet? At the port (at the bank, at the theater,

στὸν κινηματογράφο).
ston kinimatográpho).
at the movies).

Τί ὥρα; Στὶς πέντε (τρεῖς, τέσσερεις, έξι, ἑφτά, ὀχτώ, ἐνηά, δέκα
Ti óra? Stis pénde (trees, tésseris, ἕξη, ephtá, ochtó, eniá, δéka,
What time? At five (three, four, six, seven, eight, nine, ten,

ἕντεκα, δώδεκα) ἀκριβῶς.
endeka, δóδeka) akrivós.
eleven, twelve) exactly.

Πόσον καιρὸ (διάστημα) σκέπτεσθε νὰ μείνετε στὴν Ἀθήνα;
Póson keró (δiástima) sképtesϑe na meénete stin Aϑína?
How long do you plan to stay in Athens?

Θὰ μείνω δεκαπέντε περίπου μέρες ἢ ἕνα μῆνα. Ἐλπίζω τότε νὰ σᾶς δῶ πάλι
Θa meéno δekapénde perípou méres i éna mína. Elpízo tóte na sas δó páli
I will stay about fifteen days or one month. I hope then to see you again.

Χαίρετε. (σᾶς χαιρετῶ). Ἀντίο. Γειά σας.
Chérete. (sas cheretó). Andío. Yá sas.
Good-by. (I salute you). Good-by. So long.

11. STRANGER IN TOWN

XÉNOS SE PÓLI
ΞΕΝΟΣ ΣΕ ΠΟΛΗ

Μιλᾶτε 'Αγγλικά;
Miláte Angliká?
Do you speak English?

Μιλᾶ κανένας ἐδῶ ἀγγλικά;
Milá kanénas eδó angliká?
Does anyone here speak English?

Ποῦ εἶναι ἡ Τράπεζα;
Poù eéne i Trápeza?
Where is the bank?

Ποῦ εἶναι τὸ ταχυδρομεῖο;
Poù eéne to taheeδromeéo?
Where is the post office?

Ποῦ εἶναι ἡ 'Αμερικανικὴ Πρεσβεία;
Poù eéne i Amerikanikí Prezveéa?
Where is the American Embassy?

Ποῦ εἶναι τὸ 'Αμερικανικὸ Προξενεῖο;
Poù eéne to Amerikanikó Proxeneéo?
Where is the American Consulate?

'Εδῶ κοντά.
Eδó kondá.
Nearby.

Δεξιά, δυὸ μπλόκοι.
δexiá, δyô blókee.
Two blocks to the right.

Τί λέτε;
Tí léte?
What did you say?

Πέστε το πάλι, παρακαλῶ.
Pêste to páli, parakalóé
Say it again, please.

Ἔχασα τὸ πορτοφόλι μου.
Échasa to portophóli mou.
I lost my wallet.

Μοῦ ἔκλεψαν τὸ διαβατήριο.
Mou éklepsan to δiavatírio.
They have stolen my passport.

Ποῦ εἶναι τὸ 'Αστυνομικὸ Τμῆμα;
Poù eéne to Astinomikó Tmíma?
Where is the police station?

Εἶμαι 'Αμερικανός ('Αμερικανίδα).
Eéme Amerikanós (Amerikaníδa).
I am an American man (American woman).

Ξέχασα τὸ παλτό μου στὸ ἀεροπλάνο (στὸ τραῖνο, στὸ πλοῖο, στὸ λεωφορεῖο)
Xéchasa to paltó mou sto aeropláno (sto tréno, sto pleéo, sto leophoreéo).
I forgot my coat in the airplane (in the train, on the ship, on the bus).

Πῶς μπορῶ νὰ τὸ βρῶ;
Pós boró na to vró?
How can I find it?

Ἔχασα τὸ ξενοδοχεῖο (μου).
Échasa to xenoδocheéo (mou).
I cannot find the (my) hotel.

Μπορεῖτε νὰ μὲ βοηθήσετε;
Boreéte na me voiϑísete?
Can you help me?

Ἔχασα τὴν βαλίτσα μου, τὴν ὀμπρέλλα μου.
Échasa tin valitsa mou, tin ombrélla mou.
I lost my suitcase and umbrella.

Ἔχουν τὰ ἀρχικά: Μ.Ρ.
Échoun ta arhiká: M.P.
They have the initials: M.P.

Μοῦ δίνετε, σᾶς παρακαλῶ, τὸ ὄνομα καὶ τὴ διεύθυνσή σας;
Mou δínete, sas parakaló, to ónoma ke ti δiéfϑinsí sas?
Would you please give me your name and address?

Ἐπίσης τὸ τηλέφωνό σας;
Epísis to tiléphonó sas?
Also your telephone number?

Ἂν βρεθῇ ἡ βαλίτσα μου,
An vreϑí i valítsa mou,
If my suitcase is found,

παρακαλῶ νὰ μοῦ τηλεφωνήσετε στὸ ΕΣΠΕΡΙΑ ΠΑΛΑΣ, ἀριθμὸ 238-009.
parakaló na mou telephonísete sto ESPERIA PALACE, ariϑmó 238-009.
please call me at the ESPERIA PALACE, number 238-009.

12. GUEST AT DINNER

PROSKALESMÉNOS SE TRAPÉZI
ΠΡΟΣΚΑΛΕΣΜΕΝΟΣ ΣΕ ΤΡΑΠΕΖΙ

Φιλοξενῶν: Θὰ ἤθελα νὰ σᾶς ἔχω τραπέζι αὔριο βράδυ.
Philoxenón: Θa íϑela na sas écho trapézi ávrio vráδee.
Host: I would like to invite you to dinner tomorrow evening.

Προσκαλεσμένος: Πολὺ εὐχαρίστως.
Proskalezménos: Polí efcharístos.
Guest: With great pleasure.

Τιμή μου
Timí mou.
My honor.

Φιλοξενῶν: Τί φαγητὸ σᾶς ἀρέσει;
Philoxenón: Ti phayitó sas arésee?
Host: What food do you like?

Τί φαγητὸ προτιμᾶτε;
Ti phayitó protimáte?
What food do you prefer?

Προσκαλεσμένος: Ὤ, δὲν θὰ ἤθελα νὰ σᾶς βάλω σὲ κόπο.
Proskalezménos: Oh, δén θa iθela na sas válo se kópo.
Guest: Oh, I would not like to put you to trouble.

Ἐξ ἄλλου δὲν εἶμαι ἰδιότροπος στὸ φαγητό.
Ex állou δen eéme iδiótropos sto phayitó.
After all I am not fussy about my food.

Ὅ,τιδήποτε.
Otiδípote.
Anything.

Φιλοξενῶν: Καλῶς ἤλθατε.
Philoxenón: Kalós ílθate.
Host: Welcome.

Προσκαλεσμένος: Καλῶς σᾶς βρῆκα.
Proskalezménos: Kalós sas vríka.
Guest: Happy to be here.

Φιλοξενῶν: Ὀρεῖστε (κοπιᾶστε).
Philoxenón: Oreéste (kopyáste).
Host: Help yourself.

Μὴ ντρέπεστε.
Mi ndrépeste.
Don't be bashful.

Προσκαλεσμένος: Εὐχαριστῶ.
Proskalezménos: Efcharistó.
Guest: Thank you.

Φιλ. ἢ Προσκ.: Καλὴ ὄρεξη.
Phil. or Prosk.: Kalí órexi.
Host or Guest: Bon appetit!

Εὐχαριστῶ, ἐπίσης.
Efcharistó, epísis.
Thank you, same to you.

Φιλοξενῶν: Τί πιοτὸ πίνετε;
Philoxenón: Tí pyotó pínete?
Host: What would you like to drink?

Προσκαλ.: Κρασὶ (μπύρα), παρακαλῶ.
Proskalezm.: Krasi (beéra), parakaló.
Guest: Wine (beer), please.

Στὴν ὑγειὰ σας (εἰς ὑγείαν σας).
Stin iyá sas (ees iyeéan sas).
To your health.

Φιλοξ.: Ὑγιαίνετε (στὴν ὑγειά μας).
Philoxénon: Iyiénete (stin iyá mas).
Host: Be healthy (to our health).

Προσκαλ.: Ἡ κυρία σας μαγειρεύει θαυμάσια (ἐξαίσια).
Proskal.: I keería sas mayeerévi θavmásia (exésia).
Guest: Your wife cooks wonderfully.

Γειὰ στὰ χέρια της
Yá sta chéria tis.
Congratulations (for something made with hands).

Μοῦ ἄρεσε πάρα πολὺ τὸ φαγητό σας.
Mou árese pára poli to phayitó sas.
I liked your food very, very much.

Συγχαρητήρια.
Synharitíria.
Congratulations (for good cooking).

Φιλοξενῶν: Καλὴ χώνεψη.
Philoxenón: Kalí hónepsi.
Host: May you digest it well.

Προσκαλ.: Εὐχαριστῶ, ἐπίσης (παρομοίως).
Proskal.: Efcharistó, epísis (paromeéos).
Guest: Thank you, same to you.

Φιλοξενῶν: Τί προτιμᾶτε γιὰ γλυκὸ (ἐπιδόρπιο);
Philoxenón: Ti protimáte ya ghlikó (epiδórpio)?
Host: What do you prefer for dessert?

Φροῦτα, κομπόστο, γιαούρτι, μπακλαβᾶ, καταΐφι, γαλαχτομπούρικο, μπουγάτσα, ριζόγαλο;
Froùta, kompósto, yaoùrti, baklavá, kataífi, ghalahtomboùriko, boughátsa, rizóghalo?
Fruits, stewed fruit, yogurt, baklava, kataif, custard with filo, bougatsa, rice pudding?

Προσκαλ.: Εὐχαριστῶ τίποτε ἀπ' αὐτά.
Proskal.: Efcharistó, típote ap' aftá.
Guest: Thank you, none of those.

Θὰ ἤθελα μόνο ἕναν Ἑλληνικὸν καφέ, ἂν εἶναι δυνατόν.
Θa íθela móno énan Ellinikón kafé, an eéne δeenatón.
I would like only Greek coffee, if it is possible.

Φιλοξενῶν: Πῶς θέλετε τὸν καφέ: γλυκό, βαρύγλυκο, μέτριο, σκέτο;
Philoxenón: Pos θélete ton gafé: ghlikó, varighliko, métrio, skéto?
Host: How would you like your coffee: sweet, very sweet, medium, plain?

Προσκαλ.: Μέτριον, παρακαλῶ.
Proskal.: Métrion, parakaló.
Guest: Medium, please.

Φιλοξενῶν: Ἐν τάξει, ἔγινε.
Philoxenón: En dáxee, éyine.
Host: All right.

Προσκαλ.: Σᾶς εὐχαριστῶ θερμὰ γιὰ ὅλα.
Proskal.: Sas efcharistó θermá ya óla.
Guest: I thank you warmly for everything.

13. AT THE HOTEL

STO XENOδOCHEÉO
ΣΤΟ ΞΕΝΟΔΟΧΕΙΟ

Κρατεῖστε μου ἕνα δωμάτιο, παρακαλῶ.
Krateéste mou éna δomátio, parakaló.
Please reserve a room for me.

Θέλω μονὸ δωμάτιο (διπλὸ δωμάτιο) μὲ (χωρὶς) μπάνιο.
Θélo monó δomátio (δipló δomátio) me (chorís) bánio.
I wish a single room (double room) with (without) bath.

Ἔχετε ἕνα δωμάτιο μὲ διπλὸ κρεβάτι (δύο κρεβάτια);
Échete éna δomátio me δipló kreváti (δyó krevátia)?
Do you have a room with a double bed (twin beds)?

Πόσο κοστίζει τὴν ἑβδομάδα (τὸν μῆνα, τὴν ἡμέρα);
Póso kostízee tin evδomáδa (tón mína, tin iméra)?
What is the rate per week (per month, per day)?

Θὰ ἤθελα ἕνα φθηνότερο δωμάτιο (φωτεινότερο, μεγαλύτερο, μικρότερο).
Θa íϑela éna phϑinótero δomátio (photeenótero, meghaleétero, mikrótero).
I would like a cheaper room (brighter, larger, smaller).

Παρακαλῶ, φέρτε μου τὶς βαλίτσες ἐπάνω.
Parakaló, phérte mou tis valítses epáno.
Please, bring up my bags.

Ποῦ εἶναι τὸ μπάνιο (τὸ μέρος, τὸ ἰδιαίτερο, γυναικεῖο);
Poù eéne to bánio (to méros, to iδiétero, yeenekeéo)?
Where is the bathroom (the men's room, the rest room, the ladies' room)?

Τί ὥρα σερβίρουν γεῦμα (πρωϊνό, δεῖπνο);
Ti óra servíroun yévma (proinó, δeépno)?
At what time is lunch served (breakfast, dinner)?

Στεῖλτε μου τὸ πρόγευμα στὶς ὀκτὼ αὔριο.
Steélte mou to próyevma stis októ ávrio.
Send me breakfast at eight tomorrow.

Μπορῶ νὰ ἔχω πετσέτες καὶ σαπούνι;
Boró na écho petsétes ke sapoùni?
May I have towels and soap?

Τὸν λογαριασμό, παρακαλῶ.
Ton logharyazmó, parakaló.
The bill, please.

Φωνάξετε ἕνα ταξί, παρακαλῶ.
Phonáxete éna taxí, parakaló.
Please call a taxi.

Πάρτε τὶς ἀποσκευές μου στὸ ἀεροδρόμιο (τραῖνο, πλοῖο, λεωφορεῖο).
Párte tis aposkevéz mou stó aeroδrómio (tréno, pleéo, leophoreéo).
Take my luggage to the airport (train, ship, bus).

Χαίρετε.
Chérete.
Good-by.

Ἀντίο.
Adio.
So long (good-by).

14. AT THE RESTAURANT

STO ESTIATORIO
ΣΤΟ ΕΣΤΙΑΤΟΡΙΟ

Γκαρσόν, ἕνα τραπέζι γιὰ τρεῖς, παρακαλῶ.
Garsón, éna trapézi ya treés, parakaló.
Waiter, a table for three, please.

Δῶστε μου τὸν Κατάλογο (τὸ μενού), παρακαλῶ,
δóste mou ton Katálogho (to menoù), parakaló.
Give me the menu, please.

Φέρτε μας τὰ ὀρεκτικὰ (σοῦπα, ἐπιδόρπιον, κρέας, καφέ).
Phérte mas ta orektiká (soùpa, epiδórpion, kréas, kafé).
Bring us the appetizers (soup, dessert, meat, coffee).

Μπορῶ νὰ δῶ τὸν Κατάλογο κρασιῶν;
Boró na δó ton Katálogho krasión?
May I see the wine list?

Γκαρσόν, λίγο κρασὶ ἀκόμα (μπύρα, νερό, βούτυρο, ψωμί, φρυγανιά, σάλτσα, μαρμελάδα).
Garsón, lígho krasí akóma (beéra, neró, voùtiro, psomí, phreeghaniá, sáltsa, marmeláδa).
Waiter, a little more wine (beer, water, bread, toast, sauce, jam).

Μποροῦμε νὰ ἔχωμε μερικὰ φροῦτα;
Boroùme na échome meriká phroùta?
May we have some fruit?

Μοῦ δίδετε, παρακαλῶ, τὸ λογαριασμό;
Mou δίδete, parakaló to logharyazmó?
Will you please give me the check?

15. GREEK FOOD AND DISHES

ELLINIKÀ PHAYITÀ
ΕΛΛΗΝΙΚΑ ΦΑΓΗΤΑ

DRINKS

Χυμοί, Cheemeè

Πορτοκάλι.	Ντομάτα.	Λεμονάδα.	Πορτοκαλάδα.	Γάλα.	Τσάϊ
Portokáli.	Domáta.	Lemonáδa.	Portokaláδa.	Ghála.	Tsái.
Orange.	Tomato.	Lemonade.	Orange juice.	Milk.	Tea.

EGGS

Αὐγά, Avghá

'Ομελέτα.	Τηγανιτά.	Κτυπητά.	Ποσέ.	Αὐγὰ μὲ λουκάνικα.
Omeléta.	Tighanitá.	Ktypeetá	Posé.	Avghá me loukánika.
Omelet.	Fried.	Scrambled.	Poached.	Sausage and eggs.

Αὐγὰ μὲ ζαμπόν.	Αὐγὰ μὲ μπέϊκον.	Βραστὰ μελάτα.	Βραστὰ σκληρά.
Avghá me zambón.	Avghá me bacon.	Vrastá meláta.	Vrastá sklirá.
Ham and Eggs.	Bacon and eggs.	Soft-boiled.	Hard-boiled.

BREAD

Ψωμί, Psomí

Φρυγανιά.	"Ασπρο.	Τσουρέκι.	Κουλούρα.	Σταρένιο.
Phreeghaniá.	Àspro.	Tsouréki.	Kouloùra.	Starénio.
Toast.	White.	Buns.	Roll.	Whole wheat.

APPETIZERS

'Ορεκτικά, Orektiká

Πεπόνι.	Γαρίδες.	Σαρδέλλες.	Ταραμάς.	Τυρί.
Pepóni.	Gharíδes.	Sarδélles.	Taramás.	Teerí.
Melon.	Shrimps.	Sardines.	Tarama.	Cheese.

Τυρόπητα.	Σπανακόπητα.	Ντολμάδες.
Teerópita.	Spanakópita.	Ndolmáδes.
(Greek) Cheese pie.	(Greek) Spinach pie.	Stuffed grapeleaves.

'Ιμὰμ μπαϊλντί.	Φασόλια πιὰζ (πλακί).
Imám mbaildí.	Phasólia pyaz (plakí).
Stuffed eggplants.	Beans pyaz (plaki).

SOUPS

Σοῦπες, Soùpes

Αὐγολέμονο.	Κοτόσουπα.	Ψαρόσουπα.	Κρεατόσουπα.
Avgholémono.	Kotósoupa.	Psarósoupa.	Kreatósoupa.
Egg and lemon soup.	Chicken soup.	Fish soup.	Meat soup.
Πατσά.	Φασόλια (φασουλάδα).	Φακές.	Ρίζι.
Patsá.	Phasólia (phasouláδa).	Phakés.	Rízi.
Patsa (tripe soup).	Bean soup.	Lentil soup.	Rice soup.

SALADS

Σαλάτες, Salátes

Ντοματοσαλάτα. Ndomatosaláta. Tomato salad.	Χωριάτικη. Choriátiki. Greek salad.	Μουστάρδα. Moustárδa. Mustard.	Μαγιονέζα. Mayonéza. Mayonnaise.

Ἀστακός. Astakós. Lobster.	Λάδι. Láδi. Salad oil.	Ξύδι. Xeéδi. Vinegar.	Ἁλάτι. Aláti. Salt.	Πιπέρι. Pipéri. Pepper.

FISH

Ψάρι, Psári

Καλαμάρι. Kalamári. Squid.	Τσιπούρα. Tsipoùra. Porgie.	Ἀστακός. Astakós. Lobster.	Μπαρμπούνι. Barboùni. (Red) mullet.
Συναγρίδα. Seenaghríδa. Red snapper.	Κολιός. Koliós. Mackerel.	Γαρίδα. Gharíδa. Shrimp.	Μαρίδα. Maríδa. Smelt.

MEAT

Κρέας, Kréas

Μπιφτέκι στὴ σκάρα. Biftéki sti skára. Broiled steak.	Κεφτέδες. Keftéδes. Meat balls.	Ντομάτες γεμιστές. Ndomátes yemistés. Stuffed tomatoes.	Βοδινό. Voδinó. Roast beef.
Πιπεριές. Piperiés. Peppers.	Βοδινὸ βραστό. Voδinó vrastó. Boiled beef.	Ἀρνὶ πιλάφι. Arní piláfi. Lamb with rice.	Μουσακάς. Mousakás. Mousakas.

Μπριζόλες (ἀρνήσιες, μοσχαρίσιες, χοιρινές).
Brizóles (arnísyes, moscharísyes, cheerinés).
Chops (lamb, veal, pork).

Ψητὸ ἀρνί. Psitó arní. Roast lamb.	Κοτόπουλο. Kotópoulo. Chicken.	Γαλοπούλα. Ghalopoùla. Turkey.	Ἀρνὶ τῆς σούβλας. Arní tis soùvlas. Barbecued lamb.
Σουβλάκια. Souvlákia. Shish-kebab.	Βοδινὸ γιαχνί. Voδinó yachní. Beef stew.	Μπουτάκι ἀρνήσιο. Boutáki arnísio. Leg of lamb.	Σπάλα ἀρνήσια. Spála arnísya. Breast of lamb.
Κοκορέτσι. Kokorétsi. Intestines.	Σπάλα μοσχαρίσια. Spála moscharísya. Breast of veal.	Λαγὸ στιφάδο. Laghó stifáδo. Rabbit stew.	

Κρέας μὲ χόρτα
Kréas me chórta.
Stewed meat with vegetable greens.

'Αρνὶ μὲ φασολάκια.
Arní me phasolákia.
Lamb with string beans.

'Αρνὶ μὲ ἀγγινάρες.
Arní me anginares.
Lamb with artichokes.

'Αρνὶ μὲ μελιτζάνες.
Arní me melitzánes.
Lamb with eggplant.

'Αρνὶ μὲ μπάμιες.
Arní me bámies.
Lamb with okra.

Γκιουβέτσι.
Giouvétsi.
Lamb with orzo.

Στιφάδο.
Stiphádo.
Beef with onions.

VEGETABLES

Χορταρικά, Chortariká

Λάχανο.
Láchano.
Cabbage.

Σπανάκι.
Spanáki.
Spinach.

Κουνουπίδι.
Kounoupíδi.
Cauliflower.

Κολοκυθάκια.
Kolokeeϑákia.
Squash.

Φασολάκια.
Fasolákia.
String beans.

Μελιτζάνες.
Melitzánes.
Eggplant.

Μπιζέλια.
Bizélia.
Peas.

'Αγγινάρες.
Anginares.
Artichokes.

Σέλινο.
Sélino.
Celery.

Κρεμμύδι.
Kremmeéδi.
Onion.

FRUIT

Φροῦτα, Phroùta

Μῆλο.
Mílo.
Apple.

Πεπόνι.
Pepóni.
Melon.

Καρπούζι.
Karpoùzi.
Watermelon.

'Αχλάδι.
Achládi.
Pear.

'Ανανάς.
Ananás.
Pineapple.

Ρόδι.
Róδi.
Pomegranate.

Φράπα.
Frápa.
Grapefruit.

Ροδάκινο.
Roδákino.
Peach.

Μανταρίνι.
Mandaríni.
Tangerine.

Κορόμηλο.
Korómilo.
Plum.

Σῦκα.
Seéka.
Figs.

Κεράσια.
Kerásya.
Cherries.

Δαμάσκηνο.
δamáskino.
Prune.

Βερύκοκο.
Vereékoko.
Apricot.

Φράουλες.
Fráoules.
Strawberries.

Σταφύλι.
Stefeéli.
Grape.

'Αμύγδαλα.
Ameéghδala.
Almonds.

Καρύδια.
Kareéδya.
Walnuts.

16. TELLING TIME

LEGHONDAS TIN ORA
ΛΕΓΟΝΤΑΣ ΤΗΝ ΩΡΑ

Τὶ ὥρα εἶναι;
Ti óra eéne?
What time is it?

Εἶναι τέσσερεις παρά τέταρτο.
Eéne tésserees para tétarto.
It is quarter of four.

Εἶναι τρεῖς παρά δέκα.
Eéne treés para δéka.
It is ten of three.

Εἶναι ἕντεκα.
Eéne éndeka.
It is eleven o'clock.

Εἶναι ὀκτὼ καὶ τέταρτο.
Eéne októ ke tétarto.
It is eight fifteen.

Εἶναι μία παρὰ εἴκοσι.
Eéne mía para eékosi.
It is twenty of one.

Εἶναι δεκάμιση.
Eéne δekámisi.
It is ten-thirty.

Εἶναι ἐννέα καὶ μισή.
Eéne ennéa ke misí.
It is nine-thirty.

WHAT TIME IS IT?

Τὶ ὥρα εἶναι; Ti óra eéne?

Τρεῖς παρὰ δέκα.
Treés para δéka.
Ten to three.

Ἕξη παρὰ ὀκτώ.
Éxi para októ.
Eight to six.

Τέσσερες παρὰ πέντε.
Tésseres para pénde.
Five to four.

Δύο παρὰ τρία.
δίο para tría.
Three to two.

Δύο ἀκριβῶς.
δίο akrivós.
Exactly two.

Πέντε παρὰ ἕνα.
Pénde para éna.
One to five.

Ἐννέα καὶ 18.
Ennéa ke 18.
18 past 9.

Ἕξη καὶ τέταρτο.
Éxi ke tétarto.
Quarter past six.

Πέντε καὶ 20.
Pénde ke 20.
20 past 5.

Μία καὶ 22.
Mía ke 22.
22 past 1.

Τρεῖς καὶ 5.
Tris ke 5.
Five past three.

Δέκα ἀκριβῶς.
δéka akrivós.
Exactly ten.

Δέκα καὶ εἴκοσι τέσσερα.
δéka ke íkosi téssera.
24 past 10.

Δεκάμιση.
δekámisi.
Half past ten.

Μία παρὰ 20.
Mía para 20.
20 to one.

Τέσσερες καὶ 10.
Téseres ke 10.
10 past 4.

Ἑφτὰ παρὰ 25.
Ephtá para 25.
25 to seven.

Δώδεκα παρὰ τέταρτο.
δóδeka para tétarto.
Quarter to twelve.

Δύο καὶ 12.
δío ke δóδeka.
12 past 2.

Ἐννέα καὶ 25.
Ennéa ke 25.
25 past nine.

17. THE CALENDAR — THE WEATHER

TO IMEROLOYIO O KEROS
ΤΟ ΗΜΕΡΟΛΟΓΙΟ Ο ΚΑΙΡΟΣ

THE CALENDAR

Ὁ χρόνος (τὸ ἔτος) ἔχει δώδεκα μῆνες.	Ὁ μήνας ἔχει τέσσερεις ἑβδομάδες.
O chrónos (to étos) échee δόδeka mínes.	O mínas échee tésserees evδomáδes.
The year has twelve months.	The month has four weeks.

Ἡ ἑβδομάδα ἔχει ἑπτὰ (ἡ)μέρες.	Οἱ μῆνες εἶναι:	Ἰανουάριος,
I evδomáδa échee eptá (i)méres.	Ee mínes eéne:	Ianouarios,
The week has seven days.	The months are:	January,

Φεβρουάριος,	Μάρτιος,	Ἀπρίλιος,	Μάϊος,	Ἰούνιος,	Ἰούλιος,	Αὔγουστος,
Fevrouários,	Mártios,	Aprílios,	Máios,	Ioùnios,	Ioùlios,	Avghoustos,
February,	March,	April,	May,	June,	July,	August,

Σεπτέμβριος,	Ὀκτώβριος,	Νοέμβριος,	Δεκέμβριος.
Septémbrios,	Októvrios,	Noémvrios,	δekémvrios.
September,	October,	November,	December.

Οἱ μέρες τῆς ἑβδομάδος εἶναι:	Δευτέρα,	Τρίτη,	Τετάρτη,	Πέμπτη,
Ee méres tis evδomáδos eéne:	δeftéra,	Tríti,	Tetárti,	Pémbti,
The days of the week are:	Monday,	Tuesday,	Wednesday,	Thursday,

Παρασκευή,	Σάββατο,	Κυριακή.
Paraskevi,	Sávato,	Keeriakí.
Friday,	Saturday,	Sunday.

Οἱ ἐποχὲς τοῦ χρόνου εἶναι:	ὁ χειμώνας,	τὸ φθινόπωρο,	ἡ ἄνοιξη,	τὸ καλοκαίρι.
Ee epohés tou chrónou eéne:	o cheemónas,	to fθinóporo,	i áneexi,	to kalokéri.
The seasons of the year are:	winter,	autumn,	spring,	summer.

THE WEATHER

Τὶ καιρὸς εἶναι;	Πῶς εἶναι ὁ καιρός;	Εἶναι πολὺ ὡραῖος.
Ti kerós eéne?	Pos eéne o kerós?	Eéne polí oréos.
What is the weather like?	How is the weather?	It is very beautiful.

Εἶναι ἀνοιξιάτικος. Eéne aneexiátikos. It is like spring.

Εἶναι χειμωνιάτικος. Eéne cheemoniátikos. It is like winter.

Εἶναι καλοκαιρινός. Eéne kalokerinós. It is like summer.

Εἶναι παγωνιά. Eéne paghoniá. It is freezing.

Βρέχει (χιονίζει). Vréchee (chionizi). It is raining (snowing).

Βρέχει ραγδαία. Vréchee raghδéa. It is pouring.

Ψιχαλίζει. Psihalízee. It is drizzling.

Κάνει ζέστη. Kánee zésti. It is hot.

Εἶναι (κάνει) ψύχρα. Eéne (kánee) pseéhra. It is chilly.

Κάνει κρύο. Kánee kreéo. It is cold.

Τὸ κλῖμα τῆς 'Αθήνας εἶναι ξηρὸ καὶ ὑγιεινό.
To klíma tis Aϑínas eéne xiró ke eeyieenó.
The climate of Athens is dry and healthy.

'Ο οὐρανὸς τῆς 'Αθήνας εἶναι πάντα γαλανὸς καὶ λαμπρός.
O ouranós tis Aϑínas eéne pánda ghalanós ke lambrós.
The sky of Athens is always blue and bright.

Στὰ νησιὰ κάνει ὑγρασία λόγῳ τῆς θάλασσας.
Sta nisiá kánee eeghrasía lógho tis ϑálassas.
It is damp on the islands because of the sea.

'Ο χειμώνας στὴν 'Ελλάδα διαρκεῖ μόνο δύο μῆνες.
O cheemónas stin Ellaδa δiarkeé móno δeéo mines.
Winter in Greece lasts only two months.

Εἶναι μαλακὸς τὸν Δεκέμβριο κάποτε.
Eéne malakós ton δekémvrio kápote.
It is sometimes mild in December.

Κάνει τσουχτερὸ κρύο τὸν 'Ιανουάριο καὶ Φεβρουάριο.
Kánee tsouchteró kreéo ton Ianouário ke Fevrouário.
It is bitterly cold in January and February.

18. TRAVELING BY PLANE

TAXIδÉVONDAS ME AEROPLÁNO
ΤΑΞΙΔΕΥΟΝΤΑΣ ΜΕ ΑΕΡΟΠΛΑΝΟ

"Εχει ἀεροπλάνο γιὰ Ρόδο σήμερα (αὔριο);
Échee aeropláno ya Róδo símera (ávrio)?
Is there an airplane for Rhodes today (tomorrow)?

Μπορῶ νὰ ἔχω μιὰ θέση κοντὰ στὸ παράθυρο;
Boró na écho miá θési kondá sto paráθeero?
May I have a seat near the window?

Πόσο κάνει τὸ εἰσιτήριο;
Póso kánee to eesitírio?
How much does the ticket cost?

Πότε φεύγει τὸ λεωφορεῖο γιὰ τὸ ἀεροδρόμιο;
Póte phévghee to leoforeéo ya to aeroδrómio?
When does the bus leave for the airport?

Πότε φθάνει τὸ ἀεροπλάνο στὴ Ρόδο;
Póte fθánee to aeropláno sti Róδo?
When does the airplane arrive in Rhodes?

Πότε θὰ φύγῃ;
Póte θa feéghi?
When does it leave?

Θὰ ἔχῃ καθυστέρηση;
Θa échi kaθeestérisi?
Will there be a delay?

Δεσποινὶς (συνοδός), τί ὥρα φθάνει τὸ ἀεροπλάνο στὴν Ἀθήνα;
δespeenís (seenoδós), ti óra fθánee to arepláno stin Aθína?
Miss (stewardess), what time does the airplane arrive in Athens?

Σωφέρ, πάρτε με στὸ ξενοδοχεῖο "ΒΑΣΙΛΕΥΣ ΓΕΩΡΓΙΟΣ".
Sofér, párte me sto xenoδocheéo "KING GEORGE."
Chauffeur, take me to the Hotel "KING GEORGE."

19. TRAVELING BY SHIP

TAXIδÉVONDAS ME PLEÉO
ΤΑΞΙΔΕΥΟΝΤΑΣ ΜΕ ΠΛΟΙΟ

Θὰ ἤθελα πρώτη θέση, παρακαλῶ.
Θa íθela próti θési, parakaló.
I would like a first-class ticket, please.

Παίρνετε τὶς ἀποσκευές μου στὴν καμπίνα ἀριθμὸς 64, παρακαλῶ.
Pérnete tis aposkevéz mou stin kambina ariθmós 64, parakaló.
Take my luggage to cabin number 64, please.

Τί ὥρα σερβίρουν πρόγευμα, γεῦμα, δεῖπνο;
Ti óra servíroun próyevma, yévma, δeépno?
What time is breakfast, lunch, dinner, served?

Πόσο κοστίζει νὰ νοικιάσω ἕνα κάθισμα στὸ κατάστρωμα;
Póso kostízee na neekiáso éna káθizma sto katástroma?
How much does it cost to rent a deck chair?

Πότε φεύγει τὸ πλοῖο; Πότε θὰ φθάσωμε στὴν Κρήτη;
Póte phévyee to pleéo? Póte ϑa phϑásome stin Kriti?
When does the ship leave? When will we reach Crete?

Ζαλίστηκα.
Zalístika.
I have become dizzy.

Ἔχετε κάτι γιὰ τὴ ναυτία;
Échete káti ya ti naftía?
Do you have something for seasickness?

Εἶναι μεγάλη φουρτούνα (τρικυμία).
Eéne megháli fourtoùna (trikimía).
The sea is very stormy.

Ἂς πᾶμε στὸ κατάστρωμα γιὰ φρέσκον ἀέρα.
As páme sto katástroma ya fréskon aéra.
Let us go to the deck for fresh air.

Ἑτοιμᾶστε τὰ διαβατήριά σας
Eteemáste ta δiavatíria sas.
Get your passports ready.

20. TRAVELING BY TRAIN

TAXIδÉVONDAS ME TRÉNO
ΤΑΞΙΔΕΥΟΝΤΑΣ ΜΕ ΤΡΑΙΝΟ

Ποῦ εἶναι ὁ σταθμὸς τῶν σιδηροδρόμων (τραίνων);
Pou eéne o staϑmós ton siδiroδrómon (trénon)?
Where is the train station?

Δῶστε μου, παρακαλῶ, ἕνα εἰσιτήριο πρώτης (δευτέρας, τρίτης) θέσεως γιὰ Θεσσαλονίκη.
δóste mou, parakaló, éna eesitíric prótis (δeftéras, trítis) ϑéseos ya Thessaloníki.
Please give me a first-class ticket (second-class, third-class) for Salonica.

Ἁπλό.
Apló.
One way.

Μετ' ἐπιστροφῆς.
Metepistrophís.
Round trip.

Εἶναι ἡ «ὑπερταχεῖα»;
Eéne i «eepertacheéa»?
Is it the «super-express»?

Μπορῶ νὰ καπνίσω ἐδῶ;
Boró na kapníso eδó?
May I smoke here?

Ποιὰ εἶναι αὐτὴ ἡ πόλη;
Pya eéne aftí i póli?
What is this city?

Σὲ πόση ὥρα θὰ φθάσωμε στὴ Θεσσαλονίκη;
Se pósi óra ϑa fϑásome sti Thessaloníki?
In how much time will we reach Salonica?

Ποῦ εἴμαστε;
Pou eémaste?
Where are we?

Τὸ τραῖνο ἔχει καθυστέρηση;
To tréno échee kaϑeestérisi?
Does the train have a delay?

21. AT THE CUSTOM HOUSE

STO TELONEÉO
ΣΤΟ ΤΕΛΩΝΕΙΟ

Ἐπιθεωρητής: Τὸ διαβατήριό σας, παρακαλῶ.
Epiϑeoritis: To δiavatírió sas, parakaló.
Inspector: Your passport please.

Τουρίστης: Ὁρίστε.
Touristis: Oríste
Tourist: Here it is.

Ἐδῶ εἶναι καὶ τὰ πράματά μου.
Eδó eéne ke ta prámatá mou.
Here is my baggage also.

Εἶμαι τουρίστης.
Eéme touristis.
I am a tourist.

Ἔρχομαι ἀπὸ τὴν Ἀμερικὴ (Εὐρώπη, Ἀγγλία, Ἰταλία).
Érchome apó tin Amerikí (Evrópi, Anglía, Italía).
I am coming from America (Europe, England, Italy).

Ἐπιθεωρητής: Ἀνοῖξτε τὴν βαλίτσα σας.
Epiϑeoritis: Aneéxte tin valítsa sas.
Inspector: Open your suitcase.

Τουρίστης: Ὁρίστε τὰ κλειδιά.
Touristis: Oríste ta kleeδyá.
Tourist: Here are the keys.

Ἐπιθεωρητής: Ἔχετε τίποτε νὰ δηλώσετε;
Epiϑeoritis: Échete típote na δilósete?
Inspector: Do you have anything to declare?

Τουρίστης: Τίποτε, κύριε.
Touristis: Típote, keérie.
Tourist: Nothing, sir.

Ἐπιθεωρητής: Τίποτε σπίρτο (οὐΐσκι, κονιάκ); Γι' αὐτὰ πρέπει νὰ πληρώσετε τελωνεῖο.
Epiϑeoritis: Típote spírto (ouisky, konyak)? Yaftá prépee na plirósete teloneéo.
Inspector: Any spirits (whiskey, cognac)? For these you must pay duty.

Τουρίστης: Ὄχι, τίποτε ἀπ' αὐτά.
Touristis: Ochi, típote apaftá.
Tourist: No, none of those.

Μόνο λίγα δῶρα, τὰ ροῦχα μου, καὶ δύο πακέτα τσιγάρα.
Móno lígha δóra, ta roùcha mou, ke δío pakéta tsighára.
Only a few gifts, my clothes, and two packages of cigarettes.

Ἐπιθεωρητής: Αὐτὰ δὲν ἔχουν τελωνεῖο.
Epiϑeoritis: Aftá δen échoun teloneéo.
Inspector: Those things are duty free.

Εἶσθε ἐλεύθερος (ἐν τάξει).
Eésϑe eléfϑeros (en dáxee).
You are free to go (okay).

Περάστε μέσα νὰ σᾶς ἐρευνήσουμε.
Peráste mésa na sas erevnísoume.
Go inside for investigation.

Περιμένετε.
Periménete.
Wait.

22. POST OFFICE — TELEGRAMS AND CABLES

TAHEEδROMIO – TILEGHRAPHIMATA

ΤΑΧΥΔΡΟΜΕΙΟ — ΤΗΛΕΓΡΑΦΗΜΑΤΑ

POST OFFICE

Ποῦ εἶναι τὸ πλησιέστερο ταχυδρομεῖο; (γραμματοκιβώτιο).
Pou eéne to plisiéstero tachiδromeéo? (ghrammatokivótio).
Where is the nearest post office? (letter box).

Πότε κλείνει τὸ ταχυδρομεῖο;
Póte kleénee to tachiδromeéo?
When does the post office close?

Κλείνει στὶς πέντε.
Kleénee stis pénde.
It closes at five.

Πότε ἀνοίγει;
Póte aneéyi?
When does it open?

Ἀνοίγει στὶς ὀκτώ.
Aneéyi stis októ.
It opens at eight.

Θέλω ν' ἀγοράσω γραμματόσημα.
Θélo naghoráso ghrammatósima.
I want to buy stamps.

Πόσο πρέπει νὰ πληρώσω γιὰ ἕνα γράμμα ἀεροπορικῶς στὴν Ἀμερική;
Póso prépee na pliróso ya éna ghrámma stin Amerikí?
How much must I pay for an airmail letter to America?

Θέλω νὰ στείλω αὐτὸ τὸ γράμμα συστημένο, (ἐπεῖγον).
Θélo na steélo aftó to ghrámma seestiméno (epeéghon).
I want to send this letter registered (special delivery).

TELEGRAMS AND CABLES

Θέλω νὰ στείλω ἕνα τηλεγράφημα στὴν Ἀμερική.
Θélo na steélo éna tileghráfima stin Amerikí.
I want to send a telegram to America.

Πόσο στοιχίζει ἡ λέξη;
Póso steechízee i léxi?
How much is it per word?

Δῶστε μου, παρακαλῶ, ἕνα ἔντυπο τηλεγράφημα γιὰ τὸ ἐξωτερικό.
δóste mou, parakaló, éna éndeepo tileghráfima ya to exoterikó.
Give me, please, a blank for a foreign telegram.

Πόσες λέξεις μπορῶ νὰ γράψω γιὰ τὸ κατώτατο ὅριον πληρωμῆς;
Póses léxeis boró na ghrápso ya to katótato órion pliromís?
How many words may I write for the minimum rate?

Θέλω νὰ στείλω αὐτὸ τὸ δέμα ἀσφαλισμένο.
θélo na steélo aftó to δéma asfalizméno.
I want to send this package insured.

23. TELEPHONING

TILEPHONIMA
ΤΗΛΕΦΩΝΗΜΑ

Ὑπάρχει ἕνα τηλέφωνο ἐδῶ κοντά;
Eepárhee éna tiléfono eδó kondá?
Is there a telephone near here?

Παρακαλῶ, μπορεῖτε νὰ μοῦ βρῆτε τὸν ἀριθμὸ τῆς Ἀμερικανικῆς Πρεσβείας;
Parakaló, boreéte na mou vríte ton ariθmó tis Amerikanikís Prezveéas?
Please, can you find for me the number of the American Embassy?

Κέντρον, παρακαλῶ συνδέσατέ με μὲ τὸν ἀριθμὸ εἴκοσι πέντε τριακόσια πενήντα.
Kéndron, parakaló seenδésaté me me ton ariθmó triakósia penínda.
Operator, please connect me with the number 25 — 350.

Κέντρον, πῆρα λάθος τὸν ἀριθμό.
Kéndron, píra láθos ton ariθmó.
Operator, I have dialed the wrong number.

Πόσο κάνει ἕνα τηλεφώνημα στὴ Νέα Ὑόρκη;
Póso kánee éna tilephónima sti Néa Eeórki?
How much does it cost to call New York?

Ἐμπρός. Εἶναι τοῦ κυρίου Δημητρίου;
Embrós. Eéne tou keeríou δimitríou?
Hello. Is this the residence of Mr. Demetrios?

Κέντρον, συνδέσατέ με παρακαλῶ μὲ τὸ ἑστιατόριον Ἀμπασαντόρ;
Kéndron, seenδésaté me parakaló me to estiatórion Ambassador?
Operator, will you please get me the Ambassador Restaurant?

Συγγνώμη, ὅλες οἱ γραμμὲς εἶναι πιασμένες.
Seenghnómi, óles i ghrammés eéne pyazménes.
I am sorry, all the lines are busy.

Μιὰ στιγμή, παρακαλῶ· νὰ σᾶς συνδέσω.
Miá stighmí, parakaló; na sas seenδéso.
Just a moment please; I'll connect you.

Παρακαλῶ, κρατῆστε ἕνα τραπέζι γιὰ πέντε στὶς ἐννέα ἡ ὥρα.
Parakaló, kratíste éna trapézi ya pénde stis ennéa i óra.
Please, make a reservation for five at nine o'clock.

24. AT THE CAMERA SHOP

STO PHOTOGHRAPHEÉO
ΣΤΟ ΦΩΤΟΓΡΑΦΕΙΟ

Διορθώνετε φωτογραφικὲς μηχανές;
δiorθónete fotoghrafikés michanés?
Do you repair cameras?

Δῶστε μου τέσσερεις ρόλους φὶλμ γιὰ τὴν μηχανή μου
δóste mou tésserees rólous film ya tin michaní mou.
Give me four rolls of film for my camera.

Δύο κανονικὰ καὶ δύο ἔγχρωμα.
δeéo kanoniká ke δío énchroma.
Two black and white, and two color rolls.

Δῶστε μου, ἐπίσης, ἕνα φὶλμ γιὰ τὴν κινηματογραφικὴ μηχανή.
δóste mou, epísis, éna film yá tin kinimatoghraphikí mihaní.
Also give me one roll for this movie camera.

Πόσα κάνουν;
Pósa kánoun?
How much do they cost?

Ἐμφανίζετε φίλμ;
Emfanízete film?
Do you develop film?

Παρακαλῶ, κάμετε τρεῖς φωτογραφίες ἀπὸ τὴν κάθε ἀρνητική.
Parakaló, kámete treés photoghrafíes apó tin káθe arnitikí.
Please make three prints of each negative.

Πότε, θὰ εἶναι ἕτοιμες;
Póte θa eéne éteemes?
When will they be ready?

25. EXCHANGING MONEY

ALLÀZONDAS CHRIMATA
ΑΛΛΑΖΟΝΤΑΣ ΧΡΗΜΑΤΑ

Θέλω ν' ἀλλάξω (νὰ χαλάσω) μερικὰ δολλάρια (μιὰ ταξιδιωτικὴ ἐπιταγή).
Θélo nalláxo (na chaláso) meriká δolária (miá taxiδyotikí epitayí).
I want to cash some dollars (a traveler's check).

Μπορεῖτε νὰ μοῦ πῆτε, σᾶς παρακαλῶ, ποῦ εἶναι ἕνα τουριστικὸ πρακτορεῖο καμιὰ Τράπεζα;
Boreéte na mou píte, sas parakaló, pou eéne éna touristikó praktoreéo i kamiá Trápeza?
Can you tell me, please, where there is a tourist agency or a bank?

Πότε ἀνοίγει ἡ Τράπεζα;
Póte aneéyi i Trápeza?
At what time does the bank open?

Πότε κλείνει;
Póte kleénee?
At what time does it close?

Ποιὰ εἶναι ἡ τιμὴ τοῦ συναλλάγματος;
Pyá eéne i timí toù seenallághmatos?
What is the rate of exchange?

Τὸ δολλάριο ἔχει (ἰσοδυναμεῖ μὲ) τριάντα δραχμές.
To δolário échee (isoδeenameé mé) triánda δrachmés.
One dollar is equal to 30 drachmae.

Παρακαλῶ, χαλάστε μου αὐτὸ τὸ χαρτονόμισμα.
Parakaló, chaláste mou aftó to hartonómizma.
Please change this note for me.

Στὴ διπλανὴ θυρίδα.
Stí δiplaní θeerίδa.
At the next window.

Σᾶς εὐχαριστῶ.
Sas efcharistó.
Thank you.

26. AT THE BEAUTY SALON

STO KOMOTIRIO
ΣΤΟ ΚΟΜΜΩΤΗΡΙΟ

Μπορεῖτε νὰ μοῦ δείξετε (συστήσετε) ἕνα καλὸ κομμωτήριον;
Boreéte na mou δeéxete (seestísete) éna kaló kommotírion?
Can you recommend a good beauty salon to me?

Μοῦ κλείνετε, παρακαλῶ, ραντεβοὺ γιὰ τὶς δύο ἡ ὥρα σήμερα;
Mou kleénete, parakaló, randevoù ya tis δeéo i óra símera?
Will you please give me an appointment for two o'clock today?

Δυστυχῶς (λυπᾶμαι), 'η ὥρα αὐτὴ εἶναι πιασμένη.
δeesteehós (leepáme), i óra aftí eéne pyazméni.
Unfortunately (I am sorry), that hour is filled.

Θὰ περιμένω πολύ;
Θa periméno polí?
Will I wait long?

Ὄχι.
Ochi.
No.

Πόσην ὥρα;
Pósin óra?
How long?

Μέχρι τὶς τρεῖς καὶ μισὴ ἢ γρηγορότερα.
Méchri tis treés ke misí í ghrighorótera.
Until three-thirty or sooner.

Θέλω ἕνα «σαμποὺ» καὶ μιὰ «μιζαμπλί».
Θélo éna «samboù» ke miá «mizamblí».
I would like a shampoo and set.

Τὸ νερὸ εἶναι κρύο (πολὺ ζεστό, ὅ,τι πρέπει).
To neró eéne kreéo (polí zestó, ó,ti prépee).
The water is cold (very hot, just right).

Κάνετέ μου παρακαλῶ περμανὰντ (μανικιούρ, σκαλωτά).
Káneté mou parakaló permanent (manikiour, skalotá).
Please give me a permanent wave (manicure, finger wave).

Θέλω νὰ μοῦ βάψετε τὰ μαλιά μου ξανθὰ (καστανά, γκρίζα, μαῦρα).
Θélo na mou vápsete ta maliá mou xanθá (kastaná, gríza, mávra).
I would like you to tint my hair blonde (brunette, gray, black).

Θ' ἀργήσουν νὰ στεγνώσουν τὰ μαλλιά μου;
Θarghísoun na steghnósoun ta maliá mou?
Will it take long for my hair to dry?

Βιάζομαι.
Viázome.
I am in a hurry.

Κάνετε γρήγορα, παρακαλῶ.
Kánete ghríghora, parakaló.
Please be quick.

27. AT THE BARBER SHOP

STO KOUREÉO
ΣΤΟ ΚΟΥΡΕΙΟ

Σᾶς παρακαλῶ νὰ μοῦ κόψετε τὰ μαλλιά μου πολὺ κοντὰ (ἐλαφρά, στὰ πλάγια, πίσω).
Sas parakaló na mou kópsete ta maliá mou polí kondá (elaphrá, sta pláyia, píso).
Please cut my hair very short (a little, on the sides, in the back).

Θέλω ξύρισμα.
Θêlo xeérizma.
I would like a shave.

Ἔχω εὐαίσθητο δέρμα.
Écho evésϑito δêrma.
I have sensitive skin.

Κάνετέ μου μασὰζ στὸ πρόσωπο.
Kánetė mou massage sto prósopo.
Give me a face massage.

Τὸ ξυράφι σας δὲν κόβει.
To xiráfi sas δen kóvee.
Your razor blade is not sharp.

Θέλω ἕνα μεγάλο (μικρὸ) μπουκάλι κολώνια.
Θélo éna megháio (mikró) boukáli kolónia.
I want a large (small) bottle of cologne.

Πόσα σᾶς ὀφείλω;
Pósa sas ofeélo?
How much do I owe you?

28. TRAFFIC SIGNS AND DIRECTIONS

OδIGHIES SEENGEENONIAS
ΟΔΗΓΙΕΣ ΣΥΓΚΟΙΝΩΝΙΑΣ

Κίνδυνος
Kínδeenos
Danger

'Αδιέξοδος
Aδiéxoδos
Dead-end

Ἔξοδος
Éxoδos
Exit

Εἴσοδος
Eésoδos
Entrance

'Απαγορεύεται ἡ Εἴσοδος
Apaghorévete i eésoδos
Keep out

Προσοχὴ
Prosochí
Caution

Σιδηρόδρομος
Siδiróδromos
Railroad

Πρὸς τὰ τραῖνα
Prós ta tréna
To trains

'Απαγορεύεται ἡ διάβασις
Apaghorévete i δiávasis
Forbidden to cross

'Απαγορεύεται ἡ στάθμευσις
Apaghorevete i stáϑmefsis
No parking

Διασταύρωσις ὁδῶν
δiastávrosis oδón
Crossroads

Ὑπὸ κατασκευὴν
Eepó kataskevín
Under construction

Ἐμπόδιον Embóδion Obstruction	Σιγὰ (ἀργὰ) Sighá (arghá) Slow down	Κλειστὸς δρόμος Kleestós δrómos Road closed	Ἀπότομος στροφὴ Apótomos strophí Sharp curve
Ἀνώτατον ὅριον ταχύτητος Anótaton órion taheétitos Maximum speed	Σχολεῖον Scholeéon School	Νοσοκομεῖον Nosokomeéon Hospital	Σταθμὸς ταξὶ Staϑmós taxí Taxi stand
Στάσις λεωφορείων Stasis leophoreéon Bus stop	Ἀστυνομικὸν Τμῆμα Asteenomikón tmíma Police station	Ἀποσκευαὶ Aposkevé Baggage room	
Αἴθουσα ἀναμονῆς Éϑousa anamonís Waiting room	Ἀπαγορεύεται τὸ κάπνισμα Apaghorévete to kápnizma No smoking	Ἐπιτρέπεται τὸ κάπνισμα Epitrépete to kápnizma Smoking permitted	

29. LAUNDRY — SHOEMAKER

KAΘARISTIRIO – TSANGARIKO
ΚΑΘΡΙΣΤΗΡΙΟ — ΤΣΑΓΓΑΡΙΚΟ

LAUNDRY

Ἔχω δύο κοστούμια (πουκάμισα, μπλοῦζες, φοῦστες, φορέματα, παντελόνια)
Écho δío kostoùmia (poukámisa, bloùzes, foùstes, forémata, pandelónia)
I have two suits (shirts, blouses, skirts, dresses, trousers)

γιὰ τὸ καθαριστήριο.
ya to kaϑaristírio.
for the laundry.

Παρακαλῶ νὰ μὴ βάλετε κόλλα στὰ πουκάμισα.
Parakaló na mí válete kólla sta poukámisa.
Please do not starch the shirts.

Πότε θὰ εἶναι ἕτοιμα;
Póte ϑa eéne éteema?
When will they be ready?

Θὰ ἤθελα ἐπίσης νὰ τὰ σιδερώσετε ὅλα.
Θa íϑela epísis na ta siδerósete óla.
I would also like all these pressed.

Αὐτὰ τὰ μαντήλια καὶ ἐσώρουχα (πιτζάμες) εἶναι γιὰ πλύσιμο.
Aftá ta mandília ke esóroucha (pijamas) eéne ya pleésimo.
These handkerchiefs and underwear (pajamas) need laundering.

Πρέπει νὰ τὰ ἔχω αὔριο (γρήγορα).
Prépee na ta écho ávrio (ghríghora).
I must have them tomorrow (soon).

Αὐτὸ εἶναι σχισμένο.
Aftó eéne shizméno.
This is torn.

Μπορεῖτε νὰ τὸ μπαλώσετε;
Boreéte na to balósete?
Can you mend it?

Μπορεῖτε νὰ ράψετε ἕνα κουμπὶ στὸ πουκάμισο αὐτό;
Boreéte na rápsete éna koumbí sto poukámiso aftó?
Can you sew a button on this shirt?

SHOEMAKER

Ὑπάρχει ἕνα τσαγγάρικο (παπουτσίδικο);
Eepárhee éna tsangáriko (papoutsíδiko)?
Is there a shoemaker nearby?

Βάλτε σόλες (τακούνια) σ' αὐτὰ τὰ παπούτσια.
Válte sóles (takoùnia) saftá ta papoùtsia.
Put soles (heels-lifts) on these shoes.

Μοῦ γυαλίζετε παρακαλῶ τὰ παπούτσια μου;
Mou yalízete parakaló ta papoùtsia mou?
Will you please shine my shoes?

Χρειάζομαι (θέλω) ἕνα ζευγάρι κορδόνια.
Chriázome (θélo) éna zevghári korδónia.
I need (I would like) one pair of shoestrings.

30. COMMON AILMENTS

KEENES ARROSTIES
ΚΟΙΝΕΣ ΑΡΡΩΣΤΕΙΕΣ

Ποῦ μπορῶ νὰ βρῶ ἕνα καλὸν ὀδοντογιατρό;
Pou boró na vró éna kalón oδondoyatró?
Where may I find a good dentist?

Γιατρέ, ἔχω ἕνα φοβερὸ πονόδοντο (Μὲ πονεῖ τὸ δόντι τρομερά).
Yatré, écho éna foveró ponóδondo(Me poneé to δóndi tromerá).
Doctor, I have a terrible toothache.

Μπορεῖτε νὰ τὸ σφραγίσετε ἢ πρέπει νὰ τὸ βγάλω;
Boreéte na to sfraghísete í prépee na to vghálo?
Can you fill it (the tooth) or must it be pulled?

Ποιὰ εἶναι ἡ ἀμοιβή σας, γιατρέ;
Pya eéne i ameeví sas, yatré?
What is your fee, doctor?

Εἶμαι σοβαρὰ κρυωμένος.
Eéme sovará kreeoménos.
I have a bad cold.

Ἔχω πονοκέφαλο.
Écho ponokéfalo.
I have a headache.

Ἔχω πυρετό.
Écho peeretó.
I have a temperature.

Ποῦ εἶναι τὸ πλησιέστερο φαρμακεῖο;
Poù eéne to plisiéstero farmakeéo?
Where is the nearest drugstore?

Μοῦ δίδετε, παρακαλῶ, ἀσπιρίνη (ἰώδιο, βορικὸ ὀξύ);
Mou δίδete, parakaló, aspiríni (ióδio, vorikó oxeé)?
Will you give me aspirin, please (iodine, boric acid)?

Δῶστε μου λίγο βαμβάκι καὶ ἕναν ἐπίδεσμο.
δóste mou lígho vambáki ke énan epíδezmo.
Give me some cotton and a bandage.

Χρειάζομαι καινούργιο γυαλὶ γιὰ τὰ γυαλιά μου.
Chriázome kenoùryo yalí ya ta yaliá mou.
I need a new lens for my glasses.

31. VISITING THE INTERESTING PLACES IN ATHENS

EPISKÉPTONDAS TA TOPEÉA TIS ATHINAS
ΕΠΙΣΚΕΠΤΟΝΤΑΣ ΤΑ ΤΟΠΕΙΑ ΤΗΣ ΑΘΗΝΑΣ

Μπορεῖ κανεὶς νὰ δῇ τὰ πιὸ σπουδαιότατα τοπεῖα τῆς Ἀθήνας σὲ μιὰ μέρα;
Boreé kaneés na δí ta pyó spouδéa topeéa tis Athínas se miá méra?
Is it possible for someone to see the most interesting places of Athens in one day?

Σωφέρ, μᾶς παίρνετε στὴν Ἀκρόπολη καὶ στὸ Ζάππειον πρῶτα;
Sofér, mas pérnete stin Acrópoli ke sto Záppeeon próta?
Driver, would you take us to the Acropolis and the Zappeion first?

Μέχρι τί ὥρα εἶναι ἀνοιχτὸ τὸ ἀρχαιολογικὸν μουσεῖον σήμερα;
Méchri ti óra eéne aneehtó to archeologhikón mouseéon símera?
Until what time is the archaeological museum open today?

Πόσα εἶναι τὸ εἰσιτήριο;
Pósa eéne to eesitírio?
How much does the ticket cost?

Μὲ παίρνετε στὸ Κολωνάκι, καὶ μετὰ στὸ Μπενάκειον Μουσεῖον;
Me pérnete sto Kolonáki, ke metá sto Benákeeon Mouseéon?
Would you take me to Kolonaki, and afterwards to the Benakion Museum?

Μετὰ θέλομε νὰ πᾶμε στὴ Βουλιαγμένη γιὰ μπάνιο.
Metá θélome na páme sti Vouliaghméni ya bánio.
Then we would like to go to Vouliaghmeni for swimming.

Ἔπειτα ἀπὸ τρεῖς ὧρες νὰ ἔλθετε νὰ μᾶς πάρετε στὸ Πανεπιστήμιο.
Épeeta apo treés óres na élθete na mas párete sto Panepistímio.
In three hours, come to take us to the University.

Ἀπόψε θὰ πᾶμε στὶς παραστάσεις τοῦ Φιλοπάππου.
Apópse θa páme stis parastásees tou Philopápou.
Tonight we will go to the performances of Philopapou.

Θέλετε νὰ χαζέψουμε στὶς βιτρίνες;
Θélete na hazépsoume stis vitrínes?
Would you like to go window shopping?

Γιὰ φρέσκο ψάρι θὰ πᾶτε στὸ Τουρκολίμανο.
Ya frésco psári θa páte sto Tourkolímano.
For fresh fish you should go to Tourkolimano.

Ποιὰ εἶναι τὰ ἄλλα ἀξιοθέατα μέρη τῆς Ἀθήνας;
Pya eéne ta álla axioθéata méri tis Athínas?
What are the other interesting sites of Athens?

32. NIGHT LIFE AND CLUBS IN ATHENS

NEEKTERINI ZOI KE KÉNDRA STIN ATHINA
ΝΥΚΤΕΡΙΝΗ ΖΩΗ ΚΑΙ ΚΕΝΤΡΑ ΣΤΗΝ ΑΘΗΝΑ

Ἔχετε θέσεις γιὰ τὴν παράσταση ἀπόψε;
Échete θésees ya tin parástasi apópse?
Do you have seats for tonight's performance?

Σωφέρ, πάρτε μας στὸ Ἐθνικὸ Θέατρο.
Sofér, párte mas sto Eθnikó θéatro.
Driver, take us to the National Theater.

Μετὰ τὸ θέατρο, θέλομε νὰ πᾶμε στὸ νυκτερινὸ κέντρον Ἀστέρια (Δειλινά).
Metá to θéatro, θélome na páme stoneekterinó kéndron Astéria (δeeliná).
After the theater, we wish to go to the Asteria (δeelina) night club.

Τὶ ὥρα ἀρχίζει τὸ πρόγραμμα;
Ti óra archízee to próghramma?
What time does the floor show begin?

Θέλομε ἕνα τραπέζι κοντὰ στὴν πίστα.
Θélome éna trapézi kondá stin písta.
We would like a table near the dance floor.

Κοστίζει πολὺ ἀκριβά.
Kostízee polí akrivá.
It is very expensive.

Ὅλα τὰ μπροστινὰ τραπέζια εἶναι πιασμένα.
Ola ta brostiná trapézya eéne pyazména.
All the front tables are taken.

Γκαρσόν, παρακαλῶ, φέρτε μας μιὰ μποτίλια μαυροδάφνη (ροδίτικο, σαμιώτικο).
Garsón, parakaló, férte mas mía botília mavroδáfni (roδítiko, samiótiko).
Waiter, please bring us a bottle of mavrodafni (Rhodes wine, Samos wine).

Σωφέρ, πάρτε μας πίσω στὸ ξενοδοχεῖο Ὀλύμπικ (Βασίλισσα Ἀμαλία, Μεγ. Βρεττανία)
Sofér, párte mas píso sto xenoδocheéo Olympic (Vasílissa Amalía, Megh. Vretanía)
Driver, take us back to the Hotel Olympic (Queen Amalia, Grande Bretagne)

τὸ συντομώτερο.
to seendomótero.
as quickly as possible.

IDIOMS

ABSENT

Ἔλειψα ὀχτὼ μέρες.
Éleepsa ohtó méres.
I was absent (gone) eight days.

ACCIDENTALLY

Εἰκῆ κι' ὡς ἔτυχε* or στὰ κουτουροῦ.	Κατὰ τύχη.	Τυχαίως.*
Eeké kiós éteeche sta koutouroù.	Katá teéchi.	Teechéos.
Accidentally; at random.	Accidentally.	Accidentally.

ACTOR

Ξεπερασμένος ἠθοποιός.
Xeperazménos iϑopeeós.
Out of date actor (actress), passé.

ACTUALLY

Τόντις (τῷ ὄντι, πράγματι).	Ἴσα - ἴσα.
Tóndis (to óndi, prághmati).	Isa - ísa.
Actually; in fact.	In fact.

IN ADDITION

Εἰς ἐπίμετρον.*	Ἐπὶ πλέον.*	Ἐπιπροσθέτως.*
Ees epímetron.	Epi pléon.	Epiprosϑétos.
In addition to.	In addition to.	In addition to.

ADDRESS

Καλέ.	Καλέ, δὲ μοῦ λὲς τί ἔχεις;
Kalé.	Kalé, δé mou lés tí échees? (familiar mode of addressing someone)
Listen!	Please, would you tell me what is the matter with you?

ADVICE

Τὸ καλὸ ποὺ σοῦ θέλω.	Τὸ καλὸ ποὺ σοῦ θέλω (εἶναι) νὰ μὴν πᾶς σήμερα στὴ δουλειά.
To kaló poù sou ϑélo.	To kaló poù sou ϑélo (eéne) na mín pás símera sti δouliá.
Take my advice.	I would advise you not to go to work today.

AGAIN

Πάλι (ξανά).*	Ἀκόμα (η) μιὰ φορά.*
Páli (xaná).	Akóma (i) miá phorá.
Again.	Once again.

* In this section on "Idioms," the asterisk refers to idioms used in written language, journals, novels, stories, and correspondence as well as in daily conversation.

AGREE

Σύμφωνοι;*
Seémphonee?
Are we agreed?

Δὲν σοῦ λέ(γ)ω.
δén sou lé(gh)o.
I do not deny it (but...).

Τὸν ἔφερα βόλτα.
Ton éfera vólta.
I got round him.

Πάω πάσσο.
Páo pásso.
I agree.

AHEAD

Τράβα μπρός.
Tráva mbros.
Go ahead; lead the way.

ALL

Ὅλος ὁ κόσμος.
Olos ὁ kózmos.
Everybody.

ALMOST

Παρὰ λίγο (παρὰ τρίχα) νὰ (+ indefinite).
Pará lígho (pará trícha) na (+ indefinite).
Almost; nearly.

Λίγο ἀκόμα καὶ θὰ ἔπεφτα.
Lígho akóma ke θa épefta.
I almost fell.

Παρὰ τρίχα νὰ πέσω κάτω.
Pará trícha na péso káto.
I nearly fell down.

Λίγο ἤθελε νὰ πέσει.
Lígho íθele na pésee.
He (she, it) nearly fell.

ALONE

Ἀπόμεινε κοῦκος.
Apómeene koùkos.
He (she) was left on his (her) own.
Compare LEAVE.

Ξεφορτώσου με (παράτα με).
Xefortósou me (paráta me).
Leave me in peace! (alone).

ALL RIGHT

Ἐν τάξει.*
En dáxee.
Okay.

Σύμφωνοι (πολὺ καλά).
Seémphonee (polí kalá).
All right (very well).

ALSO

Ἐπίσης.* Τὸ ἴδιο.
Epísis. To ídio.
Too (also, as well, likewise).

Ἐπίσης*
Epísis.
The same to you (used in returning greeting).

ALTHOUGH

('Ακόμη) κι' ἄν.* — (Akómi) kián. — Even if.

"Αν καί.* — Ànke. — Although.

Μ' ὅλο ποὺ εἶμαι ἄρρωστος θὰ ἔρτω στὸ πάρτι.
Mólo poù eéme árrostos θa érto sto párty.
Although I am ill, I will come to the party.

"Αν καὶ εἶμαι μακρυά σου πάντα σὲ θυμᾶμαι. Μ' ὅλο πού.
Àn ke eéme makreeá sou pánda sé θeemáme. Mólo poù.
Although I am far away from you I always remember you.

ALWAYS

Γιὰ πάντα (διὰ παντός).*
Ya pánda (δia pandós).
Always.

Παντοτεινά.
Pandotiná.
Always.

AMAZE

Μοῦ φαίνεται παράξενο.*
Mou fénete paráxeno.
I am amazed(it seems strange to me).

Κέρωσε (κοκκάλωσε) ὅταν τὸ ἄκουσε.
Kérose (kokkálose) ótan to ákouse.
He (she) was astonished when he heard it.

AMONG

'Ανάμεσα στὰ δέντρα.*
Anámesa sta δéndra.
Among the trees.

Μεταξύ μας.*
Metaxí mas.
Among us.

Μεταξὺ ἄλλων.*
Metaxí állon.
Among other things.

'Αναμεταξύ μας.
Anametaxeé mas.
Between ourselves.

Ανάμεσά μας.*
Anámesá mas.
Between us.

ANEW

'Εκ νέου.* — Ek néou. — Anew.

'Εκ δευτέρου.* — Ek δeftérou. — Again.

'Εξ ἀρχῆς.* 'Απὸ τὴν ἀρχή.
Ex archís. Apó tin archí.
From the beginning.

ANGER

Βράζει ἀπὸ θυμό.*
Vrázee apó θeemó.
He (she) was seized with anger

Θόλωσε τὸ μάτι του (της).
Θólose to máti tou (tis).
He (she) is full of anger, desire, etc.

Σκάει ἀπ' τὸ κακό του.
Skáee aptó kakó tou.
He is bursting with rage.

Τὰ κατεβάζω.*
Ta katevázo.
I pull a long face.

Φωτιὰ καὶ λάβρα.*
Fotyá ke lávra.
Strong passion; exorbitant price.

Εἶμαι πῦρ καὶ μανία μαζύ σου.
Eéme peer ke manía mazi sou.
I am extremely angry with you.

Εἶμαι ἔξω φρενῶν.
Eéme exo frenón.
I am extremely angry.

Ἔγινε μπαρούτι.*
Évine mbaroùti
He (she) got furiously angry.

APPARENTLY

Ἔτσι φαίνεται.*
Étsi phénete.
Apparently.

Ὅπως φαίνεται.
Opos phénete.
It seems so.

Κατ' ἐπιφάνειαν* (ἐξωτερικά).
Katepifáneean (exoteriká).
In appearance (but not in reality).

APPEAR

Γιὰ τὰ μάτια τοῦ κόσμου.*
Ya ta mátia toù kózmou.
For appearance sake.

Μὲ τέτοια χάλια.*
Me tétya chália.
In such (bad) state.

APPLY

Πέφτω μὲ τὸ κεφάλι (τὰ μοῦτρα).
Péfto me to kefáli (ta moùtra).
I apply myself avidly.

APPROXIMATELY

Πάνω κάτω (περίπου).*
Páno káto (perípou).
Approximately.

ARGUE

Αὐτὸς εἶναι πνεῦμα ἀντιλογίας.*
Aftós eéne pnévma andiloghías.
He always likes to argue.
Compare FIGHT and QUARREL.

ARISTOCRACY

Ἡ ἀφρόκρεμα τῆς κοινωνίας.*
I afrókrema tis keenonías.
The aristocracy of society.

Ἡ κοπέλα αὐτὴ εἶναι ἀπὸ σπίτι (σώϊ).*
I kopéla aftí eéne apo spíti (sóee).
This girl comes from a good family.

Ἀπὸ τζάκι.* Αὐτὸς εἶναι ἀπὸ τζάκι.
Apó tzáki. Aftós eéne apo tzáki.
This man comes from an aristocratic family.

AS...AS

Τόσο... ὅσο καί...*
Tóso... óso ke...
As... as...

Ἴσα μέ.
Isa me.
As far as (up to).

Τὸ κατ' ἐμέ.*
To katemé.
As for me.

ASHAMED

Τὸ μέτωπό του (της) εἶναι καθαρό.*
To métopó tou (tis) eéne kaϑaró.
He (she) has nothing to be ashamed of.

ASIDE

Κατὰ μέρος.*
Kata méros.
Aside.

Ἄφησέ τα αὐτὰ (κατὰ μέρος).
Àfisé ta aftá (kata méros).
Do not mention these things.

Αὐτὰ κατὰ μέρος.
Aftá kata méros.
Leave these aside.

Κάνε στὴ μπάντα.
Káne sti mbánda.
Stand aside.

ATTACK

Καταφέρομαι (With κατὰ or ἐναντίον + gen.)
Kataférome
I speak against; I attack.

Μὴν καταφέρεσαι ἐναντίον τοῦ ἀδελφοῦ σου.
Min kataférese enandion tou aδelphoù sou.
Don't speak against your brother.

Παίρνω σβάρνα.
Pérno zvárna.
Take advantage of.

Ἡ γλῶσσα του μᾶς πῆρε ὅλους σβάρνα.
I ghlóssa tou mas píre ólous zvárna.
He attacked all of us.

ATTENTION

Δίνω βάση σέ.
δíno vási se.
I attach importance to.

Δὲ δίνω βάση σὲ λόγια κακῶν ἀνθρώπων.
δe δíno vási se lóya kakón anϑrópon.
I don't pay attention to words of evil men.

Τὰ μάτια σου τέσσερα.
Ta mátya sou téssera.
Keep your eyes wide open.

Τ' ἀκούω βερεσέ.
Takoùo veresé.
I don't pay any attention; I take it with a grain of salt.

AVAILABLE

Εἶμαι διαθέσιμος.*
Eéme diaϑésimos.
I am available.

AVERT

Χρειάζεται ἀποσόβηση τῆς καταστάσεως.*
Chreeázete aposóvisi tis katastáseos.
It is necessary to avert the crisis.

AWAKE

Στὸ πόδι. Κάθε βράδυ εἶμαι στὸ πόδι μέχρι τὶς δύο μετὰ τὰ μεσάνυχτα.
Sto pódi. Κάϑe vrádee eéme sto pódi méchri tiz dío metá ta mesáneehta.
Awake. Every night I am awake until two in the morning.

AWARE

Ἔχω ὑπ' ὄψι (μου).* Τὸ ἔχετε ὑπ' ὄψι σας;
Écho eepópsi (mou). To échete eepópsi sas?
I am aware of. Are you aware of it?

EXERCISES

Πές το ἀκόμα μιὰ φορά. Ὁ ἀδελφός μου ἔλειψε μιὰ βδομάδα. Ὁ Κέρυ Γκράντ εἶναι ξεπερασμένος ἠθοποιός. Αὔριο θὰ πᾶμε ψάρεμα. Σύμφωνοι; Ἔπειτα ἀπὸ δύο ὧρες τὸν ἔφερα βόλτα. Μοῦ ἀρέσει αὐτὸ τὸ καπέλο. Καὶ γιὰ τὸ ἄλλο ποὺ σοῦ ἀρέσει, δὲν σοῦ λέω. Θέλεις νὰ πᾶμε κολύμπι; Πάω πάσσο. Ἡ μητέρα μου καὶ ἡ μητέρα σου κάνουν (καλὸ) χωριό. Ὁ ἀδελφός μου μὲ τὴν κόρη σου δὲν κάνουν χωριό. Τόντις εἶσαι καλός. Πράγματι, δὲν ἔχω λεφτά. Χθὲς βρῆκα πενῆντα δολλάρια στὸν δρόμο εἰκῆ κι' ὡς ἔτυχε (τυχαίως). Μὴ ξοδεύεσαι στὰ κουτουροῦ. Προχθὲς εἶδα κατὰ τύχη τὴν ἀδελφή σου μέσα στὸ λεωφορεῖο. Ὁ πατέρας σου εἶναι γενναιόδωρος, πονόψυχος, ἀλτρουϊστὴς καὶ πλούσιος. Εἰς ἐπίμετρον, εἶναι ἀξιοπρεπὴς καὶ θαυμάσιος γιατρός. Καλέ, ποῦ εἶσαι; Καλέ, δὲ μοῦ λὲς ποιὸς εἶναι αὐτός; Τὸ καλὸ ποὺ σοῦ θέλω (εἶναι) νὰ μὴν τὸν βλέπῃς συχνά. Θὰ ἔρθῃς αὔριο; Ἐν τάξει; Ναί, ἐν τάξει. Ἂν καὶ εἶμαι ἄρρωστος θὰ σὲ δῶ ἀπόψε. Μ' ὅλο ποὺ ἔχω πολλὴ δουλειὰ θὰ πάω στὸ σινεμά. Σήμερα ὅλος ὁ κόσμος θέλουν νὰ γίνουν πλούσιοι. Δὲν ἔχει φίλους, οὔτε γονεῖς καὶ γυναίκα. Ἀπόμεινε κοῦκος. Ἔχω πολλὴ δουλειά, παράτα με. Δὲν ὑπάρχει τίποτε ἀνάμεσά μας. Ἡ κόρη του εἶναι πολὺ καλή. Ἐπίσης καὶ ὁ γυιός του. Χρόνια πολλά. Ἐπίσης. Παρὰ τρίχα νὰ εἶχα δυστύχημα. Παρὰ λίγο νὰ μὲ σκοτώσῃ. Παρὰ τρίχα νὰ πνιγῶ (I was almost drowned). Μοῦ εἶπε μεταξὺ ἄλλων πὼς εἶσαι ψεύτης. Αὐτὰ τὰ λέμε ἀναμεταξύ μας. Φεύγω γιὰ πάντα. Ὁ προϊστάμενός μου βράζει ἀπὸ θυμό. Ἀπὸ τὸν μεγάλο του θυμὸ θόλωσε τὸ μάτι του. Ἔσκασε ἀπ' τὸ κακό του. Ἐπειδὴ (since) δὲν τῆς ἔφερα δῶρο, τὰ κατέβασε. Ὁ πατέρας μου σήμερα εἶναι φωτιὰ καὶ λάβρα. Ὁ καταστηματάρχης ἔγινε μπαρούτι μὲ τοὺς «χίππις». Ὁ ἀδελφός μου εἶναι πῦρ καὶ μανία μαζί του. Θὰ τὴν πάρω (I will call her) ἐκ νέου (πάλι, ξανά). Τὸ σοῦπερ μίνι μοῦ φαίνεται παράξενο. Κέρωσε ὅταν (σὰν) τὸν εἶδε. Θὰ βρέξη σήμερα. Ἔτσι φαίνεται. Ὅπως φαίνεται, (ἐ)φέτος (this year) θὰ ἔχωμε βαρὺ χειμῶνα (bad winter). Αὐτὸς εἶναι εὐγενὴς κατ' ἐπιφάνειαν. Πᾶμε μαζί, γιὰ τὰ μάτια τοῦ κόσμου. Ποῦ πᾶς μὲ τέτοια χάλια. Ἔπεσα μὲ τὰ μοῦτρα στὴ νέα μου δουλειά. Πόσα λεφτὰ κρατᾶς; Πάνω - κάτω εἰκοσιπέντε δολλάρια. Ὁ γυιὸς εἶναι τόσο πλούσιος ὅσο καὶ ὁ πατέρας. Πῆγα ἴσα μὲ τὴν Κίνα. Τὸ κατ' ἐμέ, δὲν μπορῶ νὰ ρθῶ ἀπόψε. Δὲν ἔδωσα βάση (I did not pay attention) στὰ λόγια σου. Αὐτὰ τὰ λόγια τ' ἀκούω βερεσέ. Ὅταν πᾶς νὰ ψωνίσεις (to shop) τὰ μάτια σου τέσσερα, νὰ μὴ σὲ γελάσουν (in order not to deceive you). Κάνε στὴ μπάντα, σὲ παρακαλῶ, νὰ περάσω (to pass by). Ὁ νέος αὐτὸς εἶναι ἀπὸ σπίτι. Ἔχει καλὲς ἀρχὲς (he has good principles). Ἡ κοπέλα αὐτὴ εἶναι ἀπὸ τζάκι. Ὁ δικηγόρος μου ὅλο καὶ (always) καταφέρεται ἐναντίον τοῦ δικαστῆ. Πῆρε σβάρνα καὶ (also) τὸν δήμαρχο. Ἔχω ὑπ' ὄψι μου ὅτι (that) καταφέρεται ἐναντίον μου.

BAD

Μοῦ κάνει κακό.
Mou kánee kakó.
It is harmful to me.

Πῆρε τὸν κακὸ δρόμο.
Píre ton kakó ðrómo.
He (she) became corrupted.

Πάλι καλά.
Páli kalá.
It's not as bad (as it might have been)

Εἶναι κρίμα.*
Eéne kríma.
That's too bad.

Κρίμα πού...
Kríma pou...
It's a pity...

Ἕνας κι' ἕνας.
Énas kiénas.
Especially good or bad.

Δὲν κάνει.
ðen kánee.
It's bad.

BANKRUPTCY

Βροντῶ κανόνι.
Vrondó kanóni.
I am bankrupt.

Τὸ γειτονικὸ κατάστημα βρόντηξε κανόνι.
To yeetonikó katástima vróndixe kanóni.
The neighboring store went bankrupt.

BARGAIN

Κάνω παζάρι (α).
Káno pazári(a).
I bargain.

BATH

Κάνω μπάνιο.*
Káno mbánio.
I take a bath.

Κάνεις μπάνιο;
Kánees mbánio?
Do you take baths?

BE

Έκανε στὴν 'Αμερικὴ.*
Ékane stin Amerikí.
He (she) has been in America.

Πόσον καιρὸ ἔκανες στὴν 'Ελλάδα;
Póson keró ékanes stin Elláδa?
How long did you live in Greece?

BEAT

Δὲν τοῦ βγαίνει κανεὶς στὰ χαρτιά.
δen dou vghénee kaneés sta chartyá.
No one can beat him at cards.

Τὸν ἔκανα μαῦρο στὸ ξύλο.*
Ton ékana mávro sto xeélo.
I gave him a good beating.

BEGIN

Πρῶτα - πρῶτα.*
Próta - próta.
First of all; to begin with.

Πρῶτα ἀπ' ὅλα.*
Próta apóla.
First of all.

BEHAVIOR

Δὲν μοῦ ἀρέσουν τὰ ἔκτροπα.
δén mou arésoun ta éktropa.
I don't like unseemly behavior.

Μὲ τὸ μαλακὸ (μὲ τὸ καλό).
Me to malakó (me to kaló).
Softly, mildly (treatment).

Δὲν μ' ἀρέσουν τὰ καραγκιοζλίκια.
δén marésoun ta karagiozlíkya.
I don't like the crudely comical behavior.

BELONG

Εἶναι τοῦ (τῆς + noun).*
Eéne toù (tís).
They (it) belong(s) to.

Τὸ καπέλο αὐτὸ εἶναι τοῦ φίλου μου.
To kapélo aftó eéne tou phílou mou.
This hat belongs to my friend.

Τί μοῦ ἀναλογεῖ (ποιὸ εἶναι τὸ μερτικό μου or τὸ μερίδιό μου);
Tí mou analoyeé (pyó eéne to mertikó mou or to meríδió mou)?
What is my share?

BESIDES

'Εξ ἄλλου (ἄλλωστε).*
Ex állou (álloste).
Besides.

BET

Βάζω στοίχημα.*
Vázo steéchima.
I bet.

Βάζεις στοίχημα πὼς αὐτὸς εἶναι ἀλκοολικός;
Vázees steéchima pos aftós eéne alkoolikós?
Do you bet that he is an alcoholic?

BETTER

Τόσο τὸ καλλίτερο.
Tóso to kallítero.
So much the better.

Κάλλιο νὰ (+ indefinite).
Kálio na.
It is better.

Τελείωσαν (σώθηκαν) τὰ ψέματα.
Teleéosan (sóϑikan) ta psémata.
Things become better.

Κάλλιο νὰ πεθάνω παρὰ νὰ σὲ χωρίσω.
Kálio na peϑáno pará na se choríso.
I would prefer to die rather than to divorce you.

BIRTH

Ἐκ γενετῆς.*
Ek yenetís.
From birth.

Γέννημα καὶ θρέμμα.*
Yénnima ke ϑrémma.
Born and bred.

BLAME

Τοῦ καταλογίζω εὐθύνη.*
Tou kataloyizo efϑeéni.
I blame him.

Αὐτὴ φταίει.*
Aftí ftéi.
She is to be blamed.

BORING

Κατάντησε ἀνιαρὸς (Κατάντησε ἀνυπόφορος).*
Katándise aniarós (Katándise aneepóforos).
He became boring.

Μοῦ κόλλησε σὰ βδέλλα.
Mou kóllise sa vδélla.
He (she) became annoying.

Μὲ πέθανε στὴ φλυαρία.
Me péϑane sti phleearía.
He (she) wore me out with his (her) chatter.

Ἄλλη ἔννοια δὲν ἔχω.
Àlli énia δen écho.
I can't deal with you always; I have other work to do.

Compare ALONE.

BRAVE

Τὸ λέει ἡ καρδιά του (της).*
To léee i karδyá tou (tis).
He (she) is brave.

BRAVO

Εὖγε (σου)!
Évye (sou)!
Bravo!

BUSINESS

Κοίτα τὴ δουλειά σου.*
Keéta ti δouliá sou.
Mind your own business.

Δὲν εἶναι δουλειὰ (ὑπόθεση) δικιά σου.*
δen eéne δouliá (eepóθesi) δikiá sou.
It is none of your business.

Κάνω χρυσὲς δουλειές.*
Káno chreesés δouliés.
I do a very good business.

Κύτταξε πρῶτα τὴν καμπούρα σου.
Keétaxe próta tin kamboùra sou.
It's not your business.

Δὲν σοῦ πέφτει λόγος.
δen sou péftee lóghos.
You have no say.

BUSY

Ἔχω δουλειά.*
Écho δouliá.
I am busy.

Εἶμαι ἀπησχολημένος.*
Eéme apischoliménos.
I am busy.

Πνίγομαι στὴ δουλειά.*
Pníghome sti δouliá.
I am extremely busy.

EXERCISES

Τὸ τσιγάρο μοῦ κάνει κακό. Δὲν κάνει νὰ πίνης πάρα πολὺ (too much). Αὐτοκτόνησε (...committed suicide) ἐκείνη ἡ ὡραία κοπέλα. Εἶναι κρίμα! (Τί κρίμα!). Αὐτὴ ἡ παρέα εἶναι ἕνας κι' ἕνας. Πόσα πλήρωσες γιὰ ὅλο αὐτὸ τὸ τραπέζι. Πενῆντα δολλάρια. Πάλι καλά. Ὁ γνωστός μας (our familiar) ἔμπορος βροντᾶ κανόνι. Αὐτὸς κάνει πολλὰ παζάρια (big bargain). Θὰ κάνωμε μπάνιο (κολύμπι) σήμερα; Ἀσφαλῶς (βεβαίως). Ὁ παππούς μου ἔκανε στὴν Ἀμερικὴ δέκα χρόνια. Δὲν τῆς βγαίνει καμιὰ στὴν ὀμορφιά. Ὁ πατέρας του τὸν ἔκανε μαῦρο στὸ ξύλο. Πρῶτα - πρῶτα θέλω νὰ σ' εὐχαριστήσω πολὺ γιὰ τὴν φιλοξενία σου. Δὲν μοῦ ἀρέσουν οἱ τρόποι της (her behaviour). Τὴν ἔπιασε μὲ τὸ μαλακὸ (he handled her). Αὐτὸ τὸ παλτὸ εἶναι τοῦ πατέρα μου. Δὲν σοῦ ἀναλογεῖ τίποτε (nothing belongs to you). Αὐτὰ τὰ παπούτσια δὲν μ' ἀρέσουν. Ἐξ ἄλλου δὲν ἔχω χρήματα νὰ τ' ἀγοράσω (to buy them). Δὲν θὰ πᾶμε μὲ πλοῖο, μὰ (but) μὲ ἀεροπλάνο. Τόσο τὸ καλλίτερο. Κάλλιο ἀργὰ παρὰ ποτέ. Δὲν θὰ τὴν πάρη (he will not marry her). Βάζεις στοίχημα; Αὐτὸς εἶναι τυφλὸς ἐκ γενετῆς. Ὁ ἄντρας μου εἶναι γέννημα καὶ θρέμμα τῆς Ἑλλάδος. Τοῦ τρελλοῦ δὲν μπορεῖς νὰ καταλογίσῃς εὐθύνη. Αὐτὸς μιλᾶ πολλὰ καὶ καταντᾶ ἀνιαρός. Ἡ γυναίκα αὐτὴ μοῦ κόλλησε σὰ βδέλλα. Τὸ μαγαζὶ τοῦ θείου μου κάνει χρυσὲς δουλειές.

CALL

Πῶς τὸ λένε (λέτε) αὐτό;*
Pós to léne (léte) aftó?
What do you call this?

Τὸν ἔβγαλαν Νῖκο.
Tón évghalan Níko.
They named him Nick.

Ἐφιστῶ τὴν προσοχή σας.*
Ephistó tin prosochí sas.
I call (draw) your attention.

Μοῦ ἔδωσε τὸν λόγο.
Mou éδose ton lógho.
He called on me to speak.

CANDIDATE

Βάζω ὑποψηφιότητα.*
Vázo eepopsifiótita.
I run for office.

CAR

Ἔχω λάστιχο.*
Écho lásticho.
I have a flat tire.

Ἡ μηχανὴ δὲν δουλεύει.*
I michaní δen δoulévee.
The motor is not working.

Δὲν ἔχω βενζίνη.*
δén écho venzíni.
I have no gas.

CARE

Σκοτούρα του.
Skoutoùra tou.
A lot he cares.

Τὸ ἔδεσε σὲ ψηλὸ μαντίλι.
To éδese se psiló mandíli.
He (she) did not pay any attention to it.

Τί μὲ κόβει;
Tí me kóvee?
What do I care?

Τὸ ρίχνω ἔξω.*
To ríchno éxo.
I don't care.

(Ἔχε) τὸ νοῦ σου.
(Éche) to noù sou.
Take care, keep your eyes open.

Καμωμένο μὲ μεράκι (γοῦστο).
Kamoméno me meráki (ghoùsto).
Made with loving care.

CAREER

Διὰ βίου.*
δia víou.
For life.

Βίος καὶ πολιτεία.*
Víos ke politía.
One who has had a corrupted career.

CASE

῞Οπως ὅπως (ὅπως κι' ὅπως).
Opos ópos (ópos kiópos).
Any (old) way.

῞Οπωσδήποτε (ἐν πάσῃ περιπτώσει).*
Opozδípote (en pási periptósee).
In any case.

᾽Ανίσως καὶ (+ indefinite).
Anísos ke
In the case that.

Βλέποντας καὶ κάνοντας.
Vlépondas ke kánondas.
As the case may be.

CATCH

Θὰ πιάσω στὰ πράσα.
Tha pyáso sta prása.
I will catch red-handed.

Τοὺς ἔπιασαν στὰ πράσα.
Tous épyasan sta prása.
They were caught red-handed.

CAUSE

Σηκώνω στὸ πόδι.*
Sikóno sto póδi.
I cause a commotion.

Τὰ μοτοσακὸ σήκωσαν στὸ πόδι ὅλη τὴ γειτονιά.
Ta motosakó síkosan sto póδi óli ti yeetoniá.
The motorcycle caused a commotion in the whole neighborhood.

CERTAINTY

Ἑκατὸ τοῖς (τὰ) ἑκατό.*
Ekató tees (ta) ekató.
One hundred per cent.

CHANGE

Τώρα τραβᾶ τὰ μαλλιά του (της).
Tóra travá ta maliá tou (tis).
Now he (she) changed his (her) mind (but it is too late).

CHARACTER

Εἶναι μάρκα.*
Eéne márka.
He (she) is a character.

Τί μάρκα!
Ti márka.
What a character!

Αὐτὸς (αὐτὴ) εἶναι ἀγρίμι (ἀκοινώνητος).
Aftós (aftí) eéne aghrími (akeenónitos).
He (she)is an unsociable (wild) person.

῎Ισιος (εὐθὺς) ἄνθρωπος.*
Isyos (efϑeés) ánϑropos.
Sincere man.

Δὲν ἔχει ἀνατροφὴ (εἶναι ἀνάγωγος).*
δen échee anatrophí (eéne anághoghos).
He (she) lacks good manners.

Κρύος μπούζι.
Kreéos mboùzi.
He is a cold person (with no sense of humor).

'Ατσαλένιος χαρακτήρας.*
Atsalénios charachtíras.
Very strong moral character.

Εἶναι γλεντζές.*
Eéne ghlentzés.
He is an entertaining person.

Τὸν ξέρω ἀπ' τὴν καλή (του).
Ton xéro aptín kalí (tou).
I knew his real character.

Κῶλος καὶ βρακί.
Kólos ke vrakí.
Hand-in-glove.

Εἶναι ἀποκρουστικὸς (τύπος).*
Eéne apokroustikós (teépos).
He is antipathetic (repulsive).

'Ατόφυος χαραχτήρας.*
Atófyos charachtiras.
Integral character.

'Αχρεῖο ὑποκείμενο.*
Achreéo eepokeémeno.
Dishonest or corrupted person.

Εἶναι ἐλαστικὸς χαραχτήρας.*
Eéne elastikós charachtíras.
He is flexible.

Τοῦ (τῆς) βρῆκα τὸ κουμπί.
Tou (tis) vríka to koumbí.
I found his (her) weak spot.

Πῆραν τὰ μυαλά του ἀέρα.*
Píran ta meealá tou aéra.
Success has gone to his head.

CHURCH

Τί ὥρα ἀπολύει ἡ ἐκκλησία;*
Tí óra apoleéi i ekklisía?
What time does the church service end?

'Απόλυσε ἡ ἐκκλησία.
Apoleése i ekklisía.
The church service ended.

CLEAR

Καθαρίζω τὸ τραπέζι.
Kaϑarízo to trapézi.
I clear the table.

Φῶς φανάρι.*
Fós phanári.
Clear as day.

CLEVER

Διαβόλου κάλτσα (διαβολεμένος, διαβολάνθρωπος).*
δyavólou káltsa (δyavoleménos, δyavolánϑropos).
Very shrewd and able person.

Τἄχει τετρακόσα.*
Táchee tetrakósa.
He (she) is extremely clever and careful.

Αὐτὸς (αὐτὴ) εἶναι τοῦ διαβόλου καὶ τοῦ παλουκιοῦ.
Aftós (aftí) eéne tou δyavólou ke tou paloukioù.
He (she) is a devil (extremely clever or able in evil business).

Κατεβάζει (κόβει) τὸ κεφάλι του.*
Katevázee (kóvee) to kepháli tou.
He is clever (intelligent).

CLIMATE

Τὸν σηκώνει τὸ κλῖμα.*
Ton sikónee to klíma.
The climate is good for him.

COLD

Κάνει κρύο.*
Kánee kreéo.
It's cold (out).

Πιάνω κρυολόγημα.*
Pyáno kreeológhima.
I am getting a cold.

Τσουχτερὸ κρύο.*
Tsouchteró kreéo.
Bitter cold.

COME

Κοπιάστε μέσα.
Kopyáste mésa.
Please come in.

Ἔλα νὰ χαρῆς!
Éla na charís!
Please come!

COMFORT

Μὲ ἄνεση (ἀνέτως).*
Me ánesi (anétos).
At leisure, in comfort.

COMPANY

Κάνε μου παρέα.
Káne mou paréa.
Keep me company.

COMPLAINT

Ἡ γκρίνια φέρνει χρουσουζιά.
I grínia férnee chrousouzyá.
Complaints bring bad luck.

COMPLETELY

Πέρα γιὰ (καὶ) πέρα.*
Péra ya (ke) péra.
Completely, wholly.

Τὸ σπίτι πῆρε φωτιὰ πέρα καὶ πέρα.
To spíti píre fotyá péra ke péra.
The house burned down completely.

Πιὸ πέρα.
Pyó péra.
Further along.

Ὅλως διόλου.*
Olos δiólou.
Completely.

Παντελῶς.*
Pandelós.
Entirely.

Ἐντελῶς.*
Endelós.
Entirely.

CONFUSION

Ἄκρες μέσες.*
Àkres méses.
Confused knowledge; disjointedly.

Τὰ θόλωσε.*
Ta θólose.
He (she) confused the situation.

Τἄχω χαμένα.*
Tácho chaména.
I'm lost (extremely confused).

Φύρδην - μίγδην.*
Feérδin - míghδin.
Mixed up, in absolute confusion.

Χαλάει ὁ κόσμος.*
Chaláee o kózmos.
Great storm, great noise and confusion

Δὲν χάλασε ὁ κόσμος.*
δen chálase o kózmos.
Things are not so serious.

CONSEQUENCE

Κατ' ἀκολουθίαν (συνεπῶς, κατὰ συνέπειαν).*
Katakolouθían (seenepós, kata seenépeean).
Consequently.

CONTRARY

Ἀπ' ἐναντίας.*
Apenandías.
On the contrary.

Ἀντιθέτως.*
Andiθétos.
On the contrary.

Ἴσα - ἴσα.
Isa - ísa.
Exactly, precisely; on the contrary, actually.

CONTROL

Δὲ βαστιέμαι.
δé vastyéme.
I cannot control myself.

Δὲν μπορῶ νὰ κρατηθῶ.
δén mboró na kratiθó.
I cannot control myself.

CONVENIENT

Ἂν σοῦ εἶναι βολικά.
An sou eéne voliká.
If it is convenient for you.

Δὲν ἔρχεται βολικά.
δen érchete voliká.
It is not convenient.

Ποιὲς ὧρες εἶναι βολικὲς γιὰ σένα (ποιὲς ὧρες σὲ βολεύουν);
Pyés óres eéne volikés ya séna (pyés ores se volévoun)?
Which hours are convenient for you?

CONVERSATION

Πιάνω κουβέντα.*
Pyáno kouvénda.
I get into a conversation.

CORRUPTED

'Αχρεῖο ὑποκείμενο.*
Achreéo eepokeémeno.
Dishonest or corrupted person.

Κάθαρμα τῆς κοινωνίας.*
Káϑarma tis keenonías.
Extremely corrupted person.

Ξώλης καὶ προώλης.*
Xólis ke proólis.
A thoroughly bad lot; extremely corrupted man.

Εἶναι μοῦτρο.
Eéne moùtro.
He (she) is a crook.

Compare CHARACTER.

COST

Πόσο κάνει (πόσα κοστίζει);*
Póso kánee (pósa kostízee)?
How much does it cost?

Πόσο ἔχει;
Póso échee?
How much does it cost?

Μὲ κάθε τρόπο.*
Me káϑe trópo.
By all means, at all costs.

COUNT

Αὐτὸ δὲν πιάνεται.
Aftó δen pyánete.
That does not count.

COURAGE

Δὲν ἔχεις ψυχὴ (καρδιὰ) μέσα σου;
δen échees psichí (karδyá) mésa sou?
Aren't you courageous?

"Εχασα τὸ ἠθικό μου.*
Échasa to iϑikó mou.
My courage fails me.

Καρδιὰ (ψυχή, κουράγιο, θάρρος)!
Karδyá (psichí, kouráyo, ϑárros)!
Have courage! Be courageous!

Κάνω καρδιά.
Káno karδyá.
I take courage.

Δὲν βαστᾶ ἡ καρδιά μου.
δen vastá i karδyá mou.
I have not the courage or the heart (to).

CRAZY

Τή ψώνισες.*
Ti psónises.
You became crazy.

Ἔμπλεξες (τὴν ἔπαθες).*
Émblexes (tin épaϑes).
You are involved.

Σάλεψε ὁ νοῦς του.*
Sálepse o noùs tou.
He became crazy.

Τοῦ ἔστριψε (ἡ βίδα).*
Tou éstripse (i vída).
He became crazy.

Αὐτὸς εἶναι γιὰ δέσιμο.
Aftós eéne ya δésimo.
He is crazy.

Εἶναι (ἔχει) βίδα.
Eéne (échee) vída.
He is crazy.

Δὲν εἶσαι μὲ τὸ νοῦ σου.
δen eése me to noù sou.
You must be mad.

Κάνω τὸν τρελλό.
Káno ton trelló.
I pretend to be mad.

Εἶναι γιὰ τὰ πανηγύρια.*
Eéne ya ta paniyírya.
He (she) is quite crazy.

Χρωστᾶ τῆς Μιχαλοῦς.
Chrostá tis Michaloùs.
He (she) is dumb, foolish.

Δὲν εἶναι μὲ τὰ σωστά του.*
δen eéne me ta sostá tou.
He is not in his right mind.

CUSTOMARY

Εἶναι καθιερωμένο (συνηθισμένο, σύνηθες).
Eéne kaϑieroméno (seeniϑizméno, seéniϑes).
It is customary (usual).

EXERCISES

Ἐφιστῶ τὴν προσοχή σας στὸ ζήτημα αὐτό. Τοῦ ἔδωσε τὸν λόγον ἔπειτα ἀπὸ πολλὴ ὥρα. Μετὰ ποὺ χώρισε τὸ 'ριξεν ἔξω. Σκουτούρα μου, γι' αὐτοὺς ποὺ μὲ ζηλεύουν. Μέ 'βρισε στὰ γερὰ (he or she insulted me seriously) μὰ καὶ ἐγὼ τὸ ἔδεσα σὲ ψηλὸ μαντίλι. Ἔγινε ρεζίλι (he or she was made ridiculous) καὶ δὲν τὴν κόβει. Τί σὲ κόβει; Ἐγὼ θὰ σὲ βοηθήσω. Κύτταξε, τί ὡραῖο κουστούμι. Εἶναι καμωμένο μὲ μεράκι. Μαγείρευε (cook) ἀλλὰ ἔχε τὸν νοῦ σου καὶ στὸ παιδί. Θὰ τὸ τελειώσω ὅπως ὅπως. Εἶμαι κουρασμένος, ἀλλὰ θὰ εἶμαι στὴ διάλεξη ὁπωσδήποτε. Ἂν ἴσως καὶ δὲν ἔρθης σήμερα, τηλεφώνησέ μου. Ἐπειδὴ εἶμαι πολὺ ἀπησχολημένος δὲν θἄρθω στὸ χορό. Καὶ πάλι, βλέποντας καὶ κάνοντας. Ἔχετε ἰδέα ἀπὸ αὐτοκίνητο; Ἔχω λάστιχο. Ἕνας σκύλος τὴν νύχτα μᾶς σήκωσε στὸ πόδι. Ὁ ἐξάδελφός μου ἔβαλε ὑποψηφιότητα γιὰ βουλευτὴς (is runnig for congressman). Τοὺς ἔπιασαν στὰ πράσα. Θὰ σὲ δῶ ἀπόψε, ἑκατὸ τὰ ἑκατό. Τὸν ἤθελε τόσο πολὺ νὰ τὸν παντρευτῇ. Τὸν πῆρε, καὶ τώρα τραβᾶ τὰ μαλλιά της. Αὐτὸς εἶναι βίος καὶ πολιτεία. Ὁ φίλος μου εἶναι μάρκα. Πώ, πώ, πώ! Αὐτὴ εἶναι μάρκα. Τί μάρκα, αἴ! Ὁ συνέταιρός μου εἶναι ἴσιος ἄνθρωπος. Ὁ φίλος μου εἶναι ἀγρίμι. Ὁ ἄνθρωπος αὐτὸς δὲν ἔχει ἀνατροφή. Ὁ κύριος αὐτὸς εἶναι κρύος μπούζι. Ἡ κοπέλα ἐκείνη εἶναι ἀποκρουστική. Ὁ γιατρός μου εἶναι ἀτόφυος χαραχτῆρας. Ὁ ἄντρας μου εἶναι ἀτσαλένιος χαραχτῆρας. Αὐτὸς ὁ ἄντρας εἶναι ἀχρεῖο ὑποκείμενο. Ὁ ἀδελφός μου εἶναι γλεντζές. Ὁ ἄντρας της εἶναι ἐλαστικὸς χαρακτῆρας. Τὸν γείτονα τὸν ξέρω ἀπ' τὴν καλή του. Μόλις πῆρε καλύτερη δουλειά, πῆραν τὰ μυαλά του ἀέρα. Δὲν τὸν σηκώνει τὸ κλῖμα τῆς Νέας Ὑόρκης. Μόλις τρῶμε, ἡ γυναίκα μου καθαρίζει τὸ τραπέζι. Δὲν εἶμαι τσιγκούνης. Ἴσα - ἴσα κάθε 6δομάδα τρώγω τρεῖς φορὲς ἔξω. Ὁ μαθητὴς αὐτὸς εἶναι διαβόλου κάλτσα. Ὁ παππούς μου, ἂν καὶ (although) 85 χρονῶν, τἄχει τετρακόσια. Ἡ φιλενάδα μου εἶναι τοῦ διαβόλου καὶ τοῦ παλουκιοῦ. Τὸ κεφάλι του δὲν κόβει (he is not smart). Μ' ἔπιασε κουβέντα καὶ ἔχασα τὸ τραῖνο (and I missed the train). Γιατὶ περιμένετε ἔξω; Κοπιάστε μέσα. Ἔλα νὰ χαρῇς, μὴ μὲ πειράζῃς (please do not tease (bother) me). Ὁ φίλος μου κάνει καλὴ παρέα. Σήμερα κάνει κρύο. Συχνὰ πιάνω κρυολόγημα. Αὐτὸς ποτὲ δὲν πιάνει κρυολόγημα. Πέρσυ ἔπιασα δεκαπέντε κρυολογήματα. Ἐφέτος κάνει τσουχτερὸ κρύο. Στὴν Ἑλλάδα, ὅταν ἔχεις χρήματα, ζεῖς μὲ ἄνεση. Τὸ διαμέρισμά μου πῆρε φωτιὰ πέρα γιὰ πέρα. Αὐτὸς εἶναι τρελλὸς ὅλως διόλου. Βράχηκα (I was wet) ὅλως διόλου. Πολλὲς φορὲς δὲ 6αστιέμαι καὶ μιλῶ ἄσχημα. Ὁ γείτονάς μου δὲν 6αστιέται. Ἔλα τὴν Τετάρτη ἂν σοῦ εἶναι 6ολικά. Δὲν μοῦ ἔρχεται 6ολικά. Ποιὰ μέρα σὲ 6ολεύει; Μὴ γκρινιάζεις (do not complain). Εἶμαι φτωχός, συνεπῶς πρέπει νὰ δουλεύω. Αὐτὸ τὸ πουκάμισο πόσο κάνει; Αὐτὰ τὰ παπούτσια πόσα κοστίζουν; Θὰ 'ρθῶ στοὺς γάμους σου μὲ κάθε τρόπο (ὁπωσδήποτε). Ἡ γειτόνισσά μου εἶναι ξώλης καὶ προώλης. Αὐτὴ εἶναι μοῦτρο. Ἀπὸ τὴν κατοχὴ δὲν θυμᾶται παρὰ ἄκρες μέσες (from the foreign yoke he does not have but confused memories). Τά 'βαλε μέσ' τὴ 6αλίτσα ὅλα φύρδην - μίγδην. Ἔξω χαλάει ὁ κόσμος ἀπὸ τὴ 6ροχή. Ἀπ' τὰ πολλὰ 6άσανα σάλεψε ὁ νοῦς του. Αὐτοὶ εἶναι γιὰ δέσιμο. Αὐτὸς δὲν εἶναι μὲ τὸ νοῦ του. Αὐτὴ ἡ γυναίκα εἶναι γιὰ τὰ πανηγύρια. Κάνε καρδιὰ καὶ θὰ γίνῃς καλά. Δὲν 6αστᾶ ἡ καρδιά μου νὰ 6λέπω αἷμα. Στὴν Ἑλλάδα εἶναι καθιερωμένο νὰ κοιμᾶται ὁ κόσμος ἀπ' τὶς δύο ὥς τὶς πέντε.

DANGER

Ἐπικίνδυνος.*	Ἐπικίνδυνος εἶναι ἐκεῖνος ποὺ μπορεῖ νὰ κάμῃ μεγάλο κακό.
Epikínðeenos.	Epikínðeenos eéne ekeénos pou mboreé na kámi meghálo kakó.
Dangerous.	One who may cause great harm is dangerous.

Διατρέχω κίνδυνον.*
διatrécho kínδeenon.
I am in danger.

Διαφεύγω τὸν κίνδυνον.
διaphévgho ton kínδeenon.
I avoid danger.

Ἐκτὸς κινδύνου.*
Ektós kinδeénou.
Out of danger.

DARE

Δὲν τοῦ βαστάει.
δén tou vastáee.
He does not dare.

Ἢ τοῦ ὕψους ἢ τοῦ βάθους.*
I tou eépsous i tou váθous.
Life or death.

DARK

Ἀφοῦ σκοτεινιάσει.*
Afoù skoteeniásee.
After dark.

Στὰ σκοτεινά.
Sta skoteená.
In the dark.

DEATH

Στερνὰ λόγια.*
Sterná lóya.
The very last words (in death).

Μᾶς ἄφησε γειὰ γιὰ πάντα.*
Mas áfise yá ya pánda.
He (she) died.

Ἔμεινε τέζα.*
Émeene téza.
He (she) died.

Τὰ τέντωσε (τὰ τίναξε).
Ta téndose (ta tínaxe).
He (she) died.

Ἔμεινε στὸν τόπο.*
Émeene ston dópo.
He (she) died instantly.

Πνέω τὰ λοίσθια.*
Pnéo ta leésθia.
I take my last breath.

DECEIVE

Γελάστηκα (μὲ γέλασε).
Yelástika (me yélase).
I was deceived, mistaken.

Τὄφαγε τὸ δόλωμα.
Tófaghe to δóloma.
He (she) was deceived.

Μοῦ τὴν κατάφερε.*
Mou tin katáfere.
He played a trick on me.

DEEDS

Ἔμαθα τὰ καμώματά σου (τὰ κατορθώματά σου, τὶς βρωμιές σου).*
Émaθa ta kamómatá sou (ta katorθómatá sou, tis vromiés sou).
I am aware of your crooked (evil) deeds.

DEFEAT

Βάζω κάτω.
Vázo káto.
I defeat (person).

Τὸν ἔφαγε.
Ton éfaghe.
He (she) defeated him.

DELICATE

Αὐτὸς εἶναι μὴ μοῦ ἅπτου (πολὺ ντελικᾶτος, ἀρωστιάρης).*
Aftós eéne mí mou áptou (polí ndelikátos, arostiáris).
He is peculiar (very delicate, sickly).

DEPEND

Ἐξαρτᾶται.*
Exartáte.
It depends.

Ἐξαρτᾶται ἀπὸ σένα νά...
Exartáte apó séna na...
It is up to you to...

Ἀπὸ σένα ἐξαρτᾶται ἡ ἀπόφασις.*
Apo séna exartáte i apófasis.
The decision depends on you.

Ἀνάλογα μὲ τὶς περιστάσεις (ἀναλόγως τῶν περιστάσεων)...*
Análogha me tis peristásees (analóghos ton peristáseon)...
According to the circumstances...

Σὲ σένα ἔγκειται (ἀπόκειται) ἡ ἀπόφασις.*
Se séna éngeete (apókeete) i apófasis.
The decision rests with you.

DESERVE

Μοῦ ἀξίζει.*
Mou axízee.
I deserve it.

Μοῦ ἀξίζει νὰ κερδίσω.
Mou axízee na kerδíso.
I deserve to win.

Ἀξίζω νὰ τιμωρηθῶ.*
Axízo na timoriϑó.
I deserve to be punished.

Ἀξίζει τὸν κόπο.*
Axízee ton kópo.
It is worth the trouble.

Δὲν ἀξίζει (δεκάρα, πεντάρα).*
δén axízee (δekára, pendára).
It's no use; it's no good.

Χαλ(ν)άλι σου.*
Chal(n)áli sou.
You deserve it (only in good sense).

DESIRE

Ψοφῶ γιὰ (πεθαίνω γιά).*
Psophó yá (peϑéno yá).
I long for; I am mad about.

DETAIL

Λέξη πρὸς λέξη.*
Léxi pros léxi.
Word for word.

Διὰ μακρῶν (τὰ καθ' ἕκαστα).*
δia makrón (ta kaϑékasta).
At length (in detail).

DEVIL

Ὁ ἔξω ἀπὸ 'δῶ.*
O éxo apo δó.
The devil (folk term).

Ὁ ξορκισμένος.
O xorkizménos.
The devil (folk term).

Στὸ διάβολο!
Sto δyávolo.
Go to hell.

DIFFERENCE

Ἔχει νὰ κάνει.*
Échee na kánee.
It makes a difference.

Δὲν ἔχει νὰ κάνει.*
δen échee na kánee.
It makes no difference.

Τί μ' αὐτό;*
Tí maftó?
So what?

Τὸ ἴδιο (μοῦ) κάνει.*
To íδyo (mou) kánee.
It makes no difference to me.

Δὲν παίζει ρόλο (δὲν πειράζει).*
δen pézee rólo (δen peerázee).
It doesn't make any difference.

DIFFICULTY

Μετὰ βίας.*
Meta vías.
With difficulty.

Βλέπω καὶ παθαίνω.
Vlépo ke paθéno.
I have a hard job (to);
I meet great difficulty.

Φέρνω τὸν κατακλυσμό.
Férno ton katakleezmó.
I make difficulties about trifles.

Κουτσὰ στραβά.
Koutsá stravá.
With great difficulty.

Μᾶς τἄπε κουτσὰ στραβά.
Mas tápe koutsá stravá.
He said it with great difficulty.

Αὐτὸς εἶναι ζόρικος.*
Aftós eéne zórikos.
He is difficult.

Ἔχει σφίξες.
Échee sfíxes.
He (she) is in difficulty.

Τὰ βρῆκα σκοῦρα.*
Ta vríka skoùra.
I met with obstacles.

Μοῦ βγῆκε ἡ πίστη (ἀνάποδη).
Mou vyíke i písti (anápoδi).
I had geat difficulty.

Στένεψαν τὰ πράματα.
Sténepsan ta prámata.
Things have worsened.

Μοῦ ἔβγαλε τὴ ψυχή.*
Mou évghale ti psichí.
He (she) exhausted me.

DISAPPEAR

Ἀνελήφθη.*
Anelífθi.
It has disappeared (vanished).

Ἔγινε ἄφαντος.
Éyine áfandos.
He disappeared (vanished).

Ἔγινε καπνός.
Éyine kapnós.
He (she) vanished.

DISAPPOINTMENT

Νὰ σὲ βράσω.
Na se vráso.
Expression of vexed disappointment.

Τοῦ (τῆς) κόπηκαν τὰ φτερά.
Tou (tis) kópikan ta fterá.
He (she) became disappointed.

Ἔμεινε κόκκαλο.*
Émeene kókkalo.
He was dumbstruck.

Ἔμεινε στὰ κρύα τοῦ λουτροῦ.
Émeene sta kreéa tou loutroù.
He (she) was let down.

Μαύρισε τὸ μάτι μου.
Mávrise to máti mou.
I am driven to desperation (by poverty, etc).

Μοῦ βγῆκε ξυνό.
Mou vyíke xinó.
It turned out to be a disappointment after all.

Βάλ' του ρίγανη.*
Váltou ríghani.
Ironic comment on unfulfilled expectations.

DISAPPROVAL

Σὲ καλό σου!*
Se kaló sou!
Expression of mild disapproval.

DISGUST

Καημένε καὶ σύ!*
Kaeeméne ke seé!
Phrase of mild remonstration.

Αὐτὸς (αὐτὴ) εἶναι ἀηδία.*
Aftós (aftí) eéne aiδía.
He (she) is disgusting.

DO

Κάνω ὅ,τι μπορῶ.*
Káno ó,ti boró.
I do my best.

Βάζω τὰ καλά μου (τὰ δυνατά μου).*
Vázo ta kalá mou (ta δeenatá mou).
I put on my best clothes (I do my best).

Τὶ θὰ ἀπογίνω;*
Ti ϑa apoyíno?
What will become of me?

Ὅ,τι γίνεται δὲν ἀπογίνεται.*
O,ti yínete δén apoyínete.
Whatever is done cannot be undone.

DOCTOR

Κάνω τὸν γιατρό.*
Káno ton yatró.
I pretend to be a doctor.

DRAW

Ρίχνω κλῆρο.*
Ríchno klíro.
I draw lots.

DRINK

Τὸ τσούζω.*
To tsoùzo.
I drink heavily.

Τὰ κοπανάω.
Ta kopanáo.
I drink.

Εἶναι κουδούνι.
Eéne kouδoùni.
He (she) is drunk.

Τάβλα (τύφλα, τάπα, τέζα) στὸ μεθύσι.*
Távla (teéfla, tápa, téza) sto meϑeési.
Blind drunk.

DRIVE

Μὲ τρέλλανε!
Me tréllane!
He (she) drove me crazy!

DUE

Κάνει νὰ πάρω κι' ἄλλα λεφτά.
Kánee na páro kiálla leftá.
There is still some money due me.

DUMB

Τὸν κακό σου τὸν καιρό.
Ton kakó sou ton keró.
You are dumb.

Δὲν ἔχει κουκούτσι μυαλό.*
δén échee koukoùtsi mialó.
He is completely dumb.

'Ανεπίδεκτος μαθήσεως.*
Anepíδektos maϑíseos.
Dumb; not receptive at all.

Κάνω τὴν πάπια.
Káno tin pápya.
I play the fool.

DUTY

"Εχω ὑπηρεσία.*
Écho eepiresía.
I am on duty.

'Απαράβατο καθῆκο.*
Aparávato kaϑíko.
Very obligatory duty.

EXERCISES

'Ο τρελλὸς εἶναι ἐπικίνδυνος. 'Ο ἐπισκέπτης στὸ Βιετνὰμ διατρέχει κίνδυνον. 'Ο Μακάριος δυὸ φορὲς διέφυγε τὸν κίνδυνο νὰ σκοτωθῇ. 'Η ζώνη αὐτὴ εἶναι ἐκτὸς κινδύνου. Δὲν τοῦ βαστάει νὰ σκοτώσῃ ἄνθρωπο. Θὰ συναντηθοῦμε στὰ σκοτεινά. 'Ο πατέρας ἔμαθε τὰ καμώματά σου. Πεθαίνοντας εἶπε τὰ στερνὰ λόγια τοῦ χωρισμοῦ. 'Η γιαγιά μου πνέει τὰ λοίσθια. Τὸν πυροβόλησε κι' ἔμεινε στὸν τόπο. Μετὰ ἀπὸ μία ὥρα πόνους ἔμεινε τέζα. Τὰ τέντωσε (τὰ τίναξε) πολὺ νέος. Τὸν εἶχα (I considered him) γιὰ τίμιο, ἀλλὰ γελάστηκα. Τὴν γέλασε καὶ δὲν τὴν παντρεύτηκε. 'Η καϋμένη (the poor thing) τό'φαγε τὸ δόλωμα. Τῆς τὴν κατάφερε. 'Η κοπέλα αὐτὴ εἶναι μὴ μοῦ ἅπτου. 'Η φιλενάδα μου βάζει κάτω τὴν δικιά σου στὴν ὀμορφιὰ (in beauty).

'Από σένα ἐξαρτᾶται νὰ γίνης πλούσιος. Σὲ σένα ἔγκειται νὰ γίνης καλά. Πρέπει νὰ κάνης ἀστεῖα, ἀνάλογα μὲ τὲς περιστάσεις. Ὅ,τι ξοδεύω γιὰ σένα, χαλάλι σου. Τῆς ἀξίζει κάθε ἔπαινος. 'Αξίζει τὸν κόπο νὰ δῆς τὸ μουσεῖο τῆς Κῶ. Ἡ γυναίκα αὐτὴ ψοφᾶ γιὰ μεγαλεῖα (glory). Μοῦ μίλησε γιὰ σένα διὰ μακρῶν. Ἔμαθα τὰ καθ' ἕκαστα. Πές μου λέξη πρὸς λέξη τί σοῦ εἶπε. Τὸ τσιγάρο ἔχει νὰ κάνη μὲ τὴν ὑγεία. Εἴτε ἔρθεις εἴτε δὲν ἔρθεις τὸ ἴδιο μοῦ κάνει. Τὸν φέραμε στὸ νοσοκομεῖο μετὰ βίας Εἴδαμε καὶ πάθαμε νὰ βροῦμε τὸ σπίτι σου. Μοῦ 'φερε τὸν κατακλυσμὸ νὰ μοῦ δώση τὸ κλειδί. Κουτσὰ στραβὰ τὰ κατάφερε. Ὁ μπόσης μου εἶναι ζόρικος. Ὥς ὅτου πάρω τὸ δίπλωμα μοῦ βγῆκε ἡ πίστη ἀνάποδη. Ὁ καπετάνιος τὰ βρῆκε σκοῦρα. Τὶς μέρες αὐτὲς ἔχω σφίξεις. Σοῦ χρωστῶ 100 δολλάρια. Καλά, βρὲ ἀδελφέ, δὲν χάλασε ὁ κόσμος. Ἡ γραμματεύς μου σήμερα μοῦ'βγαλε τὴν ψυχή. Ὅταν μὲ εἶδε ἔγινε καπνός. Καημένε καὶ σύ, μὴ μὲ πειράζεις τώρα. Θὰ πᾶς στὸ Βιετνὰμ γιὰ διακοπές; Σὲ καλό σου! 'Αστειεύεσαι! Μόλις ἄκουσα τὸν θάνατο τοῦ βασιλῆᾶ ἔμεινα κόκκαλο. Στολίστηκε νὰ πάη στὸ χορὸ κι' ἔμεινε στὰ κρύα τοῦ λουτροῦ. Χορέψαμε ὅλη τὴ νύχτα μὰ μετὰ στὸ σπίτι μᾶς βγῆκε ξινό... Ὁ πατέρας μου τὸ τσούζει κάθε βράδυ. Κάθε βδομάδα τὰ κοπανάω. Ὁ φίλος μου εἶναι κουδούνι. Αὐτοὶ εἶναι τάβλα στὸ μεθύσι. Αὐτὴ ἡ γυναίκα μὲ τρέλλανε. Τόσο ἄσωτος εἶναι ποὺ δὲν τοῦ ἔμεινε οὔτε κουκούτσι.

EAT

Τρώγω τὸν περίδρομο.*
Trógho ton perídromo.
I eat excessively.

Τὴν κάνω ταράτσα.*
Tin káno tarátsa.
I eat excessively.

EFFORT

Ἔφαγα τὰ σίδερα.
Éfagha ta sídera.
I made a superhuman effort.

Πῆγε χαμένο (στὰ χαμένα).
Píye chaméno (sta chaména)
It was a wasted effort.

Μὲ τὰ ψέματα.
Mé ta psémata.
With very small outlay (but to good effect).

ELECT

Τὸν ἔβγαλαν βουλευτή.*
Ton évghalan voulefti.
They elected (made) him deputy.

Βγαίνω δήμαρχος.*
Vyéno dímarchos.
I was elected mayor.

ELSE

Ὅλα κι' ὅλα.
Ola kióla.
Anything else (but not that).

EMBARRASS

Μὴ μ' ἐκθέτεις (μὴ μ' ἐξευτελίζεις, μὴ μ' ἐντροπιάζεις).*
Mí mekθétees (mi mexeftelízees, mí mendropyázees).
Don't embarrass me.

Τὰ χάνω (τὰ μπέρδεψα, τὰ'καμα θάλασσα).*
Ta cháno (ta bérδepsa, tákama θálassa).
I become confused, embarrassed.

Γίνομαι θέατρο.
Yínome θéatro.
I become a laughing-stock.

Τὸν κάνω κουρέλι (ρεζίλι).*
Ton káno kouréli (rezíli).
I embarrass him completely; I heavily offend him.

ENJOY

Γουστάρω νὰ (+ indefinite).
Ghoustáro na.
I enjoy; I like.

Μοῦ γουστάρει νὰ (+ indefinite).
Mou ghoustáree na.
I enjoy; I like.

Πώ, πώ, νὰ σὲ χαρῶ!
Pó, pó, na se charó!
I enjoy you so much!

Κάνω κέφι.*
Káno kéfi.
I make merry.

Κάνω τὸ κέφι μου.*
Káno to kéfi mou.
I do what pleases me.

Τοῦ κουτρούλη ὁ γάμος.
Tou koutroùli o ghámos.
In cases of great confusion and entertainment.

Τὸ κάνω χάζι.
To káno cházi.
It amuses me.

ENOUGH

Ὡς ἐδῶ καὶ μὴ παρακεῖ.
Os eδó ke mí parakeé.
That is enough.

Ὡς αὐτὸ τὸ σημεῖο.*
Os aftó to simeéo.
To this point (degree).

Μ' ἔφερε μέχρι (ἕως) τὴ μύτη.
Méfere méchri (éos) ti míti.
I could take no more.

Δὲν βγαίνει τὸ ὕφασμα.*
δén vyénee to eéphazma.
The material is not enough.

Μ' ἔφερε στὸ ἀπροχώρητο.*
Méfere sto aprochórito.
I could not take any more from him.

ENTERTAINMENT

Εἶναι περιβόλι (διασκεδαστικός).
Eéne perivóli (δiaskeδastikós).
He (she) is an entertaining person.

EQUALLY

Ἐξ ἴσου.*
Ex ísou.
Equally.

ESPECIALLY

Πρὸ παντὸς (πρὸ πάντων).
Pro pandós (propándon).
Above all, especially.

EVEN

Εἴμαστε πάτσι (τὰ πατσίσαμε).*
Eémaste pátsi (ta patsísame).
We are even.

Πατσίζω.
Patsizo.
I am even (with him, her).

EVENTS

Τὰ ἐπίκαιρα.*
Ta epíkera.
Current events.

EVERYTHING

Κάθε τί.*
Káϑe tí.
Everything.

Τὸ κάθε τί μὲ πειράζει.
To káϑeti me peerázee.
Everything bothers me.

EXACTLY

Ἀκριβῶς!*
Akrivós!
Exactly! (I agree.)

Ἴσα - ἴσα.
Isa - ísa.
Exactly; precisely; on the contrary; actually.

Αὐτὸ ἀκριβῶς.
Aftó akrivós.
That is exactly what I mean.

Ἀκριβῶς ἐδῶ.
Akrivós eδó.
Right here.

EXAMINE

Ρίχνω μιὰ ματιὰ (σέ).*
Ríchno miá matyá (se).
I look around, look over, examine.

EXAMPLE

Λόγου χάρι(ν) (παραδείγματος χάριν)*
Lóghou chárin (paraδeéghmatos chárin).
For example.

Ὁ λόγος τὸ λέει.
O lóghos to léee.
In a manner of speaking.

Ποὺ λέει ὁ λόγος.
Pou léee o lóghos.
So to speak, for instance.

Φέρ' εἰπεῖν.*
Fereepeén.
For example.

EXCELLENT

Στὴν τρίχα.*
Stin trícha.
In excellent condition.

Ντύθηκε στὴν τρίχα.
Ndeéϑike stin trícha.
He (she) was dressed perfectly.

EXCEPTION

Κατ' ἐξαίρεσιν.*
Katexéresin.
By way of exception.

Κατ' ἐξοχήν.*
Katexochín.
Preeminently.

EXPECT

Ὡς ἦτο ἐπόμενον (ὡς ἀνεμένετο).*
Os eéto epómenon (ós aneméneto).
As was to be expected.

EXPENSE

Κόβω τὰ ἔξοδα.*
Kóvo ta éxoδa.
I reduce expenses.

Εἰς βάρος του (ἐναντίον του).*
Ees város tou (enandíon tou).
Against him; at his expense.

Εἶπε πολλὰ λόγια εἰς βάρος του.*
Eépe pollá lóya ees város tou.
He said many things against him.

Μίλησε πολὺ ἄσχημα ἐναντίον του.*
Mílise polí áschima enandíon tou.
He spoke very badly about him.

EXTRA

Ἐπὶ πλέον.*
Epi pléon.
Extra, in addition.

EXTREME

Στὸ ἔπακρο.*
Sto épakro.
In the highest degree.

Ἔφτασε ὁ κόμπος στὸ χτένι.
Éftase o kómbos sto chténi.
Things are coming to a head.

Δὲν κολλάει!
δen golláee!
That is a likely tale!

Τὸ παρατράβηξες τὸ σχοινί.*
To paratrávixes to scheení.
You overdid it.

Φτάνω στ' ἄκρα.*
Ftáno stákra.
I go to extremes.

Τὸ ἄλλο ἄκρο.*
To állo ákro.
The other extreme.

EXERCISES

Ἡ ὑπηρέτριά μας τρώγει τὸν περίδρομο. Ἀπόψε τὴν κάναμε ταράτσα. Ἔφαγα τὰ σίδερα νὰ σὲ βρῶ. Ὅλα τὰ λεφτὰ πῆγαν χαμένα ἀφοῦ κάηκε τὸ μαγαζί. Μὲ τὰ ψέματα ἔκαμε χρήματα. Ἡ κόρη μου εἶναι νευρικιά, ἀλλὰ δὲν εἶναι ἄτιμη (πρόστυχη). Ὅλα κι' ὅλα. Ὅταν ἡ οἰκογένεια δὲν εἶναι ἀγαπημένη, γίνεται θέατρο. Τὸν ἔκαμα κουρέλι. Ὅταν τὴν εἶδα τά'χασα. Ποιὸς βγῆκε δήμαρχος; Ποιὸν ἔβγαλαν βουλευτή; Τὸν χώρησε γιατὶ τὴν ἔφερε μέχρι τὴ μύτη. Δὲν βγαίνει τὸ ὕφασμα γιὰ σακκάκι καὶ παντελόνι. Γουστάρω νὰ φάω γιαούρτι. Μοῦ γουστάρει νὰ κάνω κολύμπι τὰ βράδυα. Χτὲς βράδυ ἔκαμα κέφι στὸ χορό. Τὶς βιτρίνες τὶς κάνω χάζι. Χθὲς βράδυ ἦταν τοῦ κουτρούλη ὁ γάμος. Αὐτὸ τὸ κορίτσι εἶναι περιβόλι. Οἱ γονεῖς ἀγαποῦν τὰ παιδιά τους ἐξ ἴσου. Ἀγαπῶ ὅλα τὰ φροῦτα, πρὸ πάντων τὰ πορτοκάλια. Πάρε 20 δολλάρια καὶ εἴμαστε πάτσι. Δὲν μπορῶ νὰ φάω τίποτε. Κάθε τί μὲ πειράζει. Πάω στὴ δουλειά μου ἀκριβῶς στὴν ὥρα. Ἦρθε πάνω στὴν ὥρα. Αὐτὸ ἀκριβῶς λέω κι' ἐγώ. Τὸ κάρο μου εἶναι στὴν τρίχα. Ἔρριξα μιὰ ματιὰ στὴν ἐφημερίδα, ἀλλὰ δὲν βρῆκα ἐκεῖνο ποὺ ἤθελα. Ἡ Ἑλλάδα ἐξάγει πολλὰ πράγματα, λόγου χάρη κρασί, ντομάτα, κλπ. Χρειάζομαι πολλὰ ἀπαραίτητα γιὰ τὴ δουλειά μου, φερ' εἰπεῖν αὐτοκίνητο, γυαλιά, μικρὴ βαλίτσα, κλπ. Ἔγινα δεκτὸς (I was accepted) κατ' ἐξαίρεσιν εἰς τὸ γραφεῖον τοῦ πρωθυπουργοῦ. Τὸ καράβι ἦρθε ἀργά, ὡς ἦτο ἑπόμενον. Ἀπὸ τὸν ἄλλο μῆνα πρέπει νὰ κόψω τὰ ἔξοδα γιατὶ δὲν ἔχω δουλειά. Δὲν θέλω νὰ ζῶ εἰς βάρος τῶν γονέων μου. Κάθε βδομάδα ξοδεύω πολλὰ γιὰ τὴ γυναίκα μου καὶ τὰ παιδιά μου. Ἐπὶ πλέον, συντηρῶ καὶ τοὺς γονεῖς μου. Ἐγὼ εἶμαι μετριοπαθής. Ὁ ἀδελφός μου (εἶναι) τὸ ἄλλο ἄκρο. Τὰ μοτοσακὸ στὴν Ἑλλάδα τὸ παρατράβηξαν τὸ σχοινί. Οἱ συχνὲς ἀπεργίες φτάνουν στ' ἄκρα. Αὐτὸς εἶναι σφιχτὸς στὸ ἔπακρο. Μὲ τὴν δυσανάλογη σήμερα αὔξηση ὅλων τῶν τιμῶν ἔφτασε ὁ κόμπος στὸ χτένι.

FAIL

Ἔπεσες ἔξω στὸν ὑπολογισμό (σου).*
Épeses éxo ston eepoloyizmó (sou).
You failed in your estimation.

Πέφτω ἔξω.*
Péfto éxo.
I fail; I'm not successful (in business).

Λάσπη ἡ δουλειά μας.*
Láspi i δouliá mas.
Our efforts have failed.

FALL

Μὲ παίρνει ὁ ὕπνος.*
Me pérnee o eépnos.
I fall asleep.

Φαρδιὰ - πλατιά.
Farδyá - platyá.
Sprawled out.

Ἔπεσα φαρδιὰ - πλατιά.
Épesa farδyá - platyá.
I fell sprawled out.

FALSE

Κροκοδείλια δάκρυα.*
Krokoδeélia δákreea.
False tears.

FAMOUS

Βγάζω ὄνομα.*
Vgházo ónoma.
I become famous (in good or bad sense).

Ἀφήνω ἐποχή.*
Aphíno epochí.
I leave my mark; I cause a stir.

Βγαίνω στὸ κλαρί.
Vyéno sto klarí.
I become known.

Ἀκούομαι.
Akoùome.
I am well known.

FASHION

Εἶναι τῆς μόδας.*
Eéne tis móδas.
It is in fashion.

FEAR

Φοβητσιάρη!*
Fovitsiári!
Coward!

Μοῦ 'κοψες τὸ αἷμα (μοῦ 'σπασες τὴν καρδιά μου).*
Moùkopses to éma (moùspases tin garδyá mou).
You frightened me to death.

FEEL

Αἰσθάνομαι μοναξιά.*
Esϑánome monaxyá.
I feel lonesome.

Αἰσθάνομαι καλλίτερα.*
Esϑánome kallítera.
I feel better.

Αἰσθάνομαι ἱκανὸς νά...*
Esϑánome ikanós ná...
I feel capable of...

Αἰσθάνομαι καλά.*
Esϑánome kalá.
I feel fit; I feel well.

Θίγω τὸν ἐγωϊσμό.*
ϑígho ton eghoeezmó.
I hurt someone's feelings.

Ἐσεῖς, τί λέτε;
Eseés tí léte?
How do you feel (about this)?

Νοιώθω μοναξιά.*
Neeótho monaxiá.
I feel lonesome.

Ἀκούω ἕνα πόνο.
Akoùo éna póno.
I feel a pain.

Μοῦ ἔρχεται νὰ (+ indefinite).
Mou érchete ná.
I feel a desire to.

Δὲν εἶναι στὰ καλά του.
ðén eéne sta kalá tou.
He is not in good mood (health, right mind).

Μοῦ κόβει τὰ χέρια.
Mou kóvee ta chérya.
I feel the loss of it.

Μοῦ κόπηκαν τὰ γόνατα.
Mou kópikan ta ghónata.
I felt stunned; upset.

FEW

Τρεῖς κι' ὁ κοῦκος
Treés kiokoùkos.
Very few (ironically).

Οὔτε κουκούτσι.
Oùte koukoùtsi.
Nothing at all.

FIGHT

Εἶναι ἕτοιμος γιὰ τσάκωμα (εἶναι καβγατζῆς).
Eéne éteemos ya tsákoma (eéne kavghatzís).
He is always ready for a fight.

Ἁρπάχτηκαν.
Arpáchtikan.
They started fighting.

Γίνηκαν μαλλιὰ κουβάρια.
Yínikan maliá kouvárya.
They quarreled wildly.

Ἦρθαν στὰ μαχαίρια.
Irθan sta machérya.
They started fighting.

Τὸν τρώγει ἡ μύτη του (ἡ ράχη του).
Ton tróyee i míti tou (i ráchi tou).
He is asking for trouble.

Πιάστηκαν (στὰ χέρια).
Pyástikan (sta chérya).
They came to blows.

Γιὰ ψύλλου πήδημα.
Ya psíllou píðima.
At the least provocation; for the merest trifle.

Compare QUARREL.

FINALLY

Ἐπὶ τέλους!*
Epi télous!
At last, after all!

Στὸ κάτω κάτω (τὸ κάτω κάτω τῆς γραφῆς).
Sto káto káto (to káto káto tis ghraphís).
At worst; in the last analysis.

Αὐτὸ μόνο ἔμενε.
Aftó móno émene.
That is the last straw.

Τέλος πάντων (ἐν τέλει, τελικά).*
Télos pándon (en délee, teliká).
After all, finally.

FIRST

Στὴν ἀρχὴ (ἀρχικά, κατ' ἀρχήν).*
Stin archí (archiká, katarchín).
At first, originally, in the beginning; earlier.

FIT

Κάθεται.
Káthete.
It sits well; it fits (e.g., of a coat).

Σοῦ πάει τὸ καπέλο.*
Sou páee to kapélo.
The hat becomes you.

Δὲν ταιριάζει.*
δen deryázee.
It is out of place; it is not suitable.

Δὲ μοῦ πάει (πηγαίνει) τὸ φόρεμα.*
δé mou páee (piyénee) to fórema.
The dress is not becoming to me.

Σᾶς ἔρχεται (πηγαίνει) καλά.*
Sas érchete (piyénee) kalá.
It suits you.

FIX

Θὰ τὸν διορθώσω (κανονίσω).
Θá ton δiorϑóso (kanoníso).
I will fix him.

Ἔνοια σου, θὰ σὲ φκιάξω.
Éneea sou, ϑa se fkiáxo.
You'll see, I will fix you.

Τοῦ κόψανε ἕνα μισθό.
Tou kópsane éna misϑó.
They gave him a fixed salary.

FLEXIBLE

Εἶναι ἐλαστικὸς χαρακτήρας.*
Eéne elastikós charactíras.
He is flexible.

Compare CHARACTER.

FOLLOW

Παίρνω ἀπὸ πίσω.*
Pérno apo píso.
I follow closely.

Τὴν πῆρε ἀπὸ πίσω.
Tin píre apo píso.
He followed her closely.

FOOD

Μπῆκε ὁ καλόγερος στὸ φαΐ.
Bíke o kalógheros sto faeé.
The food is burned.

Τῆς ὥρας.*
Tis óras.
Fresh, (cooked) to order.

FOOL

Θέλει νὰ μᾶς ρίξη στάχτη στὰ μάτια (ξεγελάσει).
Θélee na mas ríxi stáchti sta mátya (xeyelásee).
He (she) tries to fool us.

Ἀρλοῦμπες.
Arloùmbes.
Foolish talk, boasting.

Μὴ μᾶςλὲς ἀρλοῦμπες.
Mí mas les arloùmbes.
Don't tell us nonsense.

Σὲ περνῶ γιὰ χαζό.
Se pernó ya chazó.
I take you for a fool.

Βλάκας καὶ μισός.
Blákas ke misós.
A perfect fool.

Τί μὲ πέρασες, γιὰ χαζό;
Tí me pérases, ya chazó?
Do you take me for a fool?

Δὲν τρώ(γ)ει ἄχυρα.
δen tró(y)ee ácheera.
He (she) is no fool.

Παίρνω στὸ μεζὲ (στὸ ψηλό).*
Pérno sto mezé (sto psiló).
I make a fool of (someone).

FORBID

Ὃ μὴ γένοιτο!*
O mi yéneeto!
God forbid!

Θεὸς φυλάξει.!*
Θeós feeláxee!
May God save (you); God forbid!

FORCE

Διὰ τῆς βίας* (μὲ τὴ βία, μὲ τὸ στανιό).*
δia tis vías (me ti vía, me to stanió).
By force.

Μὲ τὸ ζόρι (θέλεις δὲ θέλεις).*
Me to zóri (θélees δe θélees).
By force.

Ἐξ ἀνάγκης (κατ' ἀνάγκην, ἀπὸ ἀνάγκη).*
Ex anángis (katanángin, apo anági).
Of necessity.

Ἆρον ἆρον.*
Àron áron.
By force.

Μὲ τὸ ἔτσι θέλω.
Me to étsi θélo.
By force.

Ὁ νόμος αὐτὸς εἶναι ἐν ἰσχύϊ.*
O nómos aftós eéne en ischeéi.
This law is in effect.

Ἐν ἰσχύϊ.*
En ischeéi.
In force, valid.

Σώνει (ναὶ) καὶ καλά.*
Sónee (né) ke kalá.
By force.

FORESEE

Δὲν μύρισα τὰ δάχτυλά μου.
δen meérisa ta δáchteelá mou.
I could not foresee.

FORGET

Μοῦ διαφεύγει (λησμονῶ, ξεχνῶ).*
Mou δiafévyee (lizmonó, xechnó).
It escapes me. (I forget.)

FRANKLY

Νέτα σκέτα (ντόμπρα).*
Néta skéta (ndómbra).
Plainly, frankly.

FREE

Τὸ δίνουν ἔτσι (χάρισμα).
To δínoun étsi (chárizma).
It is given away free.

FRESH

Θέλω νὰ φάω κάτι τῆς ὥρας.
Θélo na fáo káti tis óras.
I want to eat something cooked to order.

FRIEND

Κάνω τὸν (τὴν) (+ name) φίλο (φίλη).
Káno ton (tin) fílo (fíli).
I have made ... a friend of mine.

Ἐπιστήθιος φίλος.*
Epistíθios fílos.
Bosom friend.

FUN

Γιὰ γοῦστο (γιὰ πλάκα).*
Ya ghoùsto (ya pláka).
For fun.

Ἔχει γοῦστο νά...
Échee ghoùsto ná...
It would be a nice thing if (ironic)...

Ἔχει πλάκα.*
Échee pláka.
It makes you laugh.

Δὲν ἔχει γοῦστο.
δen échee ghoùsto.
There is no fun in that.

Σπάσαμε πλάκα.
Spásame pláka.
We had fun (at someone's expense).

FUNNY

Ἔχει πλάκα.*
Échee pláka.
He (she) is funny. He (she) is a comic.

FURIOUS

Ἔγινε βαπόρι.*
Éyine vapóri.
He (she) became furious.

FUTURE

Τοῦ λοιποῦ (ἀπὸ τώρα καὶ στὸ ἑξῆς).*
Tou leepoù (apo tóra ke sto exís).
In the future.

Τοῦ (τῆς) μέλλει νά...
Toù (tis) méllee ná...
He (she) is destined to...

EXERCISES

Γιατὶ ἔκλεισες τὸ μαγαζί σου; Ἔπεσες ἔξω; Ναί, λάσπη ἡ δουλειά μου. Ὅταν μιλᾶ ὁ συνέταιρός μου μὲ παίρνει ὁ ὕπνος. Δὲν τὸν παίρνει ὁ ὕπνος εὔκολα. Χθὲς ἕνα αὐτοκίνητο μ' ἐχτύπησε κι' ἔπεσα φαρδιὰ - πλατιὰ στὴ μέση τοῦ δρόμου. Ἡ γυναίκα αὐτὴ ὅταν κλαίει χύνει κροκοδείλια δάκρυα. Ὁ γείτονάς μου ἔβγαλε ὄνομα ἀπὸ γυναῖκες. Ὁ πρόεδρος Κέννεντυ ἄφησε ἐποχή. Ἀκόμη δὲν τελείωσε τὸ γυμνάσιο καὶ βγῆκε στὸ κλαρὶ (iron.). Τὸ σοῦπερ μίνι σήμερα εἶναι τῆς μόδας. Αὐτὸς εἶναι φοβιτσιάρης σὰν τὸν λαγό. Μπῆκες τόσο ξαφνικὰ ποὺ μοῦ 'κοψες τὸ αἷμα. Ἕνας πυροβολισμὸς χθὲς βράδυ μοῦ 'σπασε τὴν καρδιά μου. Κάποτε - κάποτε (once in a while) αἰσθάνομαι μοναξιά. Δὲν αἰσθάνομαι καλά. Σήμερα, αἰσθάνομαι καλλίτερα. Πῶς αἰσθάνεσαι; Μοῦ θίγεις τὸν ἐγωϊσμό μου. Εἶμαι παχειά. Ἐσεῖς τί λέτε; Ὅταν λείπεις νοιώθω μοναξιά. Ἐδῶ, γιατρέ, ἀκούω ἕνα πόνο. Μὲ αὐτὴ τὴ ζέστη μοῦ ἔρχεται νὰ βγάλω ὅλα τὰ ροῦχα μου. Ὁ σερβιτόρος αὐτὸς δὲν εἶναι στὰ καλά του. Δίπλα στὸ δικό μου ἄνοιξε ἄλλο ἑστιατόριο. Μοῦ κόβει τὰ χέρια. Μόλις ἄκουσα πὼς πέθανε ὁ πατέρας σου μοῦ κόπηκαν τὰ γόνατα. Πῶς θὰ πᾶς στὸ χορὸ μὲ τέτοια χάλια! Ἂν φύγετε καὶ σεῖς θὰ μείνουμε τρεῖς κι' ὁ κοῦκος. Αὐτὸς ὁ ἀστυφύλακας εἶναι ἕτοιμος γιὰ τσάκωμα. Ἁρπάχτηκαν στὰ γερὰ (they started a serious fight). Ἔγιναν μαλλιὰ κουβάρια. Μετὰ ἀπὸ τρία - τέσσερα πιοτὰ ἦρθαν στὰ μαχαίρια. Αὐτὸς φαίνεται πὼς τὸν τρώει ἡ μύτη του. Πιάστηκαν στὰ χέρια γιὰ ψύλλου πήδημα. Ἐπὶ τέλους, ἦρθε τὸ ἀεροπλάνο. Ἔχω πολλὴ δουλειὰ καὶ δὲν μπορῶ νὰ σὲ συνοδεύσω. Στὸ κάτω κάτω δὲν θέλω νὰ σὲ συνοδεύσω. Χθὲς μοῦ χάλασε τὸ αὐτοκίνητο (my car broke down). Σήμερα παρὰ τρίχα νὰ πάρη φωτιὰ τὸ διαμέρισμά μου. Αὐτὸ μόνο ἔμενε. Θὰ ρθῆς μαζί μου ἀπόψε, τέλος πάντων! Ἐν τέλει, τὸ ἀποφάσισες; Στὴν ἀρχὴ ἤσουν πολὺ εὐγενὴς καὶ σοβαρός, μὰ τώρα μοῦ κόλλησες σὰν βδέλλα. Τὸ καπέλλο μου δὲν κάθεται ἐκεῖ. Τί ὡραία ποὺ σοῦ πάει τὸ καπέλλο! Δὲν ταιριάζουν τ' ἀστεῖα τὴν στιγμὴν αὐτήν. Τὸ φόρεμα σοῦ πάει θαυμάσια. Τὸ παλτὸ σᾶς ἔρχεται καλά. Μὴν ἀνησυχῆς (don't worry) θὰ τὸν διορθώσω. Εἶσαι ψεύτης, θὰ σὲ φκιάξω. Ὁ μπόσης μοῦ'κοψε καλὸ μισθό. Θέλω ψάρι τῆς ὥρας. Ἡ ἐφημερίδα αὐτὴ προσπαθεῖ νὰ μᾶς ρίξη στάχτη στὰ μάτια. Τώρα, μοῦ λὲς ἀρλοῦμπες. Μὲ περνᾶ γιὰ χαζό. Μὴ μὲ περνᾶς γιὰ χαζή. Εἶσαι βλάκας καὶ μισός. Τὸν πῆραν στὸ μεζέ. Ἡ ἐξαδέλφη μου δὲν τρώει ἄχυρα. Πρόσεχε μὲ τὸ αὐτοκίνητο, νὰ μὴν κάμης δυστύχημα. Θεὸς φυλάξει. Μ' ἔφεραν ἐδῶ διὰ τῆς βίας. Ἐργάζομαι μέρα - νύχτα ἀπὸ ἀνάγκη. Παντρειὰ μὲ τὸ ζόρι δὲ γίνεται. Θέλεις δὲ θέλεις θὰ τὸ φᾶς. Σώνει καὶ καλὰ ἤθελε νὰ μὲ πάρη μαζί του. Μ' ἔβγαλε ἀπὸ τὸ σπίτι μου μὲ τὸ ἔτσι θέλω. Τί καιρὸ θὰ κάνει αὔριο; Δὲν μύρισα τὰ δάχτυλά μου. Μοῦ διαφεύγει τὸ ὄνομά σου. Μπράβο, δὲν σοῦ διαφεύγει τίποτα. Τί ὡραῖες γραβάτες. Τὶς δίνουν ἔτσι. Αὐτὸς τὰ λέει νέτα σκέτα. Ξέρεις, ἐγὼ μιλῶ ντόμπρα. Μόλις τὴν εἶδε, τὴν πῆρε ἀπὸ πίσω. Θέλω νὰ φάω κάτι τῆς ὥρας. Τὸ γλέντι αὐτὸ δὲν ἔχει γοῦστο. Τὴν ὥρα ποὺ θὰ σὲ φιλῶ, ἔχει γοῦστο νὰ παρουσιασθῆ ὁ ἀρραβωνιαστικός σου. Προχθὲς σπάσαμε πλάκα μὲ τ' ἀδέλφια σου. Αὐτὸς ὁ σερβιτόρος ἔχει πλάκα. Σ' ἀρέσει τὸ φίλμ; Αὐτὴ ἡ γριὰ ἔχει πλάκα. Μοῦ κάνει τὸν φίλο, ἀλλὰ στὴν πράγματικότητα (in reality) δὲν εἶναι. Ὁ καπετάνιος τοῦ πλοίου εἶναι ἐπιστήθιος φίλος μου. Ὅταν τοῦ εἶπα πὼς σὲ εἶδα μὲ ἄλλον, ἔγινε βαπόρι. Δὲν θὰ σ' ἐνοχλῶ τοῦ λοιποῦ. Ἀπὸ τώρα καὶ στὸ ἑξῆς θὰ εἴμαστε καλοὶ φίλοι. Τῆς μέλλει ν' ἀποθάνη ἀπὸ καρκῖνο.

GENEROUS

Εἶναι ἀνοιχτοχέρης (γαλαντόμος, γενναιόδωρος).*
Eéne aneechtochéris (galandómos, yenneóδoros).
He is generous (especially money).

GENTLEMAN

Εἶναι καθὼς πρέπει.*
Eéne kaθós prépee.
He (she) is modest, refined, proper.

Αὐτὸς εἶναι καθὼς πρέπει κύριος.
Aftós eéne kaθós prépee keérios.
This gentleman is respectable.

GET

Κάτι παίρνω μπρέφα.*
Káti pérno bréfa.
I learn of something.

Χάσου!*
Chásou!
Get lost!

Σηκώνομαι.*
Sikónome.
I get up.

Βρὲς κάποιον.
Vrés kápeeon.
Get someone.

Φτηνὰ τὴ γλύτωσε.
Ftiná ti ghleeétose.
He got off cheaply.

Τοῦ δίνω στὰ νεῦρα.
Tou δino sta névra.
I get on his nerves.

Γίνομαι λούτσα.
Yínome loùtsa.
I get drenched.

Βολεύομαι.
Volévome.
I get along.

Ἀποκά(μ)νω.*
Apoká(m)no.
I get tired; I finish off.

Βγῆκε λάδι.
Vyíke láδi.
He got off scot-free.

Τὰ βολεύω.
Ta volévo.
I get along; I make do.

Παίρνω τὴν κάτω βόλτα.
Pérno tin káto vólta.
I get worse.

Πιάνω κουβέντα.*
Pyáno kouvénda.
I get into a conversation.

Πιάνω τὰ ἔξοδά μου.*
Pyáno ta éxoδá mou.
I make (get) my expenses.

Μοῦ χτυπάει στὰ νεῦρα.*
Mou chteepáei sta névra.
It gets on my nerves.

GIFT

Γενναῖο δῶρο.*
Yennéo δóro.
Generous gift.

Δῶρον ἄδωρον.*
δóron áδoron.
Gift bringing more trouble than profit.

GO

Γιὰ ποῦ τό 'βαλες;
Ya poù tóvales?
Where are you headed?

"Αμε (στὸ καλό).*
Àme (sto kaló).
Go! (in good luck).

Τράβα στ' ἀνοιχτά.
Tráva staneechtá.
Go to the deep sea.

Μιὰ κι' ἔξω.*
Miá kiéxo.
In one go.

Πάει κορδόνι.
Páee korδóni.
It is going well.

"Αλλο πάλι!
Àllo páli!
There we go again!

Τὰ πᾶμε καλά.
Ta páme kalá.
We get along well.

Τί τρέχει (τί συμβαίνει, τί ἔγινε);*
Ti tréchee (ti seemvénee, ti éyine)?
What is going on?

GOOD

(Σοῦ) κάνει καλό.
(Sou) kánee kaló.
It is good for you.

Εἶναι ἀχαίρευτος.
Eéne achaeéreftos.
He is good-for-nothing.

Ἕνας κι' ἕνας.
Énas kiénas.
Especially good or bad.

GREETINGS

Τὰ δέοντα στὸν (στὴν) (+ name)... *
Ta δéonda ston (stin)...
My respects to...

Τὰ δέοντα στὴν κυρία σας.
Ta δéonδa stin keería sas.
My regards to your wife.

GROUND

Κατὰ γῆς.*
Kata yís.
To *or* on the ground.

GROW

Ρίχνω μπόϊ.
Ríchno bóee.
I grow taller.

"Εχει πρόωρη ἀνάπτυξη.*
Échee próori anápteexi.
He (she) is very tall for his (her) age.

GUILTY

Τὸν (τὴν) τρώει τὸ σκουλήκι.*
Ton (tin) tróee to skoulíki.
He (she) has a guilty conscience.

EXERCISES

Γιῶργο, σὲ βλέπω πολὺ βιαστικό. Γιὰ ποῦ τό'βαλες; Πάω γιὰ ψώνια, πρὶν κλείση ἡ ἀγορά. Ἄμε στὸ καλό. Καπετάνιο, τράβα στ' ἀνοιχτά, εἶναι γαλήνη ἡ θάλασσα. Ἡ ζωή μου πάει κορδόνι. Ὅλες οἱ συμβουλές μου πῆγαν περίπατο. Τί τρέχει, καὶ εἶναι τόσος κόσμος μαζεμένος; Ὁ νοικοκύρης μου εἶναι ἀνοιχτοχέρης. Αὐτὸς ὁ νέος εἶναι καθὼς πρέπει. Τὸ πῆραν μπρέφα πὼς εἶναι γυναικάς. Χάσου ἀπὸ μπροστά μου. Δὲν θέλω νὰ σὲ βλέπω. Τί ὥρα σηκώνεσαι κάθε πρωΐ; Μπορεῖς νὰ βρῆς κάποιον, σὲ παρακαλῶ, νὰ μὲ βοηθήση μὲ τὲς ἀποσκευές μου; Δὲν μπορῶ, ἀπόκαμα. Ἔκλεψε, σκότωσε καὶ στὸ δικαστήριο βγῆκε λάδι. Βολεύθηκες στὸ νέο σου διαμέρισμα; Φτηνὰ τὴ γλύτωσες στὸ χθεσινὸ δυστύχημα. Πῆγα καὶ τὸν εἶδα στὸ νοσοκομεῖο. Φαίνεται πὼς πῆρε τὴν κάτω βόλτα. Στὸ περσυνὸ ταξίδι μου κινδύνεψα νὰ πνιγῶ. Δὲν εἶχα ὀμπρέλλα μὲ τόση βροχὴ κι' ἔγινα λούτσα. Μὲ δυσκολία πιάνω τὰ ἔξοδά μου ἀπὸ τὴν ἔκδοση τῆς ἐφημερίδος. Ὁ κρότος αὐτὸς μοῦ χτυπάει στὰ νεῦρα. Μοῦ ἔφερε ἀπὸ τὴν Εὐρώπη ἕνα γενναῖο δῶρο. Τὸ δῶρο σου εἶναι δῶρον ἄδωρον. Τὸ οὐΐσκι κάνει καλὸ στὸ κρυλόγημα. Ὁ συγκάτοικός μου εἶναι ἀχαΐρευτος. Οἱ φίλοι σου εἶναι ἕνας κι' ἕνας. Τὰ δέοντα, παρακαλῶ, στὴν κυρία σας. Τὸ αὐτοκίνητο τὸν χτύπησε καὶ τὸν ἔρριξε κατὰ γῆς. Ἔρριξες μπόϊ σὲ τόσο λίγο διάστημα (time). Ἀφότου τὴν ξεγέλασε τὸν τρώει τὸ σκουλήκι.

HABIT

Κόψε αὐτὴ τὴ συνήθεια (αὐτὸ τὸ συνήθειο).*
Kópse aftí ti seeníθeea (aftó to seeníθeeo).
Give up this (bad) habit.

HANDLE

Τὸν κάνω καλά.*
Ton káno kalá.
I can handle him.

HAPPEN

Ἔγινε μέρα μεσημέρι.*
Éyine méra mesiméri.
It happened publicly.

Τὰ διατρέξαντα;*
Ta δiatréxanda?
What happened?

Τὰ διατρέχοντα;
Ta δiatréchonda?
What is going on?

Ἔλαχα (ἔτυχα) ἐκεῖ.
Élacha ekeé.
I happened to be there.

Ἔλαχε or ἔτυχε νὰ τὸν δῶ.*
Élache na ton δό.
I happened to see him.

HARDLY

Κουτσὰ στραβά.*
Koutsá stravá.
With great difficulty.

Μᾶς τἆπε κουτσὰ στραβά.
Mas tápe koutsá stravá.
He (she) said it to us with great difficulty.

Compare DIFFICULTY.

HATE

Δὲν τὸν χωνεύω.*
δen don chonévo.
I don't like him at all.

Βγάζω τὸ ἄχτι μου.
Vgázo to áchti mou.
I satisfy a longing desire (especially for vengeance).

Ἔχω στὸ μάτι.*
Écho sto máti.
I covet, desire.

Μὲ μάχεται (δὲν μὲ χωνεύει).*
Me máchete (δen me chonévee).
He (she) hates me.

Τὸν ἔχω ἄχτι.
Ton écho áchti.
I bear him a grudge.

Compare ATTACK.

HEAL

Ἔκλεισε ἡ πληγή μου.*
Ékleese i pliyí mou.
My wound has healed.

Μοῦ ἄνοιξες ἀγιάτρευτη πληγή.
Mou áneexes ayátrefti pliyí.
You have opened an incurable wound.

HEALTH

Κρατιέται καλά.
Kratyéte kalá.
He (she) looks well.

Περνᾶς καλά;
Pernás kalá?
Are you enjoying yourself?

Πῶς τὰ περνᾶς;
Pós ta pernás?
How are you getting along?

Εἶμαι μιὰ χαρά.
Eéme miá chará.
I am very fine.

Παίρνω ἀπάνω μου.
Pérno apáno mou.
I have recovered (in health).

Εἶμαι περδίκι.
Eéme perδíki.
I am quite well again.

Ἦρθα στὰ σύγκαλά μου (συνῆλθα).*
Irϑa sta seéngalá mou (seeníl϶a).
I returned to normal health.

HENCEFORTH

Ἀπὸ δῶ κι' ἐμπρὸς (ἀπὸ τώρα καὶ στὸ ἑξῆς).*
Apo δó kiembrós (apo tóra ke sto exís).
From now on; henceforth.

HERE - THERE

Ἐδῶ κι' ἐκεῖ.
Eδó kiekeé.
Here and there.

Νά τος (= Νὰ αὐτός).
Nátos (= Na aftós).
Here he is.

Νά τη.
Náti.
Here she is.

Νά τοι.
Nátoi.
Here they are.

HICCUP

Ἔχω λόξυγγα.
Écho lóxeenga.
I have the hiccups.

HINT

Κάνω νύξη.*
Káno neéxi.
I hint.

Ἀπ' ἔξω ἀπ' ἔξω.
Apéxo apéxo.
In a roundabout way.

HOPE

Παρ' ἐλπίδα (παρὰ πᾶσαν προσδοκίαν).*
Parelpíδa (para pásan prosδokían).
Contrary to expectation.

HOT

Κάνει ζέστη.*
Kánee zésti.
It is hot (weather).

Εἶναι κουφόβραση.*
Eéne koufóvrasi.
It is hot and humid.

HOUR

Τὸ ρολόϊ μου πάει μπροστὰ (πίσω).*
To rolóee mou páee brostá (piso).
My watch is fast (slow).

HOWEVER

Ἐν τούτοις (παρὰ ταῦτα, ἐν πάσῃ περιπτώσει).*
Endoùtees (paratáfta, en pási periptósee).
However, yet, in any case.

HUNGER

Ξελιγώθηκα.
Xelighóϑika.
I am very hungry.

HURRY

Βιάσου (τσακίσου).
Viásou (tsakísou).
Hurry up.

Μὴ βιάζεσαι.*
Mi viázese.
Take your time.
Don't hurry.

Κάνε γρήγορα.*
Káne ghríghora.
Hurry up.

Τό 'στριψε.
Tóstripse.
He (she) beat it (left in a hurry).

HURT

Θίγω τὸν ἐγωϊσμό.*
Θígho ton eghoeezmó.
I hurt his (her) feelings.

Μοῦ κακοφαίνεται.
Mou kakofénete.
It offends me.

Μοῦ καλοφαίνεται.
Mou kalofénete.
I am pleased.

Μὲ κόβουν τὰ παπούτσια.
Me kóvoun ta papoùtsia.
My shoes hurt.

HUSH

Τὰ κάνω πλακάκια.*
Ta káno plakákia.
I keep quiet.

EXERCISES

Δὲν μπορεῖ νὰ κόψῃ τὴ συνήθεια τοῦ καπνίσματος. Θὰ κόψω αὐτὸ τὸ συνήθειο, ἀλλὰ βοήθα με καὶ σύ. Ἡ γυναίκα μου τὸν κάνει καλά. Ἡ κλεψιὰ ἔγινε μέρα μεσημέρι. Ἔμαθες τὰ διατρέξαντα; Ὄχι, τί ἔγινε; Ὅταν ἔγινε τὸ ἔγκλημα ἔλαχα (ἔτυχα) ἐκεῖ. Ὁ φονηᾶς ἔλαχε (ἔτυχε) νὰ περάσῃ ἀπὸ μπρός μου. Αὐτὴ ἡ γυναίκα ἔχει μεγάλο στόμα Δὲν τὴν χωνεύω. Τὸν ἔχω στὸ μάτι. Μὲ μάχεται, γιατὶ εἶμαι πιὸ ἔξυπνος ἀπὸ ἐκεῖνον. Δὲν τὸν χωνεύω τὸν μπόση μου. Ἡ πληγὴ ποὺ μοῦ ἄνοιξες δὲν θὰ κλείση ποτέ. Ὁ παππούς σου κρατιέται καλά. Πῶς τὰ περνᾶς; Ὅπως πάντα. Πῶς εἶναι ἡ οἰκογένεια; Εἶναι μιὰ χαρά. Ὑπομονή, σιγὰ - σιγὰ τὰ παίρνεις ἀπάνω σου. Εἶναι περδίκι. Ἔπειτα ἀπὸ μισὴ ὥρα ἦρθε στὰ σύγκαλά του. Τώρα εἶναι μιὰ χαρά. Δὲν ἡσυχάζει, πηγαινοέρχεται ἐδῶ κι' ἐκεῖ. Νάτος πάλι. Ἀπὸ δῶ κι' ἐμπρὸς θὰ εἶσαι ὁ πιὸ καλός μου φίλος. Σοῦ ἔκαμε νύξη γιὰ μένα; Μοῦ μίλησε ἀπ' ἔξω ἀπ' ἔξω γιὰ τὸ ζήτημά σου. Πάει καλὰ τὸ ρολόϊ σου; Νομίζω, πάει μπροστὰ πέντε λεπτά. Παρ' ἐλπίδα, τὸ τραῖνο ἔφθασε στὴν ὥρα του. Σήμερα κάνει ζέστη (κουφόβραση). Ὅλη τὴν ἡμέρα δὲν ἔφαγα καθόλου. Ξελιγώθηκα ἀπὸ τὴν πεῖνα. Βιάσου, θὰ χάσωμε τὸ πλοῖο. Μὴ βιάζεσαι, ἔχομε ἀρκετὴ ὥρα. Τὸ πλοῖο φεύγει μετὰ ἀπὸ μισὴ ὥρα. Μὰ πρέπει νὰ τσιμπίσουμε (to eat) καὶ κάτι. Κάνε γρήγορα. Μόλις μπῆκα στὸ γραφεῖο της, τό'στριψε. Τσακίσου, Ἑλένη, δὲν προλαβαίνουμε τὸ ἀεροπλάνο. Εἶναι φτωχός, ἐν τούτοις εἶναι χουβαρδᾶς καὶ φιλότιμος. Τῆς ἔθιξε τὸν ἐγωϊσμὸ ἔτσι ποὺ τῆς μίλησε. Μοῦ κακοφάνηκε ἡ κουβέντα του. Μὲ κόβουν αὐτὰ τὰ παπούτσια. Αὐτὴ ἡ γυναίκα δὲν μ' ἀρέσει. Λέει ψέματα καὶ ὅλα τὰ κάνει πλακάκια.

IGNORE

Δὲν ἔχω ἰδέα.*
δen écho iδéa.
I haven't the slightest idea.

Κρυφὰ ἀπὸ (+ accusative).*
Kreefá apó.
Without the knowledge of.

Τὸ πῆρα ἀψήφιστα (ἀψήφισα).
To píra apsífista (apsífisa).
I treated it lightly; I ignored it.

IMAGINE

Εἶναι ἡ φαντασία σου.*
Eéne i fandasía sou.
You are imagining things.

Βάλε μὲ τὸ νοῦ σου.
Vále me to noù sou.
Just imagine.

Βάλε πώς.
Vále pós.
Suppose that.

Γιὰ φαντάσου!*
Ya fandásou!
Fancy that!

Τὄλεγες αὐτό;
Tóleyes aftó?
Would you have imagined it?

IMPRESS

Προκάλεσε αἴσθηση.*
Prokálese ésθisi.
It made an impression.

Δὲν μοῦ λέει τίποτα.
δen mou léee típota.
It does not impress me.

IMPRISON

Τὸν (τὴν) βάζω μέσα.*
Ton (tin) vázo mésa.
I imprison him (her).

INABILITY

Δὲ βαστοῦν τὰ κότσια μου.
δe vastoùn ta kótsia mou.
It is beyond my strength.

INCIDENTALLY

Ἐδῶ ποὺ τὰ λέμε.
Eδó poù ta léme.
Incidentally, by the way.

Ἐπὶ τῇ εὐκαιρίᾳ (παρεμπιπτόντως).*
Epi ti efkeria (parembiptóndos).
By the way.

INCREDIBLE

Εἶναι ἄνω ποταμῶν!*
Eéne áno potamón!
It is incredible!

Δὲν τὸ βάζει ὁ νοῦς.
δen do vázee o noùs.
It is inconceivable.

INDIFFERENCE

Καρφὶ δὲν μοῦ καίγεται.
Karfí δen mou kéyete.
I do not care at all.

Κομμάτια νὰ γίνῃ.*
Kommátya na yíni.
Never mind! I do not care.

Τί μὲ κόβει;
Tí me kóvee?
What do I care?

Πέρα βρέχει!
Péra vréchee!
I couldn't care less!

Τὸ ρίχνω ἔξω.*
To ríchno éxo.
I neglect my responsibilities.

INFERIOR

Τύφλα νἄχη αὐτὸ μπροστὰ στὸ δικό σου.
Teéfla náchee aftó brostá sto δikó sou.
This one is far inferior to yours.

INFORMATION

Γιὰ τυχὸν πληροφορίες.
Ya teechón pliroforíes.
For possible need of information.

Κατὰ κεῖ.
Kata keé.
In that direction.

Δὲν μοῦ λέτε (παρακαλῶ).*
δén mou léte (parakaló).
Phrase introducing inquiry.

Τί θὰ πῆ (ἐ)τοῦτο;*
Tí θa pí (e)toùto?
What does this mean?

INSIST

Σὰ σφῆκα τριγυρνάει.*
Sa sfíka triyirnáee.
He (she) goes around like a wasp (referring to someone pressuring another continuously).

Εἶναι ἰσχυρογνώμων (πεισματάρης).*
Eéne ischeeroghnómon(peezmatáris).
He (she) is stubborn.

INSULTS

Κέρατο (βερνικωμένο).*
Kérato (vernikoméno).
Cross-grained person.

Αὐτὸς εἶναι κόπανος.
Aftós eéne kópanos.
He is a blockhead.

Τὸ κρῖμα στὸ λαιμό σου.*
To kríma sto lemó sou.
Curse (you will pay dearly for it).

INTEND

Ἔχει καλὸ σκοπό.*
Échee kaló skopó.
He (she) means well.

Ὁ σκοπὸς εἶναι νά...
O skopós eéne na...
The important thing is to...

Τί διαθέσεις ἔχει;*
Ti δiaθésees échee?
What are his intentions?

Λέω νὰ ταξιδέψω.*
Léo na taxiδépso.
I have traveling in mind.

Δὲν λέει νὰ σταματήση ἡ βροχή.
δen léee na stamatísi i vrochí.
The rain shows no sign of stopping.

INTERFERE

Κάτσε στ' αὐγά σου (πρόσεξε, μὴ βρῆς ἐσὺ τὸν μπελᾶ σου).*
Kátse stavghá sou (prósexe, mi vris eseè ton mbelá sou).
Don't be involved.

Εἶναι ἄνθρωπος ποὺ ἀνακατώνεται παντοῦ.*
Eéne ánϑropos pou anakatónete pandoù.
He is the type of man who always likes to interfere in everything.

Χώνω τὴ μύτη μου.*
Chóno ti meéti mou.
I pry into; I interfere.

INTERMEDIATOR

Κάνω τὸ διαμέσον.*
Káno to δiaméson.
I act as a go-between; an intermediator.

INVITE

Κάνω τραπέζι.*
Káno trapézi.
I invite (for dinner, lunch).

Αὔριο θὰ κάνω τραπέζι τοῦ φίλου μου.
Àvrio ϑa káno trapézi tou fílou mou.
Tomorrow I will invite my friend for dinner.

IRRITATE

Τὸν κουρδίζω.*
Ton kourδízo.
I irritate him.

Τοῦ (τῆς) βάζω φιτίλια (φιτιλιές).*
Tou (tiz) vázo fitília (fitiliés).
I irritate him (her); I inflame him (her).

EXERCISES

Πότε φεύγει τὸ λεωφορεῖο; Δὲν ἔχω ἰδέα. Αὐτὸς ζεῖ κρυφὰ ἀπὸ τὸν Θεό. Τὸν ἀψήφισα τὸν κίνδυνο καὶ πέρασα τὸ κόκκινο φῶς. Ἀκούω φωνές. Εἶναι ἡ φαντασία σου. Βάλε μὲ τὸ νοῦ σου πὼς αὐτὴ ἦταν μόνον 9 χρονῶν. Δὲν τὸ πιστεύω πὼς ἔμεινε ἔγκυος. Γιὰ φαντάσου! Τὄλεγες πὼς αὐτὸς ὁ ἀλήτης ἦταν γυιὸς βουλευτῆ; Ἡ διάλεξη τοῦ καθηγητῆ προκάλεσε αἴσθηση. Τὸ φὶλμ αὐτὸ δὲν μοῦ λέει τίποτα. Τὸν ἔβαλαν μέσα γιατὶ σκότωσε. Αὐτὸς στὰ νειᾶτα του ἔτρωγε σίδερα. Μὰ τώρα ποὺ γέρασε δὲ βαστοῦν τὰ κότσια του νὰ σταθῆ πέντε λεπτά. Εἶναι δουλευτής, δραστήριος, χουβαρδᾶς, ὅμως ἐδῶ ποὺ τὰ λέμε εἶναι μπεκρῆς καὶ ἄσωτος. Ἐπὶ τῇ εὐκαιρίᾳ, σὲ παρακαλῶ νὰ μοῦ στείλης τὸ χρέος σου. Αὐτὸς ὁ ἄνθρωπος τὰ παραλέει (he exaggerates). Τὰ κατορθώματά του εἶναι ἄνω ποταμῶν. Τὸ τί πῆρα σήμερα, δὲν τὸ βάζει ὁ νοῦς σου. Κέρδισα ἕνα «κάντιλακ» καὶ μιὰ ἔγχρωμη τηλεόραση! Ἔξω χαλάει ὁ κόσμος κι' αὐτουνοῦ καρφὶ δὲν τοῦ καίγεται. Ξέρεις κάτι, ὁ συνέταιρός σου πεθαίνει. Κομμάτια νὰ γίνῃ. Ὁ θεῖος σου φαλήρισε. Τί μὲ κόβει;

Καλὰ νὰ πάθῃ (he deserves it). Ἡ μητέρα της πεθαίνει, κι' αὐτὴ πέρα βρέχει. Αὐτὴ ἡ κοπέλα, ἀφότου τὴν γέλασαν, τό'ριξε ἔξω. Τύφλα νἄχει τὸ φουστάνι της μπροστὰ στὸ δικό σου. Στὴν ἄλλη θυρίδα, παρακαλῶ, γιὰ τυχὸν πληροφορίες. Προχωρῆστε κατὰ κεῖ καὶ θὰ τὸ βρῆτε, εἶναι ἕνα μεγάλο κτίριο, γωνιακὸ (on the corner). Δὲν μοῦ λέτε, παρακαλῶ, ποῦ εἶναι ἡ τράπεζα; Σήμερα εἶμαι νὰ πάω (I plan to go) γιὰ κολύμπι. Θέλω νὰ τὸ φκιάξω, ἀλλὰ ὁ σκοπὸς εἶναι νὰ μὴν πληρώσω πολλά. Θὰ σὲ ἀφήσῃ γιὰ τέσσερεις ἑβδομάδες διακοπές; Τί διαθέσεις ἔχει ὁ ἐργοδότης σου.; Αὐτὸ τὸ φθινόπωρο λέω νὰ ταξιδέψω σ' ὅλο τὸν κόσμο. Αὐτὸ τὸ παιδὶ ὅλο κλαίει. Δὲν λέει νὰ σταματήσῃ. Ἐκείνη ἡ κοπέλα παντοῦ χώνει τὴ μύτη της. Μὰ ἐσύ, κάτσε στ' αὐγά σου. Κύττα τὴ δουλειά σου (mind your business). Αὐτὸς ὁ ἄνθρωπος ἀνακατώνεται παντοῦ. Ἐκείνη ἡ γρηὰ τοῦ κάνει τὸ διαμέσον γιὰ νὰ τὴν παντρευτῆ. Αὐτὸς ὁ πωλητὴς σὰ σφῆκα τριγυρνάει. Τά'μαθες; (did you hear the news?). Χωρίσανε! Τὸ κρῖμα στὸ λαιμό σου. Τὴν προσεχῆ ἑβδομάδα θέλω νὰ σοῦ κάνω τραπέζι. Αὐτὸς εἶναι καλὸς καὶ πονόψυχος, ἀλλὰ αὐτὴ τοῦ βάζει φιτίλια (φιτιλιές).

JEALOUS

Τὸ μάτι του γαρίδα.
To máti tou gharída.
He is jealous.

Βάσκανος ὀφθαλμός.*
Váskanos ofϑalmós.
Evil eye.

Νὰ προφυλάγεσαι (μακρυὰ) ἀπὸ βάσκανο ὀφθαλμὸ (μάτι).
Na profeelághese (makreeá) apo váskano ofϑalmó (máti).
Guard yourself against (be far away from) an evil eye.

Ἡ γλωσσοφαγιὰ φέρνει κάποτε καταστροφή.
I ghlossofayá férnee kápote katastrofí.
Envious talk is some times destructive.

Μοῦ μπῆκε στὸ ρουθούνι.*
Mou bike sto rouϑoùni.
He exasperated me (by pestering).

JOB

Τί ἀποδοχὲς (ἀπολαβὲς) ἔχεις ἀπ' τὴν ἐργασία σου;*
Ti apoδochès (apolavès) échees aptin erghasía sou?
What do you gain from your job?

Βλέπω καὶ παθαίνω.
Vlépo ke paθéno.
I have a hard job (to); I meet great difficulty.

Τὰ βρόντηξε κάτω.*
Ta vróndexe kato.
He (she) abandoned the job.

Πιάνω δουλειά.*
Pyáno δouleeá.
I began a (new) job.

Στερεώνω σὲ μιὰ δουλειά.*
Stereóno se miá δouleeá.
I stick to one job.

Compare DIFFICULTY.

JOKE

Κάνω φάρσα.*
Káno fársa.
I play a joke (on someone).

Τὸ γύρισα στ' ἀστεῖο (στὸ καλαμπούρι).*
To yeérisa stasteéo (sto kalamboùri).
I changed the topic to a joke.

Δὲ σηκώνει χωρατὰ (ἀστεῖα).*
δe sikónee chorata (asteéa).
He (she) does not like jokes; he (she) does not have any sense of humor.

'Αστειεύεσαι (ἔλα δά, ὄχι δά, μὴ μοῦ λές, σοβαρά; Τί λές;).*
Asteeévese (éla δá, óchi δá, mí mou lés, sovará? Tí lés?).
Are you joking; are you kidding.

JUSTICE

Τὸ ἴσιο (τὸ δίκηο, τὸ σωστό).*
To ísyo (to δíkyo, to sostó).
Justice, right.

Compare RIGHT.

EXERCISES

Αὐτὸς ἔχει βάσκανον ὀφθαλμὸ (= αὐτὸς ματιάζει). Μακρυὰ ἀπ' τὴ γλωσσοφαγιά! Δὲν μὲ ἱκανοποιοῦν οἱ ἀποδοχὲς ἀπ' τὴν ἐργασία μου. Γιατὶ τὰ βρόντηξες κάτω; Δὲν ἦταν καλὴ δουλειά. Ἔβλεπα καὶ πάθαινα νὰ ζήσω τὴν φαμίλια μου. Θὰ πιάσω δουλειὰ ἀπ' τὸν ἄλλο μῆνα. Ἄϊντε, νὰ δοῦμε, (let's see), θὰ στερεώσης σὲ μιὰ δουλειά; Ὅσο στερεώνεις ἐσύ. Τί λές, φίλε μου; Μοῦ κάνεις φάρσα. Ἡ σπιτονοικοκυρά μου δὲν σηκώνει χωρατά. Μᾶς εἶπε πολλὰ προσβλητικὰ λόγια καὶ μετὰ τὸ γύρισε στὸ ἀστεῖο. Πέθανε ὁ μεγαλύτερος καλλιτέχνης τοῦ κόσμου. Ἀστειεύεσαι; Τὸ σωστὸ εἶναι πὼς ἀξίζεις πιὸ πολλὰ χρήματα. Τὸ δίκηο εἶναι πὼς βοήθησες ἀρκετὰ τ' ἀδέλφια σου.

KEEP

Κρατῶ ὑπόσχεση.*
Krató eepóschesi.
I can keep a promise.

Εἶναι στὸ λόγο του (της).*
Eéne sto lógho tou (tis).
He (she) keeps his (her) promise.

Δὲν ἔβγαλε τσιμουδιά.*
δen évghale tsimouδyá.
He (she) kept mum.

Φυλάγω (διατηρῶ) τὸ μυστικό.*
Feelágho (δiatiró) to meestikó.
I can keep the secret.

Κάνε μου παρέα.*
Káne mou paréa.
Keep me company.

Compare COMPANY, SILENCE.

KNOW

Τόσο ξέρει (iron.)!
Tóso xéree!
He (she) doesn't know any better!

Ποῦ νὰ ξέρω;
Poù na xéro?
How should I know?

Ξέρω τὸ μάθημα νερὸ (ἀπ' ἔξω, ἀπὸ στήθους).
Xéro to máϑima neró (apéxo, apo stíϑous).
I know the lesson by heart.

EXERCISES

Ὁ φίλος μου ποτὲ δὲν κρατᾶ ὑπόσχεση. Ὅ,τι σοῦ εἶπα θὰ τὸ φυλάξης μυστικό. Ἔνοια σου, θὰ φυλάξω τὸ μυστικό. Τὸ κορίτσι μου εἶναι πάντα στὸ λόγο της. Συχνὰ μοῦ κάνει παρέα στὸ γραφεῖο. Τοῦ 'πα, τοῦ 'πα, τοῦ 'πα, κι' ἐκεῖνος δὲν ἔβγαλε τσιμουδιά. Ἄνοιξε τὴν πόρτα καὶ βγῆκε πρὶν τὴν κοπέλα. Τόσο ξέρει! Ἔμαθε τὸ μάθημά του νερό. Μπῆκα στὸ δωμάτιό μου καὶ ξεγδύθηκα (I took off my clothes). Ποῦ νὰ ξέρω πὼς ἦταν μέσα ἕνας κλέφτης!

LATE

Ἀργὰ (Adv.).*
Arghá.
Late; slowly.

Εἶναι ἀργὰ (ἔχει καθυστέρηση).*
Eéne arghá (échee kaϑeestérisi).
It is late.

Εἶναι πολὺ ἀργὰ γιὰ νά*...
Eéne polí arghá ya ná...
It is too late to...

LAUGH

Μπήγω τὰ γέλια.*
Mmígho ta yélia.
I burst out laughing.

LAY

Βάζω χέρι.
Vázo chéri.
I lay hands (on).

Μὴ βάζης χέρι.
Mi vázis chéri.
Do not lay hands on.

LAZY

Εἶναι ἄχθος ἀρούρης.*
Eéne áchϑos aroùris.
He (she) is useless, lazy.

Εἶναι τεμπελοχανᾶς.
Eéne tembelochanás.
He is very lazy.

LEADER

Ἐπὶ κεφαλῆς.*
Epi kephalís.
At the head of; in charge.

Ὁ πατέρας μου εἶναι ἐπὶ κεφαλῆς τοῦ τελωνείου.
O pateraz mou eéne epikefalís tou teloneeéou.
My father is in charge of the customs office.

LEARN

Βάζω γνώση (μυαλό).*
Vázo ghnósi (mialó).
I learn (better) by experience.

LEAST

Τοὐλάχιστον.*
Touláchiston.
At least.

LEAVE

Παράτα με (ἄφησέ με ἥσυχο).*
Paráta me (áfisé me íseecho).
Leave me alone.

Τὸ βάζω στὰ πόδια.
To vázo sta pódya.
I take to my heels.

Δὲ βλέπω τὴν ὥρα νὰ φύγω.
δe vlépo tin óra na feégho.
I am impatient to leave.

'Αφήνω στὴ μέση.*
Afíno sti mési.
I have left it unfinished.

Τὸ σκάζω (τὸ στρίβω).*
To skázo (to strívo).
I escape; I leave unnoticed.

Compare ALONE.

LESSON

Κάνω μάθημα.
Káno máθima.
I take lessons.

LIE

Δὲν λέω ψέματα.
δen léo psémata.
I do not lie.

Παχιὰ λόγια.*
Pachiá lóya.
To someone who talks too much and means nothing.

Μασᾶ τὰ λόγια του (της).*
Masá ta lóya tou (tis).
He (she) does not speak the truth.

Αὐτὸ σηκώνει νερό.
Aftó sikónee neró.
It is not quite true.

Δὲν κολλάει!
δen golláee!
That is a likely tale!

Ψέματα;*
Psémata?
Do I lie? Is that a lie?

LIFE

Διὰ βίου (παντοτεινά).*
δia víou (pandoteená).
For life.

Ἐφ' ὅρου ζωῆς.*
Efórou zoeés.
For life.

LIGHT

Ἄνοιξε τὸ φῶς.*
Àneexe to fós.
Turn on the light.

Κλεῖσε τὸ φῶς.*
Kleése to fós.
Turn off the light.

LIKE

Μ' ἀρέσει (μ' ἄρεσε).*
Marésee (márese).
I like, enjoy, care for (I liked).

Μ' ἀρέσει νά*...
Marésee ná...
I like (enjoy)....

Σ' ἀρέσει;*
Sarésee?
Are you having fun?

Θέλεις, δὲ θέλεις.*
θélees, δe θélees.
Whether you like it or not.

Δὲν τὸν χωνεύω.*
δen don chonévo.
I don't like him at all.

Δὲν τὸν γουστάρω.*
δén don ghoustáro.
I do not care for him.

Δὲν τὸν κάνω γοῦστο.*
δen don káno ghoùsto.
I do not care for him.

Κάνω γοῦστο μιὰ μπύρα.
Káno ghoùsto miá beéra.
I feel like a beer.

LISTEN

Δὲν ἀκούει.*
δen akoùee.
He (she) does not listen.

Ἄκου νὰ δῆς!
Àkou na δís!
Listen now! How do you like that!

Βάζω αὐτί.
Vázo aftí.
I listen secretly.

Δὲν παίρνει ἀπὸ λόγια.*
δen pérnee apo lóya.
He (she) will not listen to reason.

LIVE

Τρώω ἀπ' τὰ ἕτοιμα.
Tróo apta éteema.
I live on capital.

LOOK

Ρίχνω μιὰ ματιὰ (σέ).*
Ríchno miá matyá (se).
I look around, look over, examine.

Γυρεύω.*
Yeerévo.
I look for (general idea).

Ψάχνω.
Psáchno.
I search for (more emphatic).

Πασπατεύω.
Paspatévo.
I look for (in the blind).

Compare EXAMINE.

LOSS

Αὐτώνω, αὔτωσα.
Aftóno, áftosa.
I am at a loss; hesitate for a word.

Τὰ χάνω.*
Ta cháno.
I am at a loss.

Τὰ ἔχασα (τἄχασα).*
Ta échasa (táchasa).
I was at a loss.

Τἄχω χάσει.*
Tácho chásee.
I am all mixed up.

Μοῦ κόβει τὰ χέρια.
Mou kóvee ta chérya.
I feel the loss of it.

Τὰ ἔχω χαμένα.*
Ta écho chaména.
I am confused; I am at a loss.

LOST

Χάσου!*
Chásou!
Get lost!

Γυρίζει ἀπὸ δῶ κι' ἀπὸ κεῖ σὰν ἀπολωλὸς πρόβατο.
Yeerízee apó δó kiapokeé san apololós próvato.
He (she) wanders here and there like a lost sheep.

Χάνω τὰ νερά μου.*
Cháno ta nerá mou.
I feel lost.

Ἔκλεισε ἡ φωνή μου (ἔχασα τὴ φωνή μου).*
Ékleese i phoní mou (échasa ti phoní mou).
I have lost my voice.

Πιάστηκε ἡ φωνή της.*
Pyástike i phoní tis.
She lost her voice.

Χάνω τὸν μπούσουλα.*
Cháno ton mboùsoula.
I have lost my mind.

LOT

Καλὸ κουμάσι.
Kaló koumási.
A bad lot.

LOVE

Τὸν (τὴν) ἔχω κλείσει στὴν καρδιά μου.*
Ton (tin) écho kleésee stin karδyá mou.
I love him (her) very deeply.

Τὸν (τὴν) ἔβλεπε ἀχόρταγα.
Ton (tin) évlepe ahórtagha.
She (he) could not take her (his) eyes from him (her).

Ὁ ἄντρας αὐτὸς εἶναι γλυκοαίματος.*
O ándras aftós eéne ghleekoématos.
This man is likeable.

Δὲν τὸν γουστάρω.*
δen don ghoustáro.
I do not care for him.

Αὐτὴ εἶναι τοῦ γλυκοῦ νεροῦ.*
Aftí eéne tou ghleekoù neroù.
This woman has a bad reputation.

Τοῦ πονεῖ τὸ δόντι γι' αὐτή.
Tou poneè toδóndi yaftí.
He is sweet on her.

Ἐρωτεύτηκε στὰ καλά.*
Erotéftike sta kalá.
He (she) fell truly in love.

Αὐτὸς εἶναι ἐρωτόληπτος.*
Aftós eéne erotóliptos.
He is amorous.

Τἄχω μαζί της (του).*
Tácho mazí tis (tou).
I am annoyed with her (him).

Τὴν (τὸν) ἐπεθύμησα.*
Tin (ton) epeθeémisa.
I miss her (him).

Εἶσαι τρέλλα!*
Eése trella!
You are extremely beautiful!

Σὲ λατρεύω.*
Se latrévo.
I love you extremely (unspeakably).

Ἡ καλή του (poetic).*
I kalí tou.
His bride; his beloved.

Κεραυνοβόλος ἔρως.*
Keravnovólos éros.
Love at first sight.

Πώ, πώ, νὰ σὲ χαρῶ!
Pó, pó, na se charó!
I enjoy you so much!

Ὁ καλός μου (poetic).*
O kalóz mou.
My lover; my beloved.

Ἔχω καρδιὰ ἀγγινάρα.
Écho karδyá anginára.
I have many love affairs.

Σὲ λαχταρῶ.*
Se lachtaró.
I long for you; I'm anxious to see you (again).

Βάζω στὸ μάτι.
Vázo sto máti.
I set my heart on.

Μάτια μου!*
Mátya mou!
My dearest!

Τὰ φτιά(χ)νω μέ.*
Ta ftyá(ch)no mé.
I start an affair with.

Μοῦ μπῆκε στὸ μάτι.
Mou bíke sto máti.
She (he) tickles my fancy.

Τὰ ταιριάσαμε (τὰ μαγειρέψαμε).*
Tá teryásame (ta mayeerépsame).
We agreed; we fell in love.

LUCK

Ἡ γκρίνια φέρνει χρουσουζιά.*
I grínia férnee hrousouzyá.
Complaints bring bad luck.

Τὄχω σὲ καλό.*
Tócho se kaló.
I think it lucky.

Βλέπω ἄσπρη μέρα.*
Vlépo áspri méra.
I am lucky.

Μοὖρθε κουτί.
Moùrϑe koutí.
It was a godsend to me; it fit me to a T.

Μοὖρθε λουκούμι.
Moùrϑe loukoùmi.
He (she, it) was a godsend to me.

LUXURY

Περνῶ μπέϊκα (ζωὴ χαρισάμενη).
Pernó mbéeeka (zoeè charisámeni).
I live in luxury.

EXERCISES

Τὸ τραῖνο εἶναι ἀργά. Τὸ πλοῖο ἔχει καθυστέρηση. Εἶναι πολὺ ἀργὰ γιὰ κολύμπι. Μίλα ἀργά. Μόλις τῆς λέω ἕνα ἀστεῖο μπήγει τὰ γέλια. Ὁ ταχυδρόμος τῆς γειτονιᾶς μου εἶναι ἄχθος ἀρούρης. Ἔπειτα ἀπὸ τόσα λάθη, ἔβαλα γνώση. Ποτὲ δὲν σὲ βλέπομε, τοὐλάχιστον γράφε μας κάποτε. Ὁ ἄντρας μου εἶναι ἐπὶ κεφαλῆς τῆς τράπεζας. Βιάζομαι, Μιχάλη, παράτα με. Αὔριο φεύγω γιὰ τὸν Καναδᾶ, ὅπου θὰ μείνω δύο μῆνες. Θὰ βάλω στὸ πόδι μου τὴν φιλενάδα μου. Μόλις ἦρθε πέντε, δὲν ἔβλεπε τὴν ὥρα νὰ φύγῃ. Ὁ δήμαρχος αὐτὸς ἄφησε ἐποχή. Ἐμένα μ' ἄφησε κατὰ μέρος. Προχθὲς ἄρχισε τὸ βάψιμο καὶ σήμερα τὸ ἄφησε στὴ μέση. Πνίγομαι (I am extremely busy) τὴν στιγμὴν αὐτή, ξεφορτώσου με. Τό 'σκασε πρὶν τὶς πέντε. Πρὶν νυχτώσει τὸ στρίβει. Πόσες ὧρες τὴν ἑβδομάδα κάνεις ἑλληνικὸ μάθημα; Κλεῖσε τὸ φῶς νὰ κοιμηθοῦμε. Θὰ σ' εὐγνωμονῶ διὰ βίου. Θὰ θυμᾶμαι τὴν καλωσύνη σου ἐφ' ὅρου ζωῆς. Ξέρεις πὼς ποτὲ δὲν λέω ψέματα. Εἶσαι καλοφαγάς, ψέματα; Μὴν ἀκοῦς (don't listen to him), παχιὰ λόγια. Δὲν τὸν πιστεύω, μασᾶ τὰ λόγια του. Τὰ λόγια του σηκώνουν νερό. Σ' ἀρέσουν οἱ κάλτσες μου; Ναί, πολύ. Αὐτὴ τὴν ὥρα κάνω γοῦστο μιὰ μπύρα. Ἡ κόρη μου εἶναι ζωηρή, δὲν παίρνει ἀπὸ λόγια. Παρόλο ποὺ (although) τὸν συμβουλεύω πάντοτε, δὲν ἀκούει. Ἡ ὑπηρέτριά μας βάζει αὐτὶ ὅταν μιλᾶμε στὴν κρεβατοκάμαρά μας. Τὰ σημερινὰ παιδιὰ τρώουν ἀπ' τὰ ἕτοιμα. Αὐτὴ ἡ γυναίκα τὰ ἔχει χαμένα. Χτὲς μὲ τὴ βροχὴ αὔτωσα ὥς ὅτου πάω σπίτι. Ὅταν μιλῶ μαζί του, τὰ χάνω. Γιατὶ τά 'χασες; Ὁ πατέρας μου εἶναι πολὺ γέρος καὶ σχεδὸν τἄχει χάσει (χαμένα). Εἶσαι σὰν ἀπολωλὸς πρόβατο.

MAKE UP

Τὸ παίρνω ἀπόφαση.*
To pérno apófasi.
I accept the inevitable; I make up my mind.

Τὰ βγάζω πέρα.*
Ta vgházo péra.
I am successful; I manage.

MANAGE

Τὰ φέρνω ἴσα - ἴσα.
Ta férno ísa - ísa.
I break even (on expenses, etc.).

Τὰ καταφέρνω (τὰ κατάφερα).*
Ta kataférno (ta katáfera).
I succeed, manage (succeeded, managed).

Ἔκαμα τὴν μπάζα μου.
Ékama tin báza mou.
I have made much money.

Βολεύομαι (τὰ βολεύω).*
Volévome (ta volévo).
I am comfortable, settled (I get along, I make do).

Τὰ φέρνω βόλτα.
Ta férno vólta.
I get along, I make do.

Ἐξοικονομῶ τὰ πράματα.*
Exeekonomó ta prámata.
I can manage my affairs.

Τὰ οἰκονομάω.
Ta eekonomáo.
I make ends meet.

Πιάνω τὰ ἔξοδά μου.*
Pyáno ta éxoδá mou.
I make my expenses.

MARRY

Θέλω νὰ σὲ κάνω δική μου (παντρευτῶ).*
Θélo na se káno δikí mou (pandreftó).
I would like to marry you.

MASS

Καλαμπαλίκι.
Kalambalíki.
Mass of people, things.

Κάθε καρυδιᾶς καρύδι.*
Káθe kareeδyás kareéδi.
All sorts and types of people.

Πατεῖς με πατῶ σε.*
Pateéz me pató se.
A crush, scrimmage.

MATCH

Βγῆκαν ἰσόπαλοι.*
Vyíkan isópalee.
They were equally matched.

EXERCISES

Ἤπια πολὺ κι' ἔχασα τὸν μπούσουλα (μου). Ἐδῶ ποὺ ἤρθαμε ἔχασα τὰ νερά μου. Ἀπὸ τὴν πολλὴ κουβέντα πιάστηκε ἡ φωνή μου. Ρίξε μιὰ ματιὰ στὴν ἐφημερίδα καὶ δός μου την πίσω. Τί γυρεύεις ἐδῶ; (What are you looking for here?). Ψάχνω νὰ βρῶ καμιὰ καλὴ δουλειά. Δὲν κέρδισα στὸ ἐθνικὸ λαχεῖο. Καλὸ κουμάσι. Ὁ φίλος μου εἶναι ἐξαιρετικὸ παιδί. Τὸν ἔχω κλείσει στὴν καρδιά μου. Πῶς τὴν ἀγαπᾶ! Τὴν βλέπει ἀχόρταγα. Μοῦ ἀρέσει ἡ κοπέλα αὐτή. Εἶναι ἀπὸ σπίτι (ἀπὸ σόϊ). Ἐκείνη ἡ ἠθοποιὸς περνάει γιὰ ὡραία. Τὸν ἀγαπῶ, τὸν ἄντραν αὐτόν. Εἶναι γλυκοαίματος. Τὸ κορίτσι αὐτὸ εἶναι τοῦ γλυκοῦ νεροῦ. Μιλάει πολλά, δὲν τὸν γουστάρω. Ἔχει μεγάλη ἰδέα γιὰ τὸν ἑαυτό του (about himself), δὲν τὸν κάνω γοῦστο (χάζι). Κύταξέ τον, τοῦ πονεῖ τὸ δόντι γι' αὐτήν. Τὴν ἐρωτεύτηκε στὰ καλά. Ὁ ἀρραβωνιαστικός μου λείπει γιὰ πολὺ καιρό, τὸν ἐπιθύμησα. Τἄχω μαζί του, γιατὶ τὸν εἶδα μὲ ἄλλην. Τὸ φουστάνι αὐτὸ σοῦ πάει θαυμάσια. Εἶσαι τρέλλα, χρυσό μου. Πώ, πώ, νὰ σὲ χαρῶ. Πίστεψέ με, σὲ λατρεύω. Ἀπόψε, περιμένω τὸν καλό μου. Τί κάνει ἡ καλή σου; Ἔχω νὰ τὴ δῶ πολὺ καιρό, δυὸ μέρες. Σὲ βλέπω μὲ πολλὲς νὰ βγαίνῃς. Ἔχεις καρδιὰ ἀγγινάρα, φαίνεται. Μόλις τὸν ἀντίκρυσα τὸν ἀγάπησα. Κεραυνοβόλος ἔρως. Κούκλα μου (my darling), σὲ λαχταρῶ. Μόλις τὴν εἶδα, τὴν ἔβαλα στὸ μάτι. Μάτια μου, σὲ ἀγαπῶ. Τὰ ταιριάσαμε σὲ δυὸ λεπτά. Βλέπω, τά 'φτιαξες μ' ἐκείνη τὴν κοπέλα. Αὐτὸς εἶναι χρουσούζης. Ἀφότου σὲ γνώρισα δὲν εἶδα ἄσπρη μέρα. Ἡ δουλειὰ αὐτὴ μοῦρθε κουτί. Αὐτὴ ἡ κοπέλα μοῦρθε λουκούμι. Στὴν Ἀθήνα πέρασα δύο μῆνες μπέϊκα.

MEAN

Τί θέλεις νὰ πῆς;*
Ti θélees na pís?
What do you mean?

Τί θὰ πῆ αὐτό;
Ti θa pi aftó?
What does this mean?

Θέλω νὰ πῶ.*
Θélo na pó.
I mean to say.

Πάει νὰ πῆ.*
Páee na pí.
It means.

Μὲ κάθε τρόπο.*
Me káθe trópo.
By all means, at all costs.

MEET

Κλείνω ραντεβοῦ.*
Kleéno randevoù.
I make an appointment.

Χαίρω πολύ;*
Chéro polí?
How do you do?

Χάρηκα πολύ.*
Chárika polí.
I am glad to have met you.

Θὰ χαιρόμουνα πολὺ νά...*
Θa cherómouna polí ná...
I would be delighted to...

MENTION

Γιὰ νὰ μὴν ἀναφέρω...*
Ya na min anaféro...
Not to mention...

Ἀκατονόμαστα (δὲν λέγονται).*
Akatonómasta (δen léghonde).
Unmentionables.

MESS

Τὰ κάνω θάλασσα (θαλασσώνω, θαλάσσωσα).*
Ta káno θálassa (θalassóno, θalássosa).
I make a mess of things.

Πάνω - κάτω.*
Páno - káto.
Approximately, more or less, up and down, upside down.

MILD

Μὲ τὸ μαλακὸ (μὲ τὸ καλό).*
Me to malakó (me to kaló).
Softly, mildly.

Τῆς φέρθηκε μὲ τὸ καλό.*
Tis férθike me to kaló.
He spoke to her with mild words.

MIND

Μοῦ ἐπιτρέπετε νά...*
Mou epitrépete ná...
Do you mind...

Κύττα τὴ δουλειά σου.*
Keéta ti δouleeá sou.
Mind your own business.

Δὲν ἔχεις μυαλό;
δen échees mialó?
Don't you have any sense?

Χάνω τὰ μυαλά (μου).
Cháno ta mialá (mou).
I lose my mind.

Καθαρὸ μυαλό.*
Kaθaró mialó.
Lucid mind.

Τοῦ τὰ εἶπα ἀπ' τὴν καλή.
Tou ta eépa aptin kalí.
I gave him a piece of my mind.

Compare CARE; INTEND.

MISS

Λείπει τίποτε;
Leépee típote?
Is anything missing?

MISTAKE

Μπῆκε στὸ καβούκι του.
Bíke sto kavoùki tou.
He realized his mistake.

Τὰ κάνω πλακάκια.
Ta káno plakákia.
I hush it up.

Πληρώνω τὰ σπασμένα.*
Pliróno ta spazména.
I pay for someone else's mistakes.

Κατὰ λάθος.*
Kata láθos.
By mistake.

MIX

Τὰ μπέρδεψα.*
Ta bérδepsa.
I mixed them up.

Μπλέχτηκα.*
Bléchtika.
I got mixed up in; I got into a jam.

Φύρδην - μίγδην.*
Feérδin - mighδin.
Mixed up; in absolute confusion.

MODESTY

Δὲν ἔχω μεγάλες βλέψεις.*
δen écho megháles vlépsees.
I do not have great aspirations, designs.

MONEY

Ἔχω ἀναπαραδιά.*
Écho anaparaδyá.
I have no money.

Κρίμα (σ)τὰ λεφτά!*
Kríma (s)ta leftá!
What a waste of money!

Πόσα τοῖς μετρητοῖς.*
Pósa teez metriteés.
How much in cash.

Κάνει νὰ πάρω κι' ἄλλα λεφτά.*
Kánee na páro kiálla leftá.
There is still some money due me.

Μεροδούλι - μεροφάϊ.*
Meroδoùli - merofáee.
From hand to mouth.

Λεφτὰ μὲ οὐρά.*
Leftá me ourá.
A lot of money.

MOOD

Δὲν ἔχω διάθεση.*
δen écho δiáθesi.
I am not in the mood.

Εἶμαι καλὰ (θαυμάσια).*
Eéme kalá (θavmásia).
I am fine (well).

Εἶμαι χάλια.*
Eéme chália.
I am miserable.

Εἶμαι στὰ κέφια μου.*
Eéme sta kéfya mou.
I feel great; I am in a good mood.

Κάνει κέφι.
Kánee kéfi.
He is in good spirits.

Δὲν ἔχεις κέφι;*
δen échees kéfi?
Do you feel depressed?

Εἶμαι λυπημένος.*
Eéme leepiménos.
I am sad.

Πῶς πᾶνε τὰ μεράκια;*
Pos páne ta merákia?
How is your mood?

Ἔχω νεῦρα.*
Écho névra.
I am in an irritable mood.

Δὲν εἶναι στὰ καλά του.*
δen eéne sta kalá tou.
He is not in a good mood (health, right mind).

Εἶμαι μιὰ χαρά.*
Eéme miá chará.
I am very well.

Εἶμαι στὰ σεκλέτια μου.*
Eéme sta seklétya mou.
I am in a bad mood.

Εἶναι μὲ τὶς ὧρες του.*
Éene me tis óres tou.
He has his moods.

MORE

'Ακόμα πιὸ πολὺ (περισσότερο).*
Akóma pyó polí (perissótero).
Even more (more).

Τίποτε ἄλλο.*
Típote állo.
Nothing else; anything else.

MOST

Τὸ πολὺ - (πολύ).*
To polí - (polí).
At the most.

MOTIVE

'Απώτερος σκοπός.*
Apóteros skopós.
Ulterior motive.

MOVE

Γιὰ προχωρεῖτε.*
Ya prochoreéte.
Come on; move forward (on bus).

Φεύγα (φῦγε) ἀπ' τὴ μέση.*
Févgha (feéye) aptí mési.
Move out of the way.

Δὲν τὸ κουνάω ἀπὸ δῶ.*
δen do kounáo apoδó.
I won't budge from here.

MUSIC

Τὸ σκούζουν τὰ κλαρίνα.*
To skoùzoun ta klarína.
The musical instruments play very loudly.

EXERCISES

Τὸ πῆρε ἀπόφαση νὰ πάη στὴν 'Ελλάδα. Πῶς τὰ βγάζεις πέρα μὲ πέντε παιδιά; Τὰ φέρνω ἴσα - ἴσα. Πῶς τὰ καταφέρνεις; "Εμεινε στὴν 'Αμερικὴ μερικὰ χρόνια, ἔκαμε τὴν μπάζα του κι' ἔφυγε στὴν 'Ελλάδα. 'Εκεῖ ποὺ δουλεύω τὰ οἰκονομάω. Αὐτὸ τὸ κατάστημα δὲν πιάνει τὰ ἔξοδά του. Κύτταξε, τί μεγάλο καλαμπαλίκι! Εἶναι καλός, ἀλλὰ ὅταν νευριάζει τὰ κάνει θάλασσα. Τὰ θαλάσσωσες πάλι, Νῖκο. Τὸ διαμέρισμά μου εἶναι ἄνω - κάτω. Πόσα λεφτὰ θέλεις; Πάνω - κάτω πεντακόσιες δραχμές. Στὶς μεγάλες πόλεις συναντᾶς κάθε καρυδιᾶς καρύδι. Στὸ θέατρο, χθὲς βράδυ, ἦταν πολὺς κόσμος, πατεῖς με πατῶ σε. Καὶ οἱ δύο ὁμάδες ἔπαιξαν ὡραῖα. Βγῆκαν ἰσόπαλες. Πόσων χρονῶν εἶσαι; Τριάντα - ἐννέα. Ὦ, δὲν εἶστε μεγάλος! Θέλω νὰ πῶ, δὲν εἶστε καὶ πολὺ νέος. Τί πάει νὰ πῆ ἐκείνη ἡ πινακίς; Τὸ ἐρχόμενον καλοκαίρι θὰ πάω στὴν Εὐρώπη, μὲ κάθε τρόπο. Κλείσαμε ραντεβοὺ γιὰ τὶς ἑπτά, ἀπόψε. Ἀπ' ἐδῶ εἶναι ἡ κόρη μου. Χαίρω πολύ, δεσποινίς. Θὰ χαιρόμουνα πολὺ νὰ σᾶς εἶχα τραπέζι τὸ βράδυ. Εἶναι πολὺ κόλακας, γιὰ νὰ μὴν ἀναφέρω πὼς εἶναι καὶ κλέφτης. Ὅλο ξεχνᾶς τὴν ὀμπρέλλα σου, δὲν ἔχεις μυαλό; Ἔχασε τὰ μυαλά του μὲ τὴν γυναίκα αὐτή. Σοῦ τὰ εἶπε ἀπ' τὴν καλὴ γιὰ μιάμιση ὥρα. Πότε λὲς νὰ φύγης γιὰ τὰ νησιά; Συγγνώμην, κατὰ λάθος πῆρα τὸ καπέλο σου Ποιὸς πλήρωσε τὰ σπασμένα; Τὸ δωμάτιό μου εἶναι φύρδην - μίγδην. Σοῦ λείπει τίποτε; Κύτταξε καλὰ τὴν βαλίτσα σου. Ἔχεις μεγάλες βλέψεις (ἀξιώσεις) στὴν ζωή; Σήμερα ἔχω ἀναπαραδιά. Πόσα ἄλλα λεφτὰ κάνει νὰ πάρω; Αὐτὴ ἡ δουλειὰ εἶναι μεροδούλι - μεροφάϊ. Πόσα τοῖς μετρητοῖς θὰ μοῦ δώσης; Αὐτὸς ἔχει λεφτὰ μὲ οὐρά! Δὲν εἶναι στὰ καλά της σήμερα, γιατὶ δὲν πῆρε γράμμα ἀπὸ τὸν φίλον της. Πῶς πᾶνε τὰ μεράκια; Δὲν εἶμαι στὰ καλά μου. Εἶναι στὰ σεκλέτια του. Αὐτὴ ἡ γυναίκα εἶναι μὲ τὶς ὧρες της. Τί θὰ σοῦ κάνη; Τὸ πολὺ - πολὺ νὰ σὲ διώξη ἀπ' τὴν δουλειά. Ἔχεις νὰ μοῦ πῆς τίποτε ἄλλο; Ἀπώτερος σκοπός μου, ποὺ βρίσκομαι στὴν Ἀμερικὴ εἶναι νὰ πάρω τὸ δοκτορᾶτο μου. Περίμενέ με. Μὴν τὸ κουνήσης ἀπὸ δῶ. Εἶσαι στὰ κέφια σου; Δὲν ἔχεις κέφι; Ὁ φίλος μου κάνει κέφι. Μοῦ ἐπιτρέπετε νὰ καπνίσω; Μὴ μᾶς ἐνοχλῆς, κύττα τὴ δουλειά σου.

NAP

Τὸ κόβω δίπλα (τὸν παίρνω ἕνα χεράκι).
To kóvo δípla (ton bérno éna cheráki).
I take a nap.

NARROW

Εἶναι στενῆς (πλατειᾶς, φαρδιᾶς) ἀντιλήψεως ἄνθρωπος.*
Eéne stenís (platyás, farδyás) andilípseos ánϑropos.
He (she) is narrow- (broad-) minded.

Εἶναι στενόμυαλος.*
Eéne stenómialos.
He is narrow - minded.

NATURALLY

Ἐννοεῖται (φυσικά.).*
Ennoeéte (pheesiká).
Naturally; it is understood.

Αὐτὸ εἶναι εὐνόητον.*
Aftó eéne evnóeeton.
Naturally; it is understood.

NECESSARY

Ἐν ἀνάγκῃ.*
En anángi.
If necessary.

Δὲν ἔχω τ' ἀπαιτούμενα.*
δen écho tapetoùmena.
I don't have the necessary means.

Εἶναι ἐπείγουσα ἀνάγκη.*
Eéne epíghousa anángi.
It is very urgent.

NEED

Κάνω χωρὶς κι' ἐσένα.*
Káno chorís kieséna.
I can live without you.

Θέλω (χρειάζομαι) μιὰ ἀλλαξιὰ (ἕνα κοστούμι).*
Θélo (chreeázome) miá allaxyá (éna kostùmi).
I need a suit of clothes.

NEVERTHELESS

Μ' ὅλα ταῦτα.*
Móla táfta.
Anyway; nevertheless.

Ὡστόσο.*
Ostóso.
However; nevertheless.

Compare ALTHOUGH.

NEWS

Τί νέα;*
Ti néa?
What's new?

Τίποτα νεώτερο.
Típota neótero.
Nothing new.

Θ' ἀναμένω νεώτερά σου.*
Θanaméno neóterá sou.
I am waiting for your news.

NICE

Τί ὡραῖα!*
Ti oréa!
How nice!

NOISE

Χτυπάει στὰ νεῦρα (μου).*
Chteepàee sta névra (mou).
It gets on my nerves.

Ἔγινε μεγάλος σαματάς.
Éyine meghálos samatás.
It caused great noise.

Χαλάει ὁ κόσμος.*
Chaláee o kózmos.
Great storm; great noise and confusion.

NONE

Κανένας (κανεὶς), καμμιά, κανένα (with negative).*
Kanénas (kaneés), kamiá, kanéna.
Someone, anyone (no one, nobody, none).

Κανένας δὲν ἦρθε.
Kanénas δen írϑe.
No one came.

Καμιὰ φορά.*
Kamiá forá.
Once in a while.

Καμιὰ φορὰ καπνίζω.
Kamiá forá kapnízo.
I smoke sometimes.

Καμιὰ φορὰ (with negative).
Kamiá forá.
Never.

Δὲν σὲ εἶδα καμιὰ φορὰ στὸ θέατρο.
δen se eéδa kamiá forá sto θéatro.
I never saw you at the theater.

Περιμένετε κανένα;*
Periménete kanéna?
Do you expect someone?

Δὲν περιμένω κανένα.*
δen periméno kanéna.
I don't expect anyone.

NONSENSE

Λόγια τῆς καραβάνας.*
Lóya tis karavánas.
Nonsense.

Κολοκύθια!
Kolokeéθya!
Nonsense!

Κοπανίζω ἀέρα.
Kopanízo aéra.
I talk nonsense.

Ἀέρας κοπανιστός.
Aéras kopanistós.
Nonsense.

Πράσινα ἄλογα.
Prásina álogha.
Nonsense.

Μὴ λὲς σαχλαμάρες.*
Mí les sachlamáres.
Don't talk nonsense.

Τρίχες!
Triches!
Nonsense, lies!

Δὲν χαρίζω κάστανα.*
δen charízo kástana.
I will stand for no nonsense.

NOTE

Κρατῶ σημειώσεις.*
Krató simeeósees.
I take (down) notes.

NOTICE

Τὸν (τὴν) πῆρε τὸ μάτι μου.
Ton (tin) píre to máti mou.
I noticed him (her).

Παίρνω εἴδηση.*
Pérno eéδisi.
I get wind of, notice.

Τὸ παίρνω χαμπάρι.
To pérno chambári.
I notice it.

NUMBER

Ἕως (μέχρι, adv. with numbers).*
Éos (méchri).
About.

Ἕως εἴκοσι πέντε.
Éos eékosi pénde.
About twenty-five.

Κάπου (+ number).*
Kápou.
About.

Κάπου ἐκεῖ.*
Kápou ekeé.
Somewhere around there.

Κάπου τριάντα.
Kápou triánda.
About thirty.

NUMEROUS

Κόσμος καὶ κοσμάκης.*
Kózmos ke kozmákis.
Numerous people.

Χάθηκε μὲ τὸ σεισμὸ κόσμος καὶ κοσμάκης.
Cháθike me to seezmó kózmos ke kozmákis.
Numerous people were lost in the earthquake.

EXERCISES

Τὸν πῆρε ἕνα χεράκι. Δὲν εἶναι πλατειᾶς ἀντιλήψεως ἄνθρωπος. Αὐτὴ ἡ γυναίκα εἶναι στενόμυαλη. Θὰ πᾶμε στὸ μπάνιο σήμερα; Ἐννοεῖται. Ἐν ἀνάγκῃ θὰ πουλήσω καὶ τὸ αὐτοκίνητό μου γιὰ νὰ σώσω τὴν μάνα μου. Θέλω νὰ γυρίσω τὸν κόσμο, μὰ δὲν ἔχω τ' ἀπαιτούμενα. Εἶναι ἐπείγουσα ἀνάγκη νὰ τοῦ μιλήσω σήμερα. Δὲν σ' ἔχω ἀνάγκη. Κάνω χωρὶς κι' ἐσένα. Χρειάζομαι μιὰ καθημερινὴ ἀλλαξιά. Εἶναι φτωχός, μ' ὅλα ταῦτα δὲν καταδέχεται νὰ τὸν κερνοῦν. Ἄργησα κάπως, ὡστόσο ἦρθα. Γειά σου. Τί κάνεις; Τίποτα νεώτερο; Αὐτὸς ὁ κρότος χτυπάει στὰ νεῦρα. Αὐτὴ ἡ παρέα κάνει μεγάλο σαματά. Τὰ αὐτοκίνητα στὴν Ἀθήνα καὶ τὰ τρόλλεϋ χαλᾶνε τὸν κόσμο. Στὴν ἐποχή μας, σχεδὸν κανένας δὲν εἶναι φιλότιμος. Αὐτὰ ποὺ μοῦ λὲς εἶναι λόγια τῆς καραβάνας. Τὰ πιστεύεις αὐτά; Κολοκύθια! Μὴν τὸν πιστεύεις. Κοπανίζει ἀέρα. Μιλάει πολύ. Ὅ,τι λέει εἶναι πράσινα ἄλογα. Λὲς πολλὲς σαχλαμάρες. Ὅλ' αὐτὰ εἶναι τρίχες. Ὁ πεθερός μου δὲν χαρίζει κάστανα. Κάπου, ἐκεῖ κάτω, τὴν πῆρε τὸ μάτι μου. Πῆρες εἴδηση τὸν καυγᾶ; Δὲν τὸν πῆρα χαμπάρι πότε μπῆκε στὸ δωμάτιό μου. Κάπου - κάπου λέει τὴν ἀλήθεια. Ἐδῶ χάνεται κόσμος καὶ κοσμάκης κάθε μέρα καὶ σὺ κλαίεις ἑκατὸ δολλάρια!

OATH

Βάζω τὸ κεφάλι μου!
Vázo to kefáli mou!
I swear by my life!

Μὰ τὴν ἀλήθεια!*
Ma tin alíthya!
In truth!

Στὴ ζωή μου!*
Sti zoeé mou!
On my life!

OBJECT

Φέρνω ἀντίρρηση.*
Férno andírrisi.
I object (to).

OBLIGATION

Εἶμαι ὑποχρεωμένος.*
Eéme eepochreoménos.
I am obliged.

OBSERVE

Κοιτάζω (παρατηρῶ, stronger).*
Keetázo (paratiró).
I observe, look at.

Βλέπω.*
Vlépo.
I see (a general idea of vision).

Κοιτάζω μὰ δὲ βλέπω τίποτε.
Keetázo ma ðe vlépo típote.
I look, but I see nothing.

Δὲν παρατηρῶ τίποτε.
ðen paratiró típote.
I do not observe anything.

OCCASION

Ἐπὶ τῇ εὐκαιρίᾳ.*
Epi tí efkería.
By the way, on the occasion of.

Κάπου κάπου.*
Kápou kápou.
Now and then.

Ποῦ καὶ ποῦ.*
Poù ke poù.
Occasionally.

OFF

Γιὰ ποῦ;*
Ya poù?
Where are you off to?

Κάτω τὰ χέρια.*
Káto ta chérya.
Hands off.

Ἂς τὰ λοῦσα.
Às ta loùsa.
Come off it.

OFTEN

Ἀρκετὲς φορές.*
Arketés forés.
More than once; several times.

OMEN

Τὸ ἔχω σὲ κακό.*
To écho se kakó.
I think it a bad omen.

ONCE

Μὲ μιᾶς (διὰ μιᾶς).*
Me miás (δia miás).
At once; at one go.

Ἄλλη μιὰ φορά.
Àlli miá forá.
Once more.

Μιὰ φορά.*
Miá forá.
Once.

OTHER

Ὁ ἄλλος.*
O állos.
The other one.

Κάποιος ἄλλος.*
Kápyos állos.
Someone else.

Πιὸ πολὺ ἀπ' τοὺς ἄλλους.*
Pyó polí aptous állous.
More than the others.

OTHERWISE

Εἰδάλλως (εἰδαλιῶς).*
Eeδállos (eeδaliós).
If not; otherwise.

OUTSPOKEN

Τὰ λέω ξάστερα (σταράτα).*
Ta léo xástera (staráta).
I am outspoken.

Ὀρθὰ κοφτά.*
Orϑá koftá.
Straight, outspokenly.

Μοῦ τὰ εἶπε ὀρθὰ κοφτά.*
Mou ta eépe orϑá koftá.
He talked to me outspokenly.

Τοῦ τἄπα ἀνοιχτὰ καὶ ξάστερα (ντόμπρα).*
Tou tápa aneechtá ke xástera (ndómbra).
I spoke to him openly and freely.

Μιλῶ ἔξω ἀπὸ τὰ δόντια.*
Miló éxo apo ta δóndya.
I speak straightforwardly, severely.

Τοῦ τὰ εἶπα χύμα.*
Tou ta eépa cheéma.
I told him straightforwardly.

OVER

Ἐκεῖ πέρα.*
Ekeé péra.
Over there.

Ἐδῶ πέρα.*
Eδó péra.
Over here.

EXERCISES

Φέρνεις ἀντίρρηση νὰ φᾶμε ἔξω στὴν αὐλή; Ὄχι, δὲν φέρνω καμιὰ ἀντίρρηση. Εἶμαι ὑποχρεωμένος στὸν γιατρό μου. Ἐπὶ τῇ εὐκαιρίᾳ, θέλω νὰ σὲ συγχαρῶ γιὰ τὴν νέα σου ἐπιχείρηση. Ποῦ καὶ ποῦ τὸν βλέπομε. Σὲ περιμένουμε τόση ὥρα. Ἄς τὰ λοῦσα. Σὲ βλέπω βιαστική. Γιὰ ποῦ; Περνᾶ ἀρκετὲς φορὲς ἀπ' τὸ χωριό μας. Μιὰ φορὰ εἴχαμεν ἡσυχία, τώρα κάθε μέρα φασαρίες. Πές το ἄλλη μιὰ φορὰ γιατὶ δὲν σ' ἄκουσα. Θὰ μὲ παντρευτῇς εἰδάλλως δὲν θὰ μὲ βλέπῃς. Θέλω ἕνα «κάντυλακ» εἰδαλιῶς θὰ σὲ χωρίσω. Δῶσε μου κι' ἄλλο κρασί. Τὸ κάρο παίρνει ἄλλον ἕνα. Ὁ δημοσιογράφος αὐτὸς τὰ λέει ξάστερα. Ἡ ἐφημερίδα αὐτὴ τὰ γράφει ὀρθὰ κοφτά. Μᾶς τἄπε ἀνοιχτὰ καὶ ξάστερα. Ὁ ἀντιπρόεδρος τῆς Ἀμερικῆς μιλᾶ ἔξω ἀπὸ τὰ δόντια. Τί τρέχει (What is going on) ἐκεῖ πέρα; Ὅταν θύμωσε τοῦ τὰ εἶπε χύμα.

PARDON

Μὲ τὸ συμπάθειο (τὴν ἄδειά σας).*
Me to seembáϑyo (tin áδeeá sas).
Begging your pardon; with your permission.

PARTLY

Ἐν μέρει ἔχεις δίκηο.*
En méree échees δíkio.
You are partially correct.

Ἐν μέρει.*
En méree.
Partly.

Ὡς ἐπὶ τὸ πλεῖστον.*
Os epi to pleéston.
For the most part.

PATIENT

Εἶναι πολὺ ἀνεχτικός.*
Eéne polí anechtikós.
He is very patient.

Εἶναι ὑπομονετικός.*
Eéne eepomonetikós.
He is tolerant.

PAY

Δίνω βάση σέ.*
δίno vási se.
I attach importance to.

T' ἀκούω βερεσέ.*
Takoùo veresé.
I don't pay any attention;
I take it with a grain of salt.

Τί εἶναι ὁ κόπος σου;*
Ti eéne o kópos sou?
How much should I pay you
(for your service)?

Τοῦ (τῆς) κόστισε ὁ κοῦκος ἀηδόνι.*
Toù (tis) kóstise o koùkos aeeδóni.
He(she) paid for it through the nose.

PECULIAR

Αὐτὸς εἶναι μή μου ἅπτου (ἰδιότροπος, παράξενος)!*
Aftós eéne mí mou áptou (iδiótropos, paráxenos)!
He is peculiar!

PITY

Εἶναι κρῖμα!*
Eéne kríma!
That's too bad!
It is a shame!

Κρίμα πού...
Kríma poù...
It is a pity that...

Εἶναι ἁμαρτία (ἀπὸ τὸ Θεό)!*
Eéne amartía (apo to Θeó)!
It is a pity!

PLAN

Ἔχω σκοπὸ νά...
Écho skopó ná...
I intend (mean) to...

Ἔχω στὸ νοῦ (μου).
Écho sto noù (mou).
I intend to.

Μοῦ τὰ χάλασες.*
Mou ta chálases.
You have ruined my plans.

Μοῦ ἔκαναν χαλάστρα.*
Mou ékanan chalástra.
They spoiled my plans.

PLEASE

Μοῦ καλοφαίνεται.*
Mou kalofénete.
I am pleased.

Κάνω τὸ κέφι μου.*
Káno to kéfi mou.
I do what pleases me.

PLENTY

Κέρας τῆς 'Αμαλθείας.*
Kéras tis Amalθeéas.
Horn of plenty.

POINT

Πάτησες τὴν πίτα.*
Pátises tin píta.
You have come to the point.

Τοῦ (τῆς) βρῆκα τὸ κουμπί.
Toù (tis) vríka to koumbí.
I found his (her) weak spot.

POLITE

Ἔχει λεπτότητα.*
Échee leptótita.
He (she) is tactful.

Γιὰ τὰ (μαῦρα) μάτια.*
Ya ta (mávra) mátia.
For the sake of politeness.

POLITICS

Ἐπαμφοτερίζουσα πολιτική.*
Epamfoterízousa politikí.
Of doubtful or changing politics.

POSE

Κορδώνεται.*
Korδónete.
He (she) poses.

Κρατῶ πόζα.*
Krató póza.
I am standoffish.

POSSIBILITY

Ὅσο τὸ δυνατὸ (+ comparative).*
Oso to δeenató.
As ... as possible.

Ἴσως νὰ (+ indefinite).*
Isos ná.
It is possible, may happen.

Μπορεῖ νὰ (+ indefinite).*
Boreé ná.
It is possible, may happen.

Ἴσως νὰ φύγουν.
Isos na feéghoun.
They may leave.

Μπορεῖ νὰ ἔλθουν.
Boreé na élϑoun.
They may come.

Δὲν περνᾶ ἀπὸ τὸ χέρι μου.*
δen perná apo to chéri mou.
It does not depend on me.

Ἀποκλείεται.*
Apokleéete.
It is an impossibility.

Μὲ κάθε τρόπο.*
Me káϑe trópo.
By all means; at all costs.

POWERFUL

Δίνω καὶ παίρνω.*
δíno ke pérno.
I am influential.

Τὄχω δίπορτο.
Tócho δíporto.
I am capable.

Κόβει καὶ ράβει.*
Kóvee ke rávee.
He (she) has influence;
He (she) talks incessantly.

Ἔχω πέραση.*
Écho pérasi.
I am influential;
I am sought after.

PRAISE

Τὸν (τὴν) ἀνεβάζω στὰ οὐράνια.
Ton (tin) anevázo sta ouránia.
I praise him (her) to the skies.

PREFER

Καλύτερα ἔχω νὰ (+ verb).*
Kaleétera écho na.
I prefer to.

PREGNANT

Ἔμεινε ἔγκυος.*
Émeene éngeeos.
She is pregnant.

PREMATURE

Ἀκόμη δὲ βγῆκε ἀπὸ τ' αὐγό.*
Akómi de vyíke apo tavghó.
He (she) has not yet matured.

PRESENT

Πρὸς τὸ παρόν.*
Prós to parón.
At present.

Ἐπὶ τοῦ παρόντος.*
Epi tou paróndos.
For the time-being.

Γιὰ τὴν ὥρα.*
Ya tin óra.
For the present.

PRETEND

Κάνω πώς...*
Káno pós...
I pretend that...

Κάνω τὸν ἀνήξερο (κάνω τὸν ἀνίδεο).*
Káno ton aníxero (káno ton anídeo).
I pretend not to know.

Κάνω τὸν τρελλὸ (ἄρρωστο).*
Káno ton drelló (árrosto).
I pretend to be mad (sick).

Κάνω στραβὰ μάτια.*
Káno stravá mátia.
I pretend not to see.

PRICE

Τιμὴ ξεκομμένη.*
Timi xekomméni.
Fixed price.

Φωτιὰ καὶ λάβρα.*
Fotyá ke lávra.
Strong passion (referring to people); exorbitant price (referring to merchandise).

PROBABILITY

Ἐνδέχεται νὰ μὴν ἔρθη.*
Endéchete na min érϑi.
It may be that he (she) will not come.

Ἴσως (μπορεῖ) νὰ ἔρθη.*
Isos (boreé) na érϑi.
Perhaps he (she) will come.

PROMISE

Κρατῶ ὑπόσχεση.*
Krató eepóschesi.
I keep a promise.

Τάζω λαγοὺς μὲ πετραχήλια.
Tázo laghoùs me petrachília.
I make wonderful but empty promises.

Εἶναι στὸ λόγο του (της).*
Eéne sto lógho tou (tis).
He (she) keeps his (her) promise.

Μοῦ 'δωσε τὸ λόγο του.*
Moùdose to lógho tou.
He promised me.

PROPOSE

Κάνω πρόταση.*
Káno prótasi.
I propose; suggest.

Εἰσηγοῦμαι (προτείνω).*
Eesighoùme (proteéno).
I propose.

PROVE

Τὸν ἔβγαλαν ψεύτη.*
Ton évghalan pséfti.
He was proved a liar.

Τοὺς ἔβγαλαν κλέφτες.*
Tous évghalan kléftes.
They were proven thieves.

PUT

Τὸν βάζω στὴ θέση του.
Ton vázo sti θési tou.
I put him in his place.

Μὴ μὲ παίρνης γιὰ χαζὸ (βλάκα).*
Mí me pérnis ya chazó (vláka).
Don't take me for a fool; don't put me on.

Βάζω μὲ τρόπο.*
Vázo me trópo.
I put (something somewhere) without being noticed.

EXERCISES

Ἐν μέρει ἔχεις δίκηο. Οἱ Ἕλληνες, ὡς ἐπὶ τὸ πλεῖστον, εἶναι φιλόξενοι καὶ φιλότιμοι. Ὁ ἐργοδότης τῆς ἑταιρίας μας εἶναι πολὺ ἀνεχτικός. Μὴ δίνης βάση στὰ λόγια του. Τὰ λόγια σου τ' ἀκούω βερεσέ. Τὸ αὐτοκίνητο αὐτὸ τοῦ κόστισε ὁ κοῦκος ἀηδόνι. Ὁ πατέρας του πληρώνει τὰ σπασμένα πάντα. Κρίμα ποὺ δὲν ἤμουνα ἐδῶ νὰ σὲ βοηθήσω! Ἔχει σκοπὸ ν' ἀγοράση σπίτι. Ἔχεις στὸ νοῦ σου νὰ πᾶς στὴν Ἑλλάδα; Ἤθελα νὰ πήγαινα, αὐτὸ τὸ καλοκαίρι, μὰ ἡ ἀρρώστεια τοῦ παιδιοῦ μου, μοῦ τὰ χάλασε. Θὰ πηγαίναμε, σήμερα, στὸ μπάνιο, μὰ ἡ βροχὴ μᾶς ἔκανε χαλάστρα. Τοῦ καλοφάνηκε ἡ κουβέντα μου. Ἔκανε τὸ κέφι του, ἀλλ' αὐτὴ τώρα ὑποφέρει. Ἡ Ἀμερικὴ εἶναι τὸ κέρας τῆς Ἀμαλθείας. Μὲ τὸ συμπάθειο, μπορεῖς νὰ μᾶς ἀφήσης μόνους; Εἶπες, εἶπες, μὰ τώρα πάτησες τὴν πίτα. Εἶχα φασαρίες ἕως τώρα, μὰ ἐπὶ τέλους τῆς βρῆκα τὸ κουμπί. Αὐτὸς παίζει ἐπαμφοτερίζουσα πολιτική. Ἡ κοπέλα αὐτὴ ἔχει λεπτότητα. Παίνεσέ την (praise her) γιὰ τὰ μάτια. Αὐτὸς κορδώνεται σὰν νὰ εἶναι ὁ Ὠνάσης. Κρατᾶ πόζα, δὲν μιλᾶ σὲ κανένα. Τὸ μυαλό του φούσκωσε (he became conceited) ἐπειδὴ ἔμεινε λίγο στὸ ἐξωτερικό. Μοῦ φωνάζετε (would you call a taxi for me) ἕνα ταξὶ ὅσο τὸ δυνατὸ πιὸ γρήγορα. Τὸ καράβι μπορεῖ νὰ ἀργήση. Τὸ ἀεροπλάνο ἀποκλείεται νὰ φύγη μὲ αὐτὴν τὴν κακοκαιρία. Αὐτὸ ποὺ μοῦ ζητᾶς, δὲν περνᾶ ἀπὸ τὸ χέρι μου. Ὁ βουλευτὴς αὐτὸς πρὶν τρία χρόνια ἔδινε κι' ἔπαιρνε. Κόβει καὶ ράβει μέσ' τὴν κυβέρνηση. Σήμερα, τὸ δολλάριο ἔχει πέραση. Καλύτερα ἔχω νὰ χάσω τὸ σπίτι μου παρὰ νὰ φύγω ἀπ' αὐτὴ τὴν δουλειά. Δὲν εἶναι καὶ τόσο σπουδαία κοπέλα γιὰ νὰ τὴν ἀνεβάζη στὰ οὐράνια. Πρὸς τὸ παρόν, δὲν ἔχω δουλειά Κάνει πὼς εἶναι ἄρρωστος, μὰ δὲν ἔχει τίποτα. Μὴν κάνεις τὸν ἀνήξερο. Μὲ εἶδε, ἀλλὰ κάνει στραβὰ μάτια. Ἀκόμη δὲ βγῆκε ἀπὸ τ' αὐγὸ καὶ μᾶς κάνει τὸν καμπόσο. Σήμερα, ὅλες οἱ τιμὲς εἶναι φωτιὰ καὶ λάβρα. Μ' ἀρέσει αὐτὸ τὸ ἐμπορικὸ γιατὶ ἔχει τιμὲς ξεκομμένες. Τὸ καράβι ἐνδέχεται νὰ μὴν ἔρθη σήμερα. Ἴσως νὰ ἔρθη αὔριο τὸ πρωΐ. Ποτέ του δὲν κρατᾶ ὑπόσχεση. Δὲν τὸν πιστεύω, μοῦ τάζει λαγοὺς μὲ πετραχήλια. Αὐτὴ ἡ κοπέλα εἶναι πάντα στὸ λόγο της. Μοῦ δίνεις τὸν λόγο σου; Ὄχι δὲν τοὔδωσε τὸν λόγο της. Αὔριο βράδυ θὰ τῆς κάνη πρόταση γιὰ γάμο. Στὸ δικαστήριο, τὸν ἔβγαλαν ψεύτη. Τὸν πῆρε γιὰ χαζό. Μὴ μὲ παίρνεις γιὰ βλάκα. Τὴν ἔβαλε στὴ θέση της.

QUALITY

Τῆς κακιᾶς ὥρας.*
Tis kakiás óras.
Of poor quality.

QUARREL

Τὰ βάζω μὲ (+ name)...*
Ta vázo mé...
I quarrel with...

Εἶναι καβγατζῆς.
Eéne kavghatzís.
He is always ready for a fight.

Τὸν ἔφερα σὲ θεογνωσία.
Ton éfera se ϑeoghnosía.
I brought him to his senses.

Compare FIGHT.

Τσουχτερὰ λόγια.*
Tsouchterá lóya.
Bitter attacks (accusations).

Κρεμῶ τὸ ζωνάρι μου.
Kremó to zonári mou.
I seek a quarrel.

Γίναμε ἀπὸ δυὸ χωριά.*
Yíname apo δyó choryá.
We quarrelled.

QUICK

Στὸ ἄψε σβύσε.*
Sto ápse zveése.
In the twinkling of an eye.

Πῆγε κι' ἦρθε στὸ ἄψε σβύσε.
Píye kírϑe sto ápse zveése.
He (she) went and returned in the twinkling of an eye.

Στὸ πῖ καὶ φῖ.*
Sto pí ke phí.
In a second.

Σβέλτα!*
Zvélta!
Quickly.

QUIET

Ἥσυχα!*
Iseecha!
Behave yourself; be quiet!

Μὴ τσιρίζης!*
Mí tsirízis!
Don't talk too much!

Δὲν βγάζω κὶχ (ἄχ).*
δén vgházo kích (ách).
I do not utter a sound.

Δὲν ἔβγαλε τσιμουδιὰ (μιλιὰ).*
δen évghale tsimouδyá (miliá).
He (she) did not utter a word.

Μιλιά!*
Miliá!
Not a word!

EXERCISES

Αὐτὸ τὸ ριζόγαλο εἶναι τῆς κακιᾶς ὥρας. Τά 'βαλα μὲ τὸν Γιάννη γιατὶ δὲν εἶναι στὸ λόγο του. Μοῦ 'πε τσουχτερὰ λόγια. Αὐτὸς ὁ ἄνθρωπος εἶναι καβγατζῆς. Κύτταξέ τον, κρεμᾶ τὸ ζωνάρι του. Τόσο θυμωμένος ἦταν, ποὺ μὲ πῆρε μισὴ ὥρα γιὰ νὰ τὸν φέρω σὲ θεογνωσία. Πά, πά, πά, εἶναι ἔξω φρενῶν, μὴν τὸν πλησιάσης. Γίνανε ἀπὸ δυὸ χωριά! Τσακωθήκανε στὰ γερὰ γιὰ ψύλλου πήδημα. Τέλειωσε τὸ διάβασμα στὸ ἄψε σβύσε. Ἦρθε στὸ πῖ καὶ φῖ. Σβέλτα, θὰ χάσωμε τὸ τραῖνο. Ἥσυχα, μὴ τσιρίζης. Πάνω στὴν ἐγχείρηση δὲν ἔβγαλε ἄχ. Τὸν στόλισε μιὰ χαρὰ καὶ ἐκεῖνος δὲν ἔβγαλε τσιμουδιά!

RAIN

Γίνομαι λούτσα.*
Yínome loùtsa.
I get drenched.

Γίνομαι παπί.*
Yínome papí.
I get soaking wet.

RATE

Ἔτσι κι' ἀλλιῶς.*
Étsi kialliós.
At any rate.

READY

Ἐπὶ τῶν ἐπάλξεων.*
Epi ton epálxeon.
Always ready for home defense.

Ἐν ἐπιφυλακῇ.*
En epipheelakí.
Always ready; on the alert.

Ἄμ' ἔπος ἄμ' ἔργον.*
Amépos amérghon.
No sooner said than done.

REASON

Γι' αὐτό.*
Yaftó.
That is why; for this reason.

Ἔρχεται σὲ λογαριασμό.
Érchete se logharyazmó.
It will just about do; he is amenable to reason.

Δὲν συντρέχει λόγος.*
δen seendréchee lóghos.
There is no reason.

Ἀποχρῶν λόγος.*
Apochrón lóghos.
Sufficient or justifiable reason.

RED CROSS

Πρῶτες Βοήθειες.*
Prótes Voeéθeees.
First aid.

REGARDLESS

Σώνει καὶ καλά.*
Sónee ke kalá.
No matter what; regardless.

Κι' ὕστερα;*
Keéstera?
So what?

Ὅ,τι καὶ νὰ γίνη (νὰ συμβῆ).*
O,ti ke na yíni (na seemví).
No matter what (in any case).

Καὶ μ' αὐτό;
Ke maftó?
What then?

Compare CASE.

RELATIONS

Τὰ χαλάσανε.*
Ta chalásane.
They broke up.

Τὰ ἔχω καλὰ μέ.*
Ta écho kalà mé.
I am on good terms with.

Τἄχω μαζί της (του).*
Tácho mazí tis (tou).
I am annoyed with her (him).

Κόψαμε τὴν καλημέρα.*
Kópsame tin kaliméra.
We are no longer on speaking terms.

Τὰ πᾶμε καλά.*
Ta páme kalá.
We get on well.

Ἔχουν προηγούμενα.*
Échoun proeeghoùmena.
They are on bad terms.

Τὰ τσούγκρισαν.*
Ta tsoùngrisan.
They had an argument;
they broke off relations.

Τά'χομε καλά.*
Táchome kalá.
We are on good terms.

RELUCTANCE

Κάνω νάζια.*
Káno názya.
I am reluctant.

REMIND

Μὴ ξαίνεις (ἀνοίγεις) πληγές.*
Mi xénees (aneéyees) pliyés.
Don't remind (me) of old troubles.

REPEAT

Κατ' ἐπανάληψιν (ἐπανειλημμένως).*
Katepanálipsin (epaneelimménos).
Repeatedly.

Τὰ ἴδια κοπανάω.
Ta íδia kopanáo.
I keep repeating the same thing.

REPLACE

Τὸν βάζω στὸ πόδι μου.
Ton vázo sto póδi mou.
I leave him in my place.

REPROACH

Τὸν βάζω μπροστὰ (πόστα, κατσάδα).*
Ton vázo brostà (pósta, katsáδa).
I reproach him; I reprimand him.

Τὸν ἔβαλα πόστα (κατσάδα).*
Ton évala pósta (katsáδa).
I scolded him.

Εὐλογημένε μου!
Evloyiméne mou!
(Epithet of mild reproach) my good fellow!

Compare ATTACK.

RESEMBLE

Μοιάζει τοῦ πατέρα της.*
Meeázee tou patéra tis.
She resembles her father.

Μοιάζει τῆς ἀδελφῆς της.*
Meeázee tis aδelphís tis.
She resembles her sister.

RESOLVE

Τὸ βάζω πεῖσμα νά.*
To vázo peézma ná.
I firmly resolve to.

RESPONSIBILITY

'Αναλαμβάνω τὴν εὐθύνη.*
Analamváno tin efθeéni.
I take charge; I assume the responsibility.

Ἄφησέ το σὲ μένα.*
Àphise to se ména.
Leave it (up) to me.

Τὰ φορτώθηκα ὅλα στὴ ράχη μου.*
Ta fortóθika óla sti ráchi mou.
I assumed all the responsibility.

Τὸν παίρνω στὸ λαιμό μου.
Ton bérno sto lemó mou.
I am responsible for his ill fortune.

Ἔχω τὴν εὐθύνη (with genitive or with νά + verb).
Écho tin efθeénee.
I am in charge of.

REVEAL

Βγάζω στὴ μέση.*
Vgházo sti mési.
I bring into the open; reveal.

Βγάζω στὴ φόρα (ξεσκεπάζω, ἀποκαλύπτω).*
Vgházo sti phóra (xeskepázo, apokaleépto).
I reveal.

REVENGE

Βγάζω τὸ ἄχτι μου.*
Vgházo to áchti mou.
I satisfy a desire (especially for vengeance).

Θὰ σοῦ φάω τὸ μάτι.
θa sou fáo to máti.
I will take revenge on you.

Τὸ φυσάει καὶ δὲν κρυώνει.*
To pheesáee ke δen kreeónee.
He (she) cannot get over his (her) chagrin.

REVOLT

Σηκώνω μπαϊράκι.*
Sikono baeeráki.
I revolt.

Καινὰ δαιμόνια.*
Kenà δemónia.
Revolutionary ideas.

RICH

Βαράει (σηκώνει) ἡ τσέπη του.*
Varáee (sikónee) i tsépi tou.
His pockets are full of money.

Δὲ βαστιέμαι.*
δe vastyéme.
I am poor.

Αὐτὸς βαστιέται.*
Aftós vastyéte.
He is rich.

Τὸ φυσάει.*
To pheesáee.
He (she) has money.

RIDE

Κάνω ποδήλατο.*
Káno poδilato.
I ride a bicycle.

RIGHT

Πάει καλά.*
Páee kalá.
All right.

Compare *JUSTICE*.

Κοντὸς ψαλμὸς ἀλληλούϊα!*
Kondós psalmós alliloùia!
That's that!

ROW

Κάνω κουπί.*
Káno koupí.
I row (a boat).

RUDE

Ξέστρωτο γαϊδούρι.
Xéstroto ghaeeδoùri.
Extremely rude person.

RUIN

Μοῦ τὰ μάσισες (ὅλα).*
Mou ta másises óla.
You ruined me completely.

Βγάζω τὰ μάτια μου.*
Vgházo ta mátya mou.
I am ruining myself.

Κατὰ δια(β)όλου.*
Katá δya(v)ólou.
To the devil.

Πάω κατὰ διαόλου.
Páo katá δyaólou.
I am heading for destruction.

RUMOR

Διαδίδεται ὅτι.*
δiaδíδete óti.
It is rumored that.

Διαδόσεις.*
δiaδósees.
Rumor.

RUN

Πάει γιὰ βουλευτής.*
Páee ya vouleftís.
He runs for Parliament.

RUSH

Τσακίστηκε νὰ (+ indefinite)...*
Tsakístike ná...
He (she) broke his (her) neck to...

EXERCISES

Ποῦ ἤσουνα κι' ἔγινες παπί; Εἶναι πολὺ ντροπαλός, γι' αὐτὸ δὲν τρώει πολύ. Αὐτὸ δὲν εἶναι ἀποχρῶν λόγος γιὰ νὰ τὸν φυλακισουν. Δὲν συντρέχει λόγος νὰ εἶσαι τόσο νευρικός. Μίλα πιὸ σιγὰ γιατὶ ἦρθε ὁ προϊστάμενός σου. Κι' ὕστερα; Ὅ,τι καὶ νὰ γίνη, θὰ σὲ παντρευτῶ. Δὲν εἶναι ἀνάγκη νὰ πᾶς σήμερα στὸ νοσοκομεῖο. Ἔτσι κι' ἀλλιῶς θὰ πᾶς αὔριο. Ὅλος ὁ στρατὸς εἶναι ἐν ἐπιφυλακῇ. Μόλις ἔγινε τὸ δυστύχημα ἦρθαν οἱ πρῶτες βοήθειες. Τώρα ξέχασε, μὴ ξαίνεις πληγές. Σοῦ τὸ εἶπα ἐπανειλημμένως. Μοῦ ἔκαμε παρατήρηση κατ' ἐπανάληψιν. Αὐτὸς ὁ ἄνθρωπος ὅλο τὰ ἴδια κοπανάει. Ὁ ἐργοδότης μου, μ' ἔβαλε στὸ πόδι του γιὰ δυὸ βδομάδες ποὺ ἔλειπε. Τὸν ἔβαλε πόστα. Μὴν τὴν βάζεις μπροστά. Εὐλογημένη μου, τί ἤθελες νὰ τὸν ἀγαπήσης! Τὸ παιδί μου μοιάζει τῆς πεθερᾶς μου. Μοιάζεις τοῦ πατέρα σου. Δὲν πέρασε πολὺς καιρός, καὶ τὰ χαλάσανε. Τἄχω καλὰ μὲ τὸν δήμαρχο. Τἄχω μαζί σου, γιατὶ χθὲς βράδυ μὲ κοροΐδεψες στὸ ραντεβοῦ μας. Εἶναι ἕνας χρόνος ποὺ κόψαμε τὴν καλημέρα. Μέχρι τώρα τὰ πᾶμε καλὰ μὲ τὸν συνέταιρο. Αὐτοὶ οἱ δύο δὲν τὰ πᾶνε καλά, ἔχουν προηγούμενα! Δὲν σᾶς βλέπω μαζί. Τί, τὰ τσουγκρίσατε; Ἀνάλαβε, σὲ παρακαλῶ, τὴν εὐθύνη νὰ προσέχης τὶς ἀποσκευὲς τοῦτες. Μὴ στενοχωριέσαι, ἄφησέ το σὲ μένα. Τὰ φορτώθηκε ὅλα στὴ ράχη του. Ἔχω τὴν εὐθύνη νὰ φυλάω τὰ πράγματα αὐτά. Τὴν πῆρε στὸ λαιμό της. Ἄφησε τὰ πράγματα ἐδῶ, ἀλλὰ δὲν ἀναλαμβάνω καμιὰ εὐθύνη. Ὁ δάσκαλος τοῦ χωριοῦ διδάσκει καινὰ δαιμόνια. Στὴν Κῶ ὅλοι κάνουν ποδήλατο. Μὴν τὸν λυπᾶσαι, βαράει ἡ τσέπη του. Ὁ νεαρὸς ἐκεῖνος βαστιέται. Αὐτὴ τὸ φυσάει. Νὰ λὲς τὸ σωστό. Ἂν ἔρθης πρὶν τὶς πέντε, πάει καλά. Ἀλλιῶς θὰ βρῆς κλειστὴ τὴν πόρτα. Κάνεις καλὸ κουπί; Αὐτὴ ἡ κοπέλλα τοῦ τὰ μάσισε ὅλα. Τὸ κατάστημα ποὺ ἄνοιξε τὸν περασμένο μῆνα πάει κατὰ διαόλου. Κάθε μέρα βγάζουν τὰ μάτια τους. Διαδίδεται ὅτι εἶναι ἄρρωστος ἀπὸ καρκῖνο. Ὁ φίλος μου πάει γιὰ βουλευτής. Τσακίστηκα νὰ προφθάσω τὸν σιδηρόδρομο. Μὴν κάνεις νάζια. Τὄβαλα πεῖσμα ν' ἀγοράσω σπίτι. Ἡ νεολαία σήμερα σηκώνει μπαϊράκι εὔκολα.

SAKE

Γιὰ τὸ χατίρι μου!*
Ya to chatíri mou!
For my sake!

Πρὸς Θεοῦ!*
Pros θeoù!
For God's sake!

SALE

Ἔπεσαν οἱ τιμές.*
Épesan ee timés.
Things are on sale.

Αὐτὴ τὴν ἑβδομάδα θὰ ἔχῃ ἔκπτωση.*
Aftí tin evδomáδa θa échi ékptosi.
This week there will be a sale.

SAVE

Βάζω στὴ μπάντα.*
Vázo sti mbánda.
I lay aside; save up (money).

Βάζω λεφτὰ στὴν ἄκρη.*
Vázo leftà stin ákri.
I save money (in the bank).

SAY

Τί νὰ σοῦ πῶ;*
Tí na sou pó?
What shall I say?

Ἔχω τὸ βέτο.*
Écho to véto.
I have the final say.

SECRET

Τοῦ παίρνει κανεὶς λόγια μὲ μεγάλη δυσκολία.*
Tou pérnee kanéees lóya me megháli δeeskolía.
He is very trustworthy.

Φυλάγω (διατηρῶ) τὸ μυστικό.*
Pheelágho (δiatiró) to meestikó.
I will keep the secret.

Λέω τὴν ἁμαρτία μου.*
Léo tin amartía mou.
I make no secret of it; I confess my weakness.

Ὑπὸ ἐχεμύθειαν.*
Eepó echemeéθeean.
Under pledge of secrecy.

Τῆς πῆρα λόγια.*
Tis píra lóya.
I wormed it out of her.

Compare KNOWLEDGE.

SEE

Ἔγινε ἀκριβοθώρητος.*
Éyine akrivoθóritos.
He rarely is seen.

Κατὰ τὸ δοκοῦν.*
Katà to δokoùn.
As one sees fit.

Ἔκανα μαῦρα μάτια νὰ τὸν δῶ.*
Ékana mávra mátia na ton δό.
I have not seen him for ages.

Compare PRETEND.

SET

Βάζω πλώρη (for boat).*
Vázo plóri.
I set sail.

Βάλθηκα νὰ μάθω Ἑλληνικά.
Válϑika na máϑo Elliniká.
I set out to learn Greek.

SHAME

Ἀναίδεια; (Ἄκου κεῖ)!*
Anéδeea? (Àkou keè)!
What nerve!

Μὴ μὲ γελοιοποιεῖς.*
Mí me yeleeopeeís.
Don't make fun of me.

Μὴ σπάνεις πλάκα μὲ μένα.*
Mi spánees pláka me ména.
Don't make fun of me.

SHARE

Τί μοῦ ἀναλογεῖ (ποιὸ εἶναι τὸ μερτικό μου, τὸ μερίδιό μου);*
Tí mou analoyeè (pyó eéne to mertikó mou. to meríδió mou)?
What is my share?

SHIPPING

Ἄγονος γραμμή.*
Àghonos ghrammí.
Unprofitable line (shipping).

SHOCK

Ἔμεινε κόκκαλο.*
Émeene kókkalo.
He was dumbstruck.

Ἔμεινε ξερὸς (μὲ ἀνοιχτὸ στόμα).*
Émeene xerós (me aneechtó stóma).
He was extremely shocked; he fell dead.

SHOP

Ἔχετε κλείσει;*
Échete kleésee?
Are you (store) closed?

Πότε ἀνοίγετε;*
Póte aneéyete?
What time do you open?

Μέχρι τί ὥρα εἶστε ἀνοιχτοί;*
Mérchri ti óra eéste aneeshteé?
Until what time are you open?

SHREWD

Δια(β)όλου κάλτσα (διαβολεμένος, διαβολάνθρωπος).*
δya(v)ólou káltsa (δyavoleménos, δyavolánϑropos).
Very shrewd and able person.

SICK

Μὲ ζάλισες.*
Me zálises.
You make me sick.

Ἔχω κοψίματα.
Écho kopsímata.
I have diarrhea.

Αὐτὸς πάσχει ἀπὸ μεγαλομανία.*
Aftós páschee apó meghalomanía.
He suffers from megalomania.

Μὲ πιάνει ἡ θάλασσα.*
Me pyánee i ϑálassa.
I become seasick.

SILENCE

Μὴ βγάλῃς ἄχνα.
Mi vghális áchna.
Do not utter a sound.

Δὲν ἔβγαλε τσιμουδιά!*
δen évghale tsimouδyá!
He (she) did not utter a word!

Τὸν (τὴν) ἔπιασε γλωσσοδέτης.*
Ton (tin) épyase ghlossoδétis.
He (she) was tongue-tied.

Compare QUIET.

SINCE

Ἀπὸ πότε;*
Apo póte?
Since when? Starting when?

Ἀφοῦ εἶναι ἔτσι.*
Afoù eéne étsi.
This being so.

SLEEP

Κλείνω τὸ μάτι.*
Kleéno to máti.
I wink, sleep.

Ἀπόψε δὲν ἔκλεισα μάτι.
Apópse δen ékleesa máti.
Last night I did not sleep at all.

SMART

Κάνω τὸν ἔξυπνο.*
Káno ton éxeepno.
I act smart.

Γερὸ κεφάλι.*
Yeró kefáli.
Very clever.

Αὐτὸς εἶναι γερὸ κεφάλι.
Aftós eéne yeró kefáli.
He is very clever (intelligent).

Θηλυκὸ μυαλό.*
ϑileekó mialó.
Creative mind.

SMELL

'Ακούω μυρωδιά.
Akoùo meeroδyá.
I smell something.

SMOKE

Κόβω τὸ τσιγάρο.*
Kóvo to tsigháro.
I quit smoking.

SO

Ἔτσι κι' ἔτσι.*
Étsi kiétsi.
So-so.

Ἔτσι μοῦ λένε.*
Étsi mou léne.
That is what they tell me.

Ἔτσι δὲν εἶναι;*
Étsi δen eéne?
Right? Isn't that so (right)?

Ὄχι ἔτσι.*
óchi étsi.
Not that way.

Ἔτσι ποὺ (ὥστε).*
Étsi poù (óste).
In such a way that.

Κι' ὕστερα;*
Keéstera?
So what? What then?

Καὶ οὕτω καθ' ἑξῆς.*
Ke oùto kaθexís.
And so on.

SOCIAL

Κοσμικὴ κίνησις.*
Kozmikí kínisis.
Social activity.

Τῆς σειρᾶς μας.*
Tis seeráz mas.
Of our (social) class.

Αὐτὸς εἶναι τῆς σειρᾶς μας.
Aftós eéne tis seeráz mas.
He is of our (social) class.

SOMEHOW

Κουτσὰ στραβὰ (ὅπως ὅπως, κάπως).*
Koutsà stravà (ópos ópos, kápos).
Somehow.

Ἦταν πολλὰ τὰ ἐμπόδια, μὰ κουτσὰ στραβὰ τὰ καταφέραμε.
Itan pollà ta embóδia, ma koutsà stravà ta kataférame.
There were many obstacles, but somehow we overcame them.

SOMEONE

Κάνω κάποιον νὰ κάνη.
Káno kápion na káni.
I force someone to do something.

Compare NONE.

SOMEWHERE

Κάπου ἐκεῖ.*
Kápou ekeé.
Somewhere there.

SORRY

Θὰ κτυπήσης τὸ κεφάλι σου.*
ϑa kteepísis to kefáli sou.
You will be sorry.

Θὰ μετανοιώσης.*
ϑa metaniósis.
You will be sorry.

SORT

Τί λογῆς;*
Ti loyís?
What sort of?

Τί λογῆς ἄνθρωπος εἶναι;
Ti loyís ánϑropos eéne?
What kind of man is he?

Ἡ σάρα κι' ἡ μάρα.*
I sára kee mára.
All kinds of people.

Λογιῶν - λογιῶν.*
Loyón - loyón.
All sorts of.

SPEECH

Βγάζω λόγο.*
Vgházo lógho.
I make a speech.

Ὁ λόγος του ἦταν θαυμάσιος.
O lóghos tou ítan ϑavmásios.
His speech was wonderful.

SPEND

Ξόδεψε ὅ,τι εἶχε καὶ δὲν εἶχε.*
Xóδepse óti eéche ke δen eéche.
He (she) spent all his (her) money.

Ξόδεψε τοῦ κόσμου τὰ λεφτά.
Xóδepse tou kózmou ta leftá.
He (she) spent a great deal of money.

Compare PAY.

SPOIL

Χαλάει τὸ κρέας (τὸ ψάρι).*
Chaláee to kréas (to psári).
The meat (the fish) spoils.

Χαλάει τὸ ψάρι ὅταν δὲν τὸ κρατᾶς στὸ ψυγεῖο.
Chaláei to psári ótan δen to kratás sto pseeyío.
Fish spoils when you do not keep it in the refrigerator.

Σαπίζουν τὰ φροῦτα.*
Sapízoun ta froùta.
The fruit rots.

Σαπίζουν τὰ φροῦτα ὅταν τὰ κρατᾶς πολὺ καιρό.
Sapízoun ta froùta. ótan ta kratás poli keró.
Fruit rots when you keep it too long.

STAND

Κάνε στὴν μπάντα.*
Káne stin mbánda.
Stand aside.

Δὲν τὸν χωνεύω.*
δèn don chonévo.
I cannot stand him.

START

Βάζω μπρός.*
Vázo mbrós.
I start (off).

Βάζω τὰ κλάματα.*
Vázo ta klámata.
I start crying.

Πιάνω δουλειά.*
Pyáno δouliá.
I start a (new) job.

STINGY

Εἶναι σφιχτὸς (τσιγγούνης).*
Eéne sfichtós (tsingoùnis).
He is a stingy person.

STRAIGHT

Ἴσια μπρὸς (εὐθεῖα).*
Isya mbrós (efθeéa).
Straight ahead.

Κατ' εὐθεῖαν (ἀπ' εὐθείας).*
Katefθeéan (apefθeéas).
Straight; direct.

STUBBORN

Ἀγύριστο κεφάλι.*
Ayeéristo kefáli.
Stubborn person.

Δὲν τὸ βάζω κάτω.
δen to vázo káto.
I will not admit defeat.

Τοῦ καρφώθηκε ἡ ἰδέα.
Tou karfóθike i iδéa.
He is possessed with the idea.

Κάνω τοῦ κεφαλιοῦ μου.
Káno tou kefalioù mou.
I go my own way; I do as I please.

STUPID

Εἶναι ἄμυαλος (ἠλίθιος).*
Eéne ámialos (iliθios).
He has no brains.

SUCCEED

Τὰ βγάζω πέρα.*
Ta vgházo péra.
I succeed; manage.

Δρέπω δάφνας.*
δrépo δáfnas.
I triumph; succeed.

Compare MANAGE.

SUDDENLY

Μὲ μιᾶς (ξαφνικά).*
Me miás (xafniká).
Suddenly, all of a sudden.

Στὰ καλὰ καθούμενα.
Sta kalá kaθoùmena.
Out of the blue; all of a sudden.

Ἐξ ἀπροόπτου (αἰφνιδίως, ἔξαφνα, ἀπροσδόκητα).*
Ex aproóptou (efniδíos, éxafna, aprosδókita).
Unexpectedly, suddenly.

SUPPOSE

Πὲς πὼς κέρδισα.*
Pés pós kérδisa.
Supposing I won.

SURE

Στὰ σίγουρα.*
Sta síghoura.
In safety.

Χωρὶς ἄλλο (δίχως ἄλλο, ἐξ ἅπαντος).*
Chorís állo (δíchos állo, ex ápandos).
For sure; without fail.

Γιὰ καλά.*
Ya kalá.
For certain, definitely.

Δὲν χωρεῖ ἀμφιβολία.*
δen chorí amfivolía.
There is no room for doubt.

Γιὰ τὰ καλά.*
Ya ta kalá.
Seriously, definitely.

SUSPECT

Μπαίνω σὲ ἰδέα.*
Béno se iδéa.
I become suspicious.

Παίρνω μυρωδιὰ (χαμπάρι).*
Pérno meercδyá (chambári).
I get wind of; suspect.

EXERCISES

Γιὰ τὸ χατήρι σου θὰ ριψοκινδυνέψω νὰ πάω στὴ φυλακή. Πρὸς Θεοῦ, μὴ λὲς τόσα ψέματα! Αὐτὴ τὴ 6δομάδα θὰ πέσουν οἱ τιμές. Πόσα 6άζεις στὴν μπάντα κάθε 6δομάδα; Τοῦ χρόνου (next year) θὰ 6άζω πολλὰ λεφτὰ στὴν ἄκρη. Τί νὰ σοῦ πῶ, δὲν εἶναι συνεπὴς οὔτε εἰλικρινής. Ἔχω νὰ σὲ δῶ γιὰ τρεῖς μῆνες, ἔγινες ἀκριβοθώρητος! Ἔκανα μαῦρα μάτια νὰ σὲ δῶ. Εἶμαι νευρικός, λέω τὴν ἁμαρτία μου. Αὐτὰ ποὺ σοῦ λέγω, ὑπὸ ἐχεμύθειαν. παρακαλῶ. Τῆς πῆρα λόγια εὔκολα. Τί ὥρα βάζεις τραπέζι; Βάλθηκα νὰ μάθω Ἑλληνικά. Ἔπειτα ἀπὸ τόσες βρισιές, ἀναίδεια νὰ μοῦ τηλεφωνήση! Δὲν σοῦ ἀναλογεῖ τίποτα. Ὅταν τὸν εἶδα ἔμεινα κόκκαλο. Ἔμεινα ξερὴ ἀπὸ τὴν συμπεριφορά του. Ἔχετε κλείσει; Ὄχι, εἶμαι ἀκόμη ἀνοιχτός. Σπάνει πλάκα μὲ σένα. Σιγά - σιγά, μὴ βγάλης ἄχνα. Πολλὰ μοῦ εἶπες, βρὲ ἀδερφέ, μὲ ζάλισες. Σὲ πιάνει ἡ θάλασσα; Λιγάκι. Δὲν τὴν πιάνει ἡ θάλασσα. Ἀπὸ πότε δουλεύεις ἐδῶ; Ἀφοῦ εἶναι ἔτσι, δὲν ἔρχομαι μαζί σου. Εἶχα στεναχωρεθῆ τόσο πολὺ ποὺ δὲν ἔκλεισα μάτι ὅλη τὴ νύχτα. Μὴν κάνεις τὸν ἔξυπνο. Ἔχεις θηλυκὸ μυαλό. Δὲν ἔχει γερὸ κεφάλι. Δὲν μπορῶ νὰ κόψω τὸ τσιγάρο. Περιμένει κανένας ἔξω; Ὄχι, δέν εἶναι κανένας. Αὐτὸς δὲν εἶναι τῆς σειρᾶς της. Κουτσὰ - στραβὰ πῆρε τὸ δίπλωμά του. Ἂν δὲ μ' ἀκούσης, θὰ κτυπήσης τὸ κεφάλι σου. Τί λογῆς ἄνθρωπος εἶναι; Στὶς μεγάλες πόλεις ζοῦν λογιῶν - λογιῶν ἄνθρωποι. Σ' αὐτὸ τὸ καφενεῖο μαζεύονται ἡ σάρα κι' ἡ μάρα. Ξόδεψε ὅ,τι εἶχε καὶ δὲν εἶχε γιὰ νὰ σπουδάση τὰ παιδιά του. Ξόδεψε τοῦ κόσμου τὰ λεφτὰ γιὰ νὰ κάμη τὴν μάνα του καλά. Αὐτὸ τὸ σπίτι τῆς κόστισε ὁ κοῦκος ἀηδόνι. Χάλασε τὸ κρέας, γιατὶ δὲν τὄβαλες στὸ ψυγεῖο. Ἡ σπιτονοικοκυρά μου εἶναι σφιχτή. Αὐτὸς εἶναι ἀγύριστο κεφάλι. Τοῦ καρφώθηκε ἡ ἰδέα ν' ἀνοίξη ἑστιατόριο. Μὴν κάνεις τοῦ κεφαλιοῦ σου. Πῆραν τὰ μυαλά της ἀέρα. Αὐτὸ τὸ κορίτσι εἶναι ἄμυαλο. Πῶς μπορῶ ν' ἀφήσω τὶς δουλειές μου καὶ στὰ καλὰ καθούμενα νὰ ταξιδέψω; Ξαφνικά, ἔνοιωσα στὶς πλάτες μου δυὸ χέρια. Ποιὸς ἦταν; Ὁ ἀδελφός μου ἀπ' τὴν Ἀμερική! Παρ' ὅλες τὶς δυσκολίες, τἄβγαλα πέρα. Ὁ ἀδελφός μου δρέπει δάφνες στὸ ἐξωτερικό. Αὐτὸς εἶναι τρελλός, στὰ σίγουρα. Θὰ σὲ περιμένω ἐξ ἅπαντος στὶς ὀκτώ. Αὐτὸ τὸ φθινόπωρο θὰ πάω στὴν Ἑλλάδα χωρὶς ἄλλο. Τὴν ψώνισε γιά καλά. Τὸ ἅρπαξε τὸ κρυολόγημα γιὰ τὰ καλά. Δὲν χωρεῖ ἀμφιβολία πὼς εἶναι δραστήριος καὶ τυχερὸς ἐπιχειρηματίας. Μᾶς πῆραν μυρωδιά. Ὑποπτεύομαι πὼς ἔχουν ἐρωτικὲς σχέσεις. Πὲς πὼς κέρδισες τρεῖς χιλιάδες δολλάρια. Τί θὰ τὰ ἔκανες; Βάλε μπρὸς τὴν μηχανὴ νὰ φύγουμε.

TAKE

Παίρνω τὸ δίκηο του.*	Τοῦ δίνω δίκηο.*	Δίνω ἐξετάσεις.
Pérno to δíkio tou.	Tou δíno δíkio.	δíno exetásees.
I take his part.	I take his part.	I take examinations.

Δράττομαι τῆς εὐκαιρίας.*
δráttome tis efkerías.
I take the opportunity.

Παίρνω ἀπὸ κακό.
Pérno apó kakó.
I take a dislike to.

Τὸν πῆρε μὲ ἄσχημο (κακὸ) μάτι _or_ τὸν κακοπῆρε.
Ton píre me áschimo (kakó) máti _or_ ton kakopíre.
He disliked him from the very beginning.

Μοῦ κατεβαίνει νά.
Mou katevénee ná.
It comes to my mind to.

Τοῦ κάπνισε νὰ (+ verb).
Tou kápnise ná.
It came to his mind to.

Τὸν πῆρα ἀπὸ καλό.*
Ton píra apó kaló.
I liked him from the very beginning.

Παίρνω (λαμβάνω) μέτρα.*
Pérno (lamváno) métra.
I take measures.

TALK

Κάνω τὸν καμπόσο.*
Káno ton gambóso.
I talk big; boastingly.

'Αρλοῦμπες.
Arloùmbes.
Foolish talk; boasting.

Τὄστρωσε στὴν κουβέντα.*
Tóstrose stin gouvénda.
He (she) talked too much.

Ἔλα νὰ σοῦ πῶ.*
Éla na sou pó.
Come here; I want to talk to you.

Μοῦ ἔφαγε τ' αὐτιά.
Mou éfaye taftyá.
He (she) talked too much.

Μὴ βγάλης ἄχνα.
Mi vghális áchna.
Do not utter a sound.

Μὴ συζητᾶς ἄτοπα.*
Mi seezitás átopa.
Don't talk of unbecoming things.

Μὴ τσιρίζεις.*
Mi tsirízees.
Don't talk too much.

Παίρνω φόρα.*
Pérno fóra.
I begin to speak without control.

Βγάζω γλώσσα.*
Vgházo ghlóssa.
I answer cheekily.

Κόβει καὶ ράβει.*
Kóvee ke rávee.
He (she) talks incessantly.

Νὰ σοῦ πῶ.*
Na sou pó.
I say; look here (also as qualified rejoinder or guarded response).

Θὰ τὰ ποῦμε.*
ϑa ta poùme.
We will have a talk.

Μίλα ρωμαίικα!*
Míla roméeeka!
Be explicit!

Ἄλλα ἀντ' ἄλλων.*
Àlla andállon.
Random talk.

Compare TELL; SAY.

TAX

Κεφαλικὸς φόρος.*
Kefalikós phóros.
Personal tax.

TEAR

Κροκοδείλια δάκρυα.*
Krokoδeélia δákreea.
False tears.

TEASE

Μὴ μὲ πειράζεις.*
Mí me peerázis.
Don't tease me.

Μὴ μὲ δουλεύεις.*
Mí me δoulévees.
Don't tease me.

Τοῦ βάζω τὰ ἑφτὰ καρφιά.
Tou vázo ta eftà karfyá.
I tease him.

TELEPHONE

Μὴν κλείσῃς τὸ ἀκουστικό.*
Mín glísis to akoustikó.
Hold the line.

TELL

Γιὰ πές μας.
Ya péz mas.
Come on, tell us.

Δὲ μοῦ λέτε.
δé mou léte.
Please tell me.

Πές μου κάτι.
Péz mou káti.
Tell me something.

Ἀραδιάζω.*
Araδyázo.
I recount (tell) quickly and without any interruption.

Ἀλλοῦ αὐτά!
Alloù aftá!
Don't tell me that!

Compare TALK; SAY.

TERRIBLE

Εἶναι ἀπελπισία (γιὰ κλάματα).*
Eéne apelpisía (ya klámata).
It is hopeless (terrible).

THANK

Δόξα σοι, ὁ Θεός!*
δóxa see, o θeós!
Glory to God!

Δόξα τῷ Θεῷ!*
δóxa to θeó!
Thank God!

THERE

Ἐκεῖ.*
Ekeé.
There.

Ἐκεῖ πέρα.*
Ekeè péra.
Over there, in the distance.

Πιὸ πέρα (παρέκει).*
Pyó péra (parekeé).
Further over.

THINK

Μοῦ φαίνεται πώς...*
Mou fénete pós...
I think, believe; it seems to me that...

Γιὰ σκέψου!*
Ya sképsou!
Just think of it!

Πῆρε ψηλὰ τὸ χερουβικὸ (τὸν ἀμανέ).
Píre psilá to cherouvikó (ton amané).
He(she) thought too much of himself (herself).

Στερνὴ γνώση.*
Sterní ghnósi.
Second thought; wise opinion.

Στερνή μου γνώση, νὰ σ' εἶχα πρῶτα.*
Sterní mou ghnósi, na seécha próta.
If only I had my second thought sooner.

Σκέψου καλά.*
Sképsou kalá.
Think hard.

Ποῦ ἀρμενίζει (ταξιδεύει) ἡ σκέψη σου;*
Pou armenízee (taxiδévee) i sképsi sou?
Where is your thought traveling?

Μόνο νὰ τὸ σκεφθῶ!*
Móno na to skefθó!
At the mere thought of it!

Τὸ ἔχει γιὰ γοῦρι.
To échee ya ghoùri.
He (she) thinks it a lucky omen.

Τὸ ἔχω σὲ κακό.
To écho se kakó.
I think it a bad omen.

Δὲ μοῦκοψε (δὲ μοῦ κατέβηκε, δὲν τό' βαλε ὁ νοῦς μου).
δe moùkopse (δé mou katévike, δen tóvale o noùz mou).
It did not occur to me (to).

THOROUGHLY

Κατὰ βάθος (κατ' οὐσίαν).*
Katà váθos (katousían).
Essentially, thoroughly.

TIME

Γιὰ τὴν ὥρα.*
Ya tin óra.
So far (of time).

Ἐδῶ καί....
Εδό ké...
...ago; for (period of time).

Ἐδῶ καὶ τρεῖς μέρες.
Εδό ke treés méres.
Three days ago.

Ἐν τῷ μεταξὺ (στὸ μεταξύ).*
En do metaxeè (sto metaxeè).
In the meantime; meanwhile.

Κάθε μέρα (καθημερινῶς).*
Κάθe méra (kaθimerinós).
Daily (adverb); every day.

Κάθε πότε;*
Κάθe póte?
How often?

Μὲ τὸν καιρό.*
Me ton geró.
In time, eventually, gradually.

Καμιὰ φορά.
Kamiá forá.
Once in a while; never (with negative).

Πόση ὥρα κάνει;
Pósi óra kánee?
How long does it take?

Κάθε λίγο καὶ λιγάκι (κάθε ὥρα καὶ στιγμή).
Κάθe lígho ke lighάki (kάθe óra ke stighmí).
Every so often.

Κάθε τόσο.*
Κάθe tóso.
Every so often.

Κάθε λίγο καὶ λιγάκι τὸν βλέπαμε.
Κάθe lígho ke lighάki ton vlépame.
Every so often we saw him.

Σὲ λίγο.
Se lígho.
In a while, shortly, soon; for a while.

Δὲν εἶναι σωστὸ νὰ μᾶς ἐνοχλῇς κάθε ὥρα καὶ στιγμή.
δen eéne sostó na más enochlís kάθe óra ke stighmí.
It isn't right to bother us every so often.

Πόσες τοῦ μηνὸς ἔχουμε σήμερα;*
Póses tou minós échoume símera?
What is the date today?

Γιὰ μερικὲς μέρες.*
Ya merikés méres.
For a few days.

Χρόνο μὲ χρόνο.*
Chróno me chróno.
Year by year.

Μέρα παρὰ μέρα.*
Méra paraméra.
Every other day.

Μιὰ καὶ καλὴ (μιὰ γιὰ πάντα).*
Miá ke kalí (miá ya pánda).
Once and for all.

Ὅπου νά 'ναι.*
Opou náne.
Any minute now.

Πάει πέντε ἡ ὥρα.
Páee pénde i óra.
It is almost five o' clock.

'Από πότε;*
Apó póte?
Since when?

Πρὶν περάσει πολλὴ ὥρα.*
Prín perási pollí óra.
Before long.

Πόσο συχνὰ (κάθε πότε);*
Póso seechnà (káϑe póte)?
How often?

Μέχρι πότε;*
Méchri póte?
Until when?

Ποτὲ πρίν!*
Potè prín!
Never before!

Ποτὲ πάλι.
Potè páli.
Never again.

Σχεδὸν ποτέ.*
Scheδón potè.
Almost never.

Μιὰ στιγμούλα.
Mià stighmoùla.
Just a minute.

Τὶς προάλλες.*
Tis proálles.
The other day, recently.

Τοῦ χρόνου.*
Tou chrónou.
Next year.

Καὶ τοῦ χρόνου!
Ke tou chrónou!
And next year!

'Από τώρα κι' ὕστερα.*
Apo tóra keéstera.
From now on; henceforth.

'Ως (τὰ) τώρα.*
Os (ta) tóra.
Till now.

Τώρα ἀμέσως.*
Tóra amésos.
Right now.

Χθὲς (χτὲς) τὸ μεσημέρι.*
Chϑés (chtés) to mesiméri.
Yesterday noon.

Χαμένος καιρός.*
Chaménos kerós.
A waste of time.

Χθὲς τὸ βράδυ.*
Chϑés to vráδee.
Last night.

Χθὲς τὸ πρωΐ (σήμερα, αὔριο, προχθές).*
Chϑés to proeè (símera, ávrio, prochϑés).
Yesterday morning (today, tomorrow, day before yesterday).

'Ωσότου νὰ (+ verb).
Osótou ná.
Until, till.

Μῆνες καὶ καιρούς.
Mínes ke keroùs.
Long time.

Ἔχω μῆνες καὶ καιροὺς νὰ σὲ δῶ.*
Écho mínes ke keroùs na sé δó.
I haven't seen you for a long time.

Χειμώνα καλοκαίρι.*
Cheemóna kalokéri.
All year round.

Ποῦ καὶ ποῦ.
Poù ke poù.
Now and then; here and there.

Μᾶς παίρνει ἡ ὥρα.*
Mas pérnee i óra.
We have time.

Οἱ βλάχοι ζοῦνε στὰ βουνὰ καὶ στὰ χαμηλώματα χειμώνα καλο καίρι.
Ee vláchee zoùne sta vounà ké sta chamilómata cheemóna kalo kéri.
Peasants live in the mountains and in the plains all year round.

('Α) πάνω πού.*
(A) páno poù.
At the moment when.

Μιὰ ὥρα ἀρχύτερα.*
Miá óra archeétera.
As soon as possible.

Αὐθημερὸν (τὴν ἴδια μέρα).*
Afϑimerón (tin íδya méra).
On the same day.

Στὸ ἑξῆς.*
Sto exís.
From now on.

Ἕως τὴν αὐγή.*
Éos tin avyí.
Until dawn.

Ἕως ὅτου νὰ (+ indefinite).
Éos ótou ná.
Until.

Κάναμε γοῦστο.*
Káname ghoùsto.
We had an amusing time.

Πόσες ἔχει ὁ μήνας;
Póses échee o mínas?
What day of the month is it?

Δὲν κατατρίβομαι μὲ μικρὰ πράγματα.*
δen gatatrívome me mikrá prághmata.
I don't waste my time with trifles.

Ἴσα μὲ τὶς τέσσερεις.
Isa me tis tésserees.
Up to (until) four o' clock.

Ἔκανε καιρὸ νὰ μᾶς γράψη.*
Ékane keró ná mas ghrápsi.
He (she) took a long time to write to us.

Κατ' ἔτος.*
Katétos.
Every year; per year.

Κοντεύει μεσημέρι.*
Kondévee mesiméri.
It is almost noon.

Σὰ(ν) σήμερα πέρσυ.*
Sa(n) símera pérsee.
A year ago today.

Ἄλλη φορά.
Àlli phorá.
Some other time.

Ὥρα μὲ τὴν ὥρα.*
Ora me tin óra.
At any moment.

TIRED

'Αποκά(μ)νω.*
Apoká(m)no.
I get tired.

Ψόφιος στὴν κούραση.*
Psófyos stin goùrasi.
Dead tired.

TOOTH

Χρειάζεται σφράγισμα τὸ δόντι μου;
Chreeázete sfráyizma to δóndi mou?
My tooth needs to be filled.

Βούλλωσα τὸ δόντι μου.*
Voùllosa to δóndi mou.
I filled my tooth;
I had my tooth filled.

TORTURE

Μοῦ 'ψησε τὸ ψάρι στὰ χείλη.*
Moùpsise to psári sta cheéli.
He (she) made me unhappy.

Μοῦ 'βγαλε τὴν ψυχὴ ἀνάποδα.*
Moùvghale tin psichí anápoδa.
He (she) tortured me to death.

Μᾶς πότισε ὅλους φαρμάκι (πίκρα).*
Mas pótise ólous farmáki (píkra).
He (she) made us all unhappy.

Compare TROUBLE.

TRICKS

Δὲ μ' ἀρέσουν οἱ κατεργαριές.*
δé marésoun ee katergharyès.
I don't like cunning acts, tricks.

Μοῦ τὴν κατάφερε.*
Mou tin gatáfere.
He played a trick on me.

Τὸν ἔκοψα.
Ton ékopsa.
I tricked him;
I did not pass him (in exam).

Μοῦ 'στησε μιὰ μηχανή.
Moùstise miá michaní.
He played a trick on me.

Τοῦ σκάρωσα μιὰ δουλειά.*
Tou skárosa miá δouliá.
I played a trick on him.

Μοῦ τὴν ἔφτιαξε.*
Mou tin éftyaxe.
He (she) played a trick on me.

TRIP

Κλείνω θέση.*
Kleéno θési.
I make a reservation.

Περάσαμε θαυμάσια.*
Perásame θavmásia.
We had a wonderful time.

Trécho na prolávo.
Τρέχω νὰ προλάβω.*
I run to catch (a train, bus, etc.).

Τράβα στ' ἀνοιχτά.*
Tráva staneechtá.
Anchors away.

Ποῦ βγάζει ὁ δρόμος;*
Pou vgházee o δrómos?
Where does the road lead?

Καθ' ὁδόν.*
Kaθoδón.
On the way.

Τί διατυπώσεις χρειάζονται;*
Ti δiateepósees chreeázonde?
What kind of formalities are necessary?

TROUBLE

Τὰ χρειάστηκα.*
Ta chreeástika.
I was in a desperate situation.

Τὸν (τὴν) ἔφαγαν τὰ βάσανα.*
Ton (tin) éfaghan ta vásana.
He (she) suffered much.

Μοῦ 'ψησε τὸ ψάρι στὰ χείλη.*
Moùpsise to psári sta cheéli.
He (she) made me unhappy.

Ἔχω φωτιὰ καὶ λάβρα στὰ στήθη μου.*
Écho fotyá ke lávra sta stíϑi mou.
I am extremely troubled (upset).

Πανικόβλητος.*
Panikóvlitos.
Panic-stricken.

Οἱ ἄνθρωποι στοὺς σεισμοὺς γίνονται πανικόβλητοι.
Eee ánϑropee stous seezmoùs yínonde panikóvlitee.
In earthquakes people become panic-stricken.

Ἔχομεν ἁμαρτίες ἀκόμη.
Échomen amartíes akómi.
We have more troubles in store.

Μὴ ξαίνεις (ἀνοίγεις) πληγές.*
Mi xénees (aneéyis) pliyès.
Don't remind (me) of old troubles.

Μ' ἔφερε στὸ ἄκρον ἄωτον.*
Méfere sto ákron áoton.
He (she) brought me to the utmost point. He (she) made me lose my patience.

Ἦρθα στὸ ἄκρον ἄωτον.*
Irϑa sto ákron áoton.
I came to the utmost point. I lost my patience.

Μὲ λόγια δὲ σώνεται ἡ κατάστασις.
Me lóya δe sónete i katástasis.
The situation will not be solved by words alone.

Μαύρισε τὸ μάτι μου.*
Mávrise to máti mou.
I am driven to desperation (by poverty, etc.).

Ἤπια πολλὰ φαρμάκια.*
Ipya pollà farmákia.
I met many troubles.

Μοῦ ἦρθε κεραμίδα.
Mou írϑe keramíδa.
It was a bombshell to me.

Μόνο νὰ τὸ σκεφθῶ!*
Móno na to skefϑó!
At the mere thought of it!

Βρῆκα τὸ μπελᾶ μου.*
Vríka to belá mou.
I got involved (in trouble).

Τὸν τρώ(γ)ει ἡ μύτη του (ἡ ράχη του).*
Ton dró(y)ee i meéti tou (i ráchi tou).
He is asking for trouble.

Ρουθούνι δὲν ἔμεινε.*
Rouϑoùni δen émeene.
Not a soul survived.

Εἶμαι πάνω σ' ἀναμμένα κάρβουνα.
Eéme páno sanamména kárvouna.
I am in hot water.

Ἄνω - κάτω.*
Àno - káto.
Upset, upside down.

Εἶμαι ἄνω - κάτω.*
Eéme áno - káto.
I am upset.

Εἶναι ἄνω - κάτω.*
Eéne áno - káto.
It is in a mess (of house, office, etc.).

Διακυβεύεις τή ζωή σου.*
δiakeevévees ti zoeé sou.
You are taking a chance on your life.

Εἴχατε φασαρία;*
Eéchate fasaría?
Did you have much trouble?

TRUTH

Μὰ τὴν ἀλήθεια!*
Ma tin alíϑya!
In truth!

Ὄνομα καὶ πρᾶμα!*
Onoma ke práma!
In very truth!

TURN

Ἄνοιξε τὸ φῶς.
Aneexe to fós.
Turn on the light.

Κλεῖσε τὸ φῶς.
Kleése to fós.
Turn off the light.

Μοῦ βγῆκε σὲ καλό.*
Mou vyíke se kaló.
It turned out well for me.

Κόβω δεξιά.
Kóvo δexiá.
I turn right.

Μὲ τὴ σειρά.*
Me ti seerá.
In turn.

EXERCISES

Ἄδικα παίρνεις τὸ δίκηο του. Ὅλοι ξέρουν πὼς αὐτὸς φταίει. Πότε δίνεις ἐξετάσεις; Μὴν τῆς δίνεις δίκηο. Δράττομαι τῆς εὐκαιρίας νὰ σᾶς εὐχαριστήσω γιὰ τὴν εὐκολία ποὺ μοῦ κάνατε. Μὲ πῆρε ἀπὸ κακὸ γιατὶ τοῦ εἶπα ὀρθὰ κοφτὰ τὶ σκεπτόμουνα. Τὸν πῆρε μὲ κακὸ μάτι. Μᾶς κακοπῆρε. Αὐτὸς κάνει τὸν καμπόσο. Ἔλα νὰ σοῦ πῶ κάτι. Τό στρώσαμε στὴν κουβέντα καὶ ξεχάσαμε νὰ πᾶμε γιὰ φαγητό. Μᾶς ἔφαγε τ' αὐτιὰ αὐτὴ ἡ γυναίκα. Αὐτὸς μιλᾶ ἄλλα ἀντ' ἄλλων. Σᾶς λέει ἀρλοῦμπες. Αὐτὸς παίρνει φόρα εὔκολα. Τὶ τσιρίζεις τόση ὥρα! Θὰ τὰ ποῦμε καμιὰ ἄλλη ὥρα. Μίλα ρωμαίηκα! Μὴ μὲ πειράζεις. Τώρα μέ δουλεύεις. Θά τῆς βάλω τὰ ἑφτά καρφιά. Μιά στιγμή, κάποιος κτυπᾶ τὴν πόρτα, μὴν κλείσης τὸ ἀκουστικό. Γιὰ πές μου πῶς πέρασες τὶς διακοπές σου; Δὲ μοῦ λές, ἔχεις γλωσσοδέτη καὶ δὲν μιλᾶς; Πές μας κάτι. Τὶ μᾶς ἀραδιάζεις τόσα ὀνόματα. Τὸ δωμάτιο ποὺ μένω, εἶναι ἀπελπισία. Τὸ φαγητὸ εἶναι γιὰ κλάματα. Μᾶς πῆρε ἀπὸ καλό. Ἐνῶ συζητούσαμε, τοῦ κάπνισε νὰ πιῆ. Κάνε καρδιά, δὲν ἔχεις τίποτα σοβαρό. Χτὲς τῆς κατέβηκε νὰ πάη στὸ Λονδῖνο γιὰ νὰ δουλέψη ἐκεῖ. Ἐδῶ γίνονται πολλὲς κλεψιές, πρέπει νά λάβης τὰ μέτρα σου. Ἔχε τὸ νοῦ σου στὶς ἀποσκευές. Πῶς εἶσαι; Εἶμαι καλά, δόξα τῷ Θεῷ! Δόξα σοι, ὁ Θεός, ἦρθες ἐπὶ τέλους! Γιὰ σκέψου, αὐτὴ τὸν ἔσωσε κι' αὐτὸς δὲν τῆς λέει οὔτε καλημέρα! Πρὶν ἀνοίξης μαγαζί, σκέψου καλά. Ἔκαμε λίγα χρήματα καὶ πῆρε ψηλὰ τὸν ἀμανέ. Γιατὶ εἶναι σιωπηλός, ποῦ ἀρμενίζει ἡ σκέψη σου; Ὅταν χύνεται τὸ κρασὶ στὸ τραπέζι, τὸ ἔχει γιὰ γούρι. Μὰ σὰν γαυγίζει λυπητερὰ ἕνα σκυλὶ σὲ σταυροδρόμι, τὸ ἔχει σὲ κακό. Δὲν μᾶς ἔκοψε νὰ βγάλωμε καὶ φέτα τυρί. Μόνο νὰ τὸ σκεφθῆς πὼς εἶναι καρδιακός! Εἶναι νευρικός, μὰ κατὰ βάθος εἶναι καλὸς καὶ πονόψυχος. Δὲν πιάνει κακία (he or she does not hate anyone). Κατ' οὐσίαν δὲν ἔχομε καμιὰ διαφορά. 'Απόκαμα πιὰ νὰ τὸν συμβουλεύω. Κάθε βράδυ πηγαίνω σπίτι ψόφιος στὴν κούραση. Περνᾶμε καλὰ γιὰ τὴν ὥρα. 'Εδῶ καὶ τρία χρόνια τὸ μέρος αὐτὸ δὲν εἶχε οὔτε ἕνα κατάστημα. Στὴν Νέα Ὑόρκη καθημερινῶς ἀκούει κανεὶς Ἑλληνικὰ ἀπ' τὰ ράδια, στοὺς δρόμους, κ.λ.π. Μὲ τὸν καιρό, ὅλα ξεχνιοῦνται. Καμιὰ φορὰ τὸν βλέπω στὸ πανεπιστήμιο. Κάθε τόσο βήχει. Κάθε πότε ἔχει ἀεροπλάνο γιά Ρόδο; Πόση ὥρα κάνει τὸ ἀεροπλάνο ἀπὸ 'Αθήνα — Θεσσαλονίκη. Σὲ λίγο, θ' ἀρχίση ἡ μουσική. Παρὰ τρίχα νὰ ἔχω δυστύχημα. Χρόνο μὲ χρόνο οἱ τιμὲς ἀνεβαίνουν. Δουλεύω μέρα παρὰ μέρα. Γιὰ μερικὲς μέρες τώρα, ἔχω πονοκέφαλο. Πόσο συχνὰ ἔχει πλοῖο γιὰ τὰ νησιά. Τώρα ἀμέσως ἔρχομαι. Ὡς τώρα δὲν ἔχω παράπονο ἀπ' τὴ δουλειά μου. Διάβασε αὐτὸ τὸ περιοδικὸ ὡσότου νὰ ἑτοιμαστῶ. Πάνω ποὺ ἔκλεινα τὴν πόρτα, νὰ ἡ Κική. Ἔλα, τέλειωνε μιὰ ὥρα ἀρχύτερα. Πότε φθάνει τὸ πλοῖο στὴν Κρήτη; Αὐθημερόν. Τὸν κάνω γοῦστο (I enjoy him). Πῆρα τὸ δίπλωμά μου ἐδῶ καὶ δυὸ χρόνια. Στὸ ἑξῆς, δὲν θέλω νὰ τὸν βλέπω. Κοντεύει μεσημέρι καὶ ἀκόμη δὲν γλυτώσαμε (we did not finish) ἀπὸ τὸν γιατρό. Μᾶς παίρνει ἡ ὥρα νὰ πάρωμε ἕνα γλυκό; Σὰ σήμερα πέρυσι ἤμασταν στὴ Θεσσαλονίκη. Ἄλλη φορὰ θὰ σὲ κεράσω ἐγώ. Ὥρα μὲ τὴν ὥρα τὸ περιμένουμε τὸ καράβι. Δὲν τῆς ἀρέσουν οἱ κατεργαριές. Μᾶς τὴν κατάφερε ἄσχημα. Μοῦ σκάρωσε μιὰ δουλειὰ ποὺ δὲν μπορῶ νὰ σοῦ πῶ! Μᾶς τὴν ἔφτιαξε. Ἂν κάνεις ἕνα ταξίδι θὰ γίνης καλά. Κλεῖστε μου θέση, παρακαλῶ, μὲ τὸ ἔξη. Περάσαμε θαυμάσια στὸ περυσινό μας ταξίδι. Τρέξε νὰ προλάβωμε τὸ λεωφορεῖο. Βγάζει αὐτὸς ὁ δρόμος στὴν ἀρχαία ἀγορά ἢ στὴν ἀκρόπολη; Τὶ διατυπώσεις χρειάζονται γιὰ νὰ βρῶ μιὰ καλὴ δουλειὰ στὴν κυβέρνηση; Συναντήσαμε τὴν θεία σου καθ' ὁδόν. Θέλω νὰ βουλλώσω τὸ δόντι μου. Μᾶς ἔψησε τὸ ψάρι στὰ χείλη. Μόνο νά τὸ σκεφθῆς μπορεῖς νὰ αὐτοκτονήσης! Δὲ φτάνει (it is not enough) ποὺ τὴν ἔσωσα, βρῆκα καὶ τὸν μπελά μου. Σὲ τρώει ἡ μύτη σου; Εἶναι πολὺ ἐνοχλητική, μὰ τὴν ἀλήθεια! Αὐτὴ εἶναι ὄνομα καὶ πρᾶμα γυναίκα! Ἡ καθυστέρηση μοῦ βγῆκε σὲ καλό. Μὲ τὴ σειρά, ὅλοι θὰ ἔχετε θέση.

UNDERSTAND

Μπῆκα στὸ νόημα.*
Bíka sto nóeema.
I grasped (understood) the idea.

UNLUCKY

Καταδρομὴ τῆς τύχης.*
Kataδromí tis teéchis.
Persistent ill fortune.

Ἀποφρὰς ἡμέρα (χρουσούζικη μέρα).*
Apofrás iméra (chrousoùziki méra).
Unlucky day.

UPSET

Τὸ φέρ(ν)ω βαριὰ (βαρέως).*
To férno varyá (varéos).
I am annoyed (upset) by it.

Μοῦ κόπηκαν τὰ γόνατα.*
Mou kópikan ta ghónata.
I felt stunned, upset.

USELESS

Δὲν εἶναι τῆς ἀνθρωπιᾶς (εἶν' ἄχρηστο).*
δen eéne tis anϑropyás (eenáchristo).
It is useless.

Εἶναι ἄχθος ἀρούρης.*
Eéne áchϑos aroùris.
He (she) is useless; lazy.

Εἶναι ἀχαΐρευτος.
Eéne achaeéreftos.
He is good-for-nothing.

Χαμένο κορμί!*
Chaméno kormí!
Useless man!

EXERCISES

Μπῆκες (στὸ νόημα); Χρουσούζικη μέρα σήμερα. Τὸ φέρνω βαριὰ νὰ μὲ βλέπη καὶ νὰ μὴ μὲ χαιρετᾶ. Μόλις κατάλαβε πὼς ξέρω ὅλες τὶς βρωμοδουλειές του, τοῦ κόπηκαν τὰ γόνατα. Αὐτὸ τὸ ποδήλατο δὲν εἶναι τῆς ἀνθρωπιᾶς. Εἶν' ἄχρηστο. Τὰ περισσότερα παιδιὰ σήμερα εἶναι ἄχθος ἀρούρης. Ὁ σπιτονοικοκύρης μου εἶναι ἀχαΐρευτος. Ἄ, αὐτὸς εἶναι χαμένο κορμί.

VACATION

Διακοπές.*
δiakopès.
Vacation; holiday.

Σᾶς εὔχομαι καλὲς διακοπές.*
Sas éfchome kalès δiakopès.
I wish you a good vacation.

VAIN

Τοῦ κάκου!
Tou kákou!
In vain!

Δὲ βαριέσαι (ἀδίκως).*
δe varyése (aδíkos).
In vain.

Κάνω μιὰ τούπα στὸ νερό.
Káno miá treépa sto neró.
I make a vain effort.

VISIT

Κάνω ἐπίσκεψη.*
Káno epískepsi.
I pay a visit.

Φέρνω βόλτα (+ accus)
Férno vólta.
I visit, walk around.

Φέρνω βόλτα τὸ λιμάνι.
Férno vólta to limáni.
I walk around the port.

'Αρμένικη ἐπίσκεψις.*
Arméniki epískepsis.
(Unduly) prolonged visit.

VITALITY

Βράζει τὸ αἷμα του.*
Vrázee to éma tou.
He is full of vitality.

VOICE

Πιάστηκε ἡ φωνή της.*
Pyástike i foní tis.
She lost her voice.

EXERCISES

Πῶς πέρασες τίς διακοπές; Ποῦ πῆγες; Τὸν συμβουλεύεις, μὰ ἐκεῖνος τοῦ κάκου. Ἄδικα προσπαθεῖς νὰ τὸν πείσῃς. Εἶναι ἰσχυρογνώμων. Δὲ βαριέσαι, κάνεις μιὰ τρύπα στὸ νερό. Πότε θὰ μοῦ κάμῃς ἐπίσκεψη; Τὸ καλοκαίρι θά φέρω βόλτα ὅσα πιὸ πολλὰ νησιὰ μπορέσω. Μᾶς ἔκαμε ἀρμένικη ἐπίσκεψη! Εἶναι νέος, βλέπεις, βράζει τὸ αἷμα του. Πιάστηκε ἡ φωνή μου νὰ σοῦ μιλῶ.

WAIT

Κάτσε νὰ δοῦμε!
Kátse na δoùme!
Let's wait and see!

Τί γυρεύεις ἐδῶ;*
Ti yeerévees eδó?
What are you waiting for here?

'Αράδα.*
Aráδa.
Continuously waiting in line.

'Αράδα - ἀράδα.*
Aráδa - aráδa.
In line.

Στὴν Ἑλλάδα περιμένουν ἀράδα γιὰ ν' ἀγοράσουν κρέας ἢ ψάρι.
Stin Elláδa periménoun aráδa ya naghorásoun kréas í psári.
In Greece they wait in line in order to buy meat or fish.

Βραδιάστηκα νὰ περιμένω.*
Vraδyástika na periméno.
I waited until nightfall.

WALK

Πηγαίνω (πῆγα) μιὰ βόλτα.*
Piyéno (pígha) miá vólta.
I go for a walk.

Κάνω μιὰ βόλτα.*
Káno miá vólta.
I take a stroll.

'Ανοίγω τὸ βῆμα μου.
Aneégho to víma mou.
I walk faster.

WASTE

Χάνω χρήματα (λεφτά).*
Cháno chrímata (leftá).
I lose money.

Κάλαθος ἀχρήστων.*
Kálaθos achríston
Wastebasket.

Δέν κατατρίβομαι μὲ μικρὰ πράγματα.*
δen gatatrívome me mikrá prághmata.
I don't waste my time with trifles.

Κρῖμα (σ)τὰ λεφτά!*
Kríma (s)ta leftá!
What a waste of money!

Πῆγε χαμένο (στὰ χαμένα).*
Píye chaméno (sta chaména).
It was a wasted effort.

Χαμένος καιρός.*
Chaménos kerós.
A waste of time.

Compare LOOSE.

WEATHER

Κάνει ζέστη (κρύο, ψύχρα, κουφόβραση, παγωνιά).*
Kánee zésti (kreéo, pseéhra, koufóvrasi, paghoniá).
It is hot (cold, chilly, humid, freezing).

Κάνει κατακλυσμό*.
Kánee katakleezmó.
It is pouring.

Ψιλὴ βροχούλα ἄρχισε.
Psilí vrochoùla árchise.
It has begun to drizzle.

Τσουχτερὸ κρύο*.
Tsouchteró kreéo.
Bitter cold.

Βρέχει, ἀστράφτει, βροντᾶ.
Vréchee, astráftee, vrondá.
It is raining, lightning, thundering.

Χαλασμὸς Κυρίου!*
Chalazmós Keeríou!
(It is) terrible weather!

Πώ, πώ, τί καιρός!
Pó, pó, ti kerós!
My God, what weather!

Σήμερα εἶναι μεγάλη κακοκαιρία.*
Símera eéne meghάli kakokería.
Today the weather is very bad.

Χαλάει ὁ κόσμος!*
Chaláee o kózmos!
What a storm! What noise and confusion!

Σήμερα κάνει κουφόβραση.*
Símera kánee koufóvrasi.
It is humid today.

Χιονίζει ἄγαρμπα.*
Chionízee ágharmba.
It is snowing very heavily.

WELCOME

Τίποτα (τίποτες).*
Típota (típotes).
You are welcome; don't mention it.

Τὸν (τὴν) ἀποθέωσαν.*
Ton (tin) apoϑéosan.
They welcomed him (her) with a great reception.

Καλῶς τονε (τηνε).*
Kalóstone (tine).
Welcome *to him* (*her*).

WELL

Ἔκαμες καλὰ κι' ἄγια ποὺ ἦρθες (ποὖρθες).
Ékames kalá kiáyia pou írϑes (poùrϑes).
You did very well to come.

Καλῶς ἐχόντων τῶν πραγμάτων.*
Kalós echóndon ton praghmáton.
All is well.

Εἶμαι περδίκι.*
Eéme perδíki.
I am quite well again.

Ἀμμὲ (ἀμ' πῶς)!
Ammè (ampós)!
Well! Of course!

Πάει κορδόνι.
Páee korδóni.
It is going well.

Ποὺ λές. Λέει.
Pou lès. Léee.
Well (resumptive). Parenthetic phrase to support narrative.

WISH

Μακάρι νά...*
Makári na...
I wish that...

Μακάρι νὰ ἤσουν ἐδῶ!
Makári na ísoun eδó!
I wish you (were, had been) here!

Ἄμποτε (adverb)...*	Ἄμποτε νὰ ἤμουνα στὸ πάρτυ σας χθὲς βράδυ.
Àmbote...	Àmbote na ímouna sto párty sas chϑés vráδee.
I wish that...	I wish that I had been at your party yesterday evening.
Ἔχει ὁ Θεός!*	Σοῦ εὔχομαι τὰ ἐλέη τοῦ Θεοῦ!
Échee o ϑeós!	Sou éfchome ta eléi tou ϑeoù!
God will provide!	I wish you the best fortune!
Καλὸ νἄχης!*	Μὲ τὸ καλό!*
Kaló náchees!	Me to kaló!
May God help you.	Go safely, with God's help!

WITHDRAW

Ἀποτραβιέμαι ἀπὸ τὴν κοσμικὴ ζωή.*
Apotravyéme apo tin kozmikí zoeé.
I withdraw from social life.

WOMAN

Παρδαλὴ γυναίκα.
Parδali yinéka.
Light-headed (foolish) woman.

Compare CHARACTER.

WONDERFUL

Δὲν λέγεται (δὲν περιγράφεται).*
δen léyete (δen perigráphete).
It is beyond description; wonderful.

WORK

Πιάνω δουλειά.*
Pyáno δouliá.
I start work.

WORRY

Δὲν βαριέσαι!*
δen varyése!
Don't worry; never mind about that!

Ἔξω νοῦ (μακριὰ οἱ σκουτοῦρες)!*
Éxo noù (makrià ee skoutoùres)!
Away with cares!

Ἔνοια σου!*
Éneea sou!
Take care! Don't worry! (Threat.)

Πάω νὰ σκάσω.*
Páo na skáso.
I am about to burst.

WRONG

Κάνω (ἔχω) λάθος.*
Káno (écho) láϑos.
I am wrong; I am mistaken.

Ἂν δὲν κάνω λάθος.
Àn δen káno láϑos.
If I am not mistaken.

Στραβὴ γνώμη.*
Stravi ghnómi.
Wrong opinion.

EXERCISES

Ἔχεις ἄδικο! Δὲν ἔχει δίκηο. Κάτσε νὰ δοῦμε θὰ ἔρθη στὴν ὥρα του; Βραδιάστηκα νὰ σὲ περιμένω. Πᾶμε μιὰ βόλτα; Ἄνοιξε τὸ βῆμα σου. Κάνεις δουλειὲς (do you good business);"Ὄχι, χάνω χρήματα. Εἶναι ἐξαιρετικὴ καλλιτέχνις. Τὴν ἀποθέωσαν. Καλῶς ἐχόντων τῶν πραγμάτων, θὰ ταξιδέψω ἀεροπορικῶς στὴν Φλώριδα τὸν ἐρχόμενο Δεκέβρη. Ἡ δουλειά μου μέχρι τώρα πάει κορδόνι. Πού λές, δὲν εἶναι καὶ πολὺ φτωχός. Σήμερα κάνει ζέστη. Χτὲς ἔκανε κρύο. Βρέχει, δὲ λὲς τίποτα, κάνει κατακλυσμό. Στὸν Καναδᾶ, κάνει τσουχτερὸ κρύο. Αὔριο θὰ κάνη κουφόβραση, ἔτσι εἶπε τὸ ράδιο. Μακάρι νὰ πήγαινα στὴν Ἱσπανία αὐτὸ τὸ καλοκαίρι. Ἄμποτε νὰ πηγαίναμε μαζὶ στὴν Εὐρώπη! Μ' ἔσωσες ἀπ' τὸν κόπο. Καλὸ νἄχης. Ἡ ἀγαπητηκιά σου (your girl friend) εἶναι παρδαλὴ γυναίκα. Δὲν λέγεται, πόσο ὄμορφα εἶναι τὰ ἔπιπλα τοῦ σπιτιοῦ της. Δὲν μπορῶ νὰ καταλάβω γιατὶ ἄργησε, πάω νὰ σκάσω.

YET

Ἐν τούτοις.*
En doùtees.
However, yet.

Καὶ ὅμως!*
Ke ómos!
And yet!

YOUTH

Βράζει τὸ αἷμα του.*
Vrázee to éma tou.
He is full of vitality.

OUTLINE OF MODERN GREEK GRAMMAR

33. THE ARTICLE

Masculine	Feminine	Neuter
ὁ (ό)	ἡ (ί)	τὸ (τό)
ὁ πατέρας	ἡ μητέρα	τὸ παιδὶ
(the father)	(the mother)	(the child)

DECLENSION OF THE ARTICLE

SINGULAR NUMBER

	Masculine	Feminine	Neuter
Nominative	ὁ (ό)	ἡ (ί)	τὸ (τό)
Genitive	τοῦ (tou)	τῆς (tis)	τοῦ (tou)
Accusative	τὸ(ν) (ton)	τὴ(ν) (tin)	τὸ (to)

PLURAL NUMBER

	Masculine	Feminine	Neuter
Nom.	οἱ (i)	οἱ (i)	τὰ (ta)
Gen.	τῶν (ton)	τῶν (ton)	τῶν (ton)
Accus.	τοὺς (tous)	τὶς (tis)	τὰ (ta)

The ν of the accusative is added whenever the following word begins with a vowel or with one of the consonants: κ, π, τ, ξ, ψ; it is dropped before nouns beginning with a continuant consonant (φ, θ, χ, σ, ζ, ρ, λ, μ, ν,) and assimilated to π, τ, κ, into mb, nd, ng respectively.

The most important *uses* of the definite article are:

a) Before proper names:

'Ο Γιῶργος εἶναι καλὸ παιδί.
O Yórghos eéne kaló peδí.
George is a good boy.

'Ο κύριος Μπενάκης δὲν εἶναι ἐκεῖ.
O keérios Benákis δen eéne ekée.
Mr. Benakis is not there.

b) Before the names of places and geographical divisions:

'Η 'Αθήνα εἶναι ἡ πρωτεύουσα τῆς 'Ελλάδος.
I Aθína eéne i protévousa tis Elláδos.
Athens is the capital of Greece.

c) Before the names of avenues, streets and squares:

Μένω στὴν ὁδὸ Σταδίου.
Méno stin oδó Staδíou.
I live on Stadium street.

d) Before titles or names of professions followed by a person's name:

'Ο γιατρὸς κύριος Εὐγενίδης εἶναι πολὺ πλούσιος.
O yatrós keérios Evyeníδis eéne poli ploùsios.
Doctor Eugenides is very rich.

e) Before nouns used in an abstract or a general sense:

'Η εἰλικρίνεια εἶναι ἡ πιὸ μεγάλη ἀρετή.
I eelikríneea eéne i pyó megháli aretí.
Sincerity is the greatest virtue.

Μοῦ ἀρέσει τὸ ψάρι.
Mou arésee to psári.
I like fish.

f) Before nouns designating parts of the body, personal articles of clothing:

Τὰ μαλλιὰ τῆς Μαρίας εἶναι ξανθά.
Ta mallià tis Marías eéne xanθá.
Mary's hair is blond.

g) Before nouns modified by a possesive adjective which follows the noun:

Ὁ ἀδελφός μου ὁ Γιάννης ἔχει καλὴ δουλειά.
O aδelphóz mou o Yánnis échee kalí δouleeá.
My brother John has a good job.

h) Before nouns modified by a demonstrative adjective. In such a case the definite article is placed between the demonstrative adjective and the noun or in the very beginning followed by the noun and the demonstrative adjective:

Αὐτὴ ἡ κοπέλα εἶναι πολὺ ὡραία.
Afti i kopéla eéne polí oréa.
This girl is very beautiful.

Or

Ἡ κοπέλα αὐτὴ εἶναι πολὺ ὡραία.
I kopéla aftí eéne polí oréa.
This girl is very beautiful.

i) Before a noun indicating a class of objects or persons:

Τὸ ψάρι εἶναι ἀκριβὸ ἐφέτος.
To psári eéne akrivó ephétos.
Fish is expensive this year.

Οἱ ἀστυνόμοι εἶναι αὐστηροί.
Ee asteenómee eéne afstireé.
Policemen are strict.

The names of cities are usually of feminine gender. The gender in Greek is grammatical; that is, it does not depend on the sex of the noun but on its ending. Nouns designating male beings, however, are normally masculine and female feminine. Names of winds, months, rivers are masculine and those of trees feminine.

INDEFINITE ARTICLE (a, an)

The indefinite article is ἕνας (for the masculine), μιὰ or μία (for the feminine), and ἕνα (for the neuter).

It is declined as follows:

SINGULAR

	Masculine	Feminine	Neuter
Nom.	ἕνας	μιὰ or μία	ἕνα
Gen.	ἑνὸς	μιᾶς or μίας	ἑνὸς
Accus.	ἕνα(ν)	μιὰ or μίαν	ἕνα

PLURAL
(some)

	Masculine	Feminine	Neuter
Nom.	κάποιοι or μερικοὶ	κάποιες or μερικὲς	κάποια or μερικὰ
Gen.	κάποιων or μερικῶν	κάποιων or μερικῶν	κάποιων or μερικῶν
Accus.	κάποιους or μερικοὺς	κάποιες or μερικὲς	κάποια or μερικὰ

The indefinite article is not used in Greek as often as in English. It mostly expresses the idea of the numeral for one, hence it has exactly the same form as the numeral.

The article as well as the indefinite article agree in gender, case, and number with the noun they modify.

34. THE DECLENSION OF NOUNS

There are three declensions in Modern Greek. FIRST, SECOND and THIRD. The third declension is hardly used in the demotic (spoken) language. Instead, the other two are used (First and Second).

There are five CASES (Nominative, Genitive, Dative, Accusative, and Vocative). In the demotic only three (Nominative, Genitive, Accusative) are in common use, though the vocative is not entirely dropped. The dative is scarcely used even in Puristic (Katharevousa). It has been replaced by the genitive or the accusative preceded by a preposition, usually εἰς, which with the definite article becomes στὸ (=εἰς τὸ), στὸν (= εἰς τὸν), στὴν (= εἰς τὴν), etc., and in front of a vowel it is written as σ', e. g. σ' ἕνα θέατρο (at or in a theater). It is equivalent to the English to, in, at, inside, with verbs of motion and location, i. e. I go to, I am in, I arrive at.

The genitive is generally used to express possesion or appurtenance, e.g.,

Τὰ παράθυρα τοῦ σπιτιοῦ μου εἶναι ἀκάθαρτα.
Ta paráθeera tou spityoù mou eéne akáθarta.
My house's windows are filthy.

Τὸ γραφεῖο τοῦ ἀδελφοῦ μου εἶναι θαυμάσιο.
To grapheéo tou aδelphoù mou eéne θavmásio.
My brother's office is wonderful.

Τὰ κτίρια τῆς πόλης αὐτῆς εἶναι πολὺ (ὑ)ψηλά.
Ta ktíria tis pólis aftís eéne polí (ee)psilá.
This city's buildings are very high.

The accusative is used after prepositions such as σὲ (to, at, in, on to, etc.); μὲ or μαζὶ μὲ (with); πάνω σὲ or πάνω ἀπὸ (on, over); κοντὰ σὲ (near); μέσα σὲ (into, inside); ἀπὸ (from); κάτω ἀπὸ (under); γιὰ (for). As an object, after verbs such as βλέπω, θέλω, παίρνω, ἔχω, τρώγω, χρεωστῶ, etc.; e. g.,

Βλέπω ἕναν ἄνθρωπο.
Vlépo énan ánθropo.
I see a man.

Παίρνω τὸν ἀδελφό μου στὴ δουλειὰ κάθε πρωΐ.
Pérno ton aδelphó mou sti δouliá káθe proí.
I take my brother to work every morning.

Ἔχω δύο ἀδελφὲς καὶ τρεῖς ἀδελφούς.
Écho δío aδelphès ké treés aδelphoùs.
I have two sisters and three brothers.

Τρώγω πολὺ κρέας καὶ πολλὰ αὐγά.
Trógho polí kréas ke pollá avghá.
I eat much meat and many eggs.

Πόσα λεφτὰ χρωστᾶτε;
Pósa leftá chrostáte?
How much do you owe?

Also after some nouns when it expresses their content, e.g.,

Θέλω ἕνα ποτήρι νερό.
θélo éna potíri neró.
I want a glass of water.

The vocative is used to address a person, etc. directly without the exclamation ὦ, e. g., ταμία, ῥάφτη, Νῖκο, Κώστα, Μαρία.

FIRST DECLENSION

comprises:	Masculines	ending in ας, ης
	Feminines	ending in α, η

EXAMPLES

Masculine ending in ας

	SINGULAR	PLURAL
Nom.	ὁ πατέρας	οἱ πατέρες
Gen.	τοῦ πατέρα	τῶν πατέρων
Accus.	τὸν πατέρα(ν)	τοὺς πατέρες

Masculine ending in ης

	SINGULAR	PLURAL
Nom.	ὁ ἐργάτης	οἱ ἐργάτες
Gen.	τοῦ ἐργάτη	τῶν ἐργατῶν
Accus.	τὸν ἐργάτη(ν)	τοὺς ἐργάτες.

Feminine ending in α

	SINGULAR	PLURAL
Nom.	ἡ μητέρα	οἱ μητέρες
Gen.	τῆς μητέρας	τῶν μητέρων
Accus.	τὴν μητέρα(ν)	τὶς μητέρες

Feminine ending in η

	SINGULAR	PLURAL
Nom.	ἡ ἀδελφὴ	οἱ ἀδελφὲς
Gen.	τῆς ἀδελφῆς	τῶν ἀδελφῶν
Accus.	τὴν ἀδελφὴ(ν)	τὶς ἀδελφὲς

SECOND DECLENSION

comprises:	Masculines	ending in ος
	Feminines	ending in ος
	Neuters	ending in ον

a) Masculines and Feminines have the same endings in all the cases. The only difference between them is in the vocative of the singular number.

b) In the demotic also, most of the nouns belonging to the second declension have been changed into the first declension, e.g., ἡ κάμηλος becomes ἡ καμήλα.

c) Neuter nouns have the same endings in the Nominative, Accusative and Vocative cases.

EXAMPLES

Masculine ending in ος

	SINGULAR	PLURAL
Nom.	ὁ θεῖος	οἱ θεῖοι
Gen.	τοῦ θείου	τῶν θείων
Accus.	τὸν θεῖο(ν)	τοὺς θείους
Voc.	(ὦ) θεῖε	(ὦ) θεῖοι

Feminine ending in ος

	SINGULAR	PLURAL
Nom.	ἡ εἴσοδος	οἱ εἴσοδοι
Gen.	τῆς εἰσόδου	τῶν εἰσόδων
Accus.	τὴν εἴσοδο(ν)	τί(ε)ς εἰσόδους
Voc.	(ὦ) εἴσοδος	(ὦ) εἴσοδοι

Neuter ending in ον

	SINGULAR	PLURAL
Nom.	τὸ δωμάτιον	τὰ δωμάτια
Gen.	τοῦ δωματίου	τῶν δωματίων
Accus.	τὸ δωμάτιον	τὰ δωμάτια
Voc.	(ὦ) δωμάτιο	(ὦ) δωμάτια

Some nouns ending in ιον (χαρτίον) drop the last syllable (ον) in the Nominative case, e. g. τὸ χαρτί, τοῦ χαρτιοῦ, τὸ χαρτί.

The THIRD DECLENSION comprises ali nouns which increase in the Genitive. In the demotic most of these nouns have their endings changed into the endings of the first declension in the singular number only. In the plural they retain their own form, e.g., ὁ ἀγών, τοῦ ἀγῶνος becomes ὁ ἀγώνας, τοῦ ἀγώνα; ἡ ἐλπίς, τῆς ἐλπίδος becomes ἡ ἐλπίδα, τῆς ἐλπίδας. Thus they are declined in the same way as πατέρας, μητέρα.

35. ADJECTIVES

Adjectives in Greek have three genders, Masculine, Feminine and Neuter, e.g., good: ὁ καλός, ἡ καλή, τὸ καλὸ; big: ὁ μεγάλος, ἡ μεγάλη, τὸ μεγάλο. The adjectives are always in agreement with the gender, case and number of the noun which they qualify.

Greek nouns are well as adjectives may be grouped also into two formal classes. Each of the two classes is then subgrouped by genders. The following table accounts for most modern Greek nouns and adjectives.

CLASS I

(Corresponding to the ancient declension)

Masculine

— ος pl. — οι	ἄνθρωπος ἄνθρωποι, καλὸς καλοὶ
— ας pl. — ες	πατέρας πατέρες, γείτονας γείτονες
— έας pl. — εῖς	κουρέας (κουρεὺς) κουρεῖς
— ης pl. — ες	ἐργάτης ἐργάτες (mostly agent nouns in —της) ράφτης ράφτες

Feminine

— α pl. — ες	μητέρα μητέρες, ὡραία ὡραῖες
— η pl. — ες	ἀδελφὴ ἀδελφές, ὄμορφη ὄμορφες
— η pl. — εις	σκέψη σκέψεις (ancient —σις)

Neuter

— ο pl. — α	νερὸ νερά, μαῦρο μαῦρα
— ι pl. — ια	παιδὶ παιδιά, σπίτι σπίτια
— ος pl. — η	ἴχνος ἴχνη
— μα pl. — ματα	χρῶμα χρώματα, ψέμα ψέματα
— σιμο pl. — σίματα	πλύσιμο πλυσίματα

CLASS II

(imparisyllabic - δ - stems)

Masculine

— ὰς pl. — άδες	φαγὰς φαγάδες, παπὰς παπάδες, ψαρὰς ψαράδες
— ὲς pl. — έδες	καφὲς καφέδες, μεζὲς μεζέδες
— οὺς pl. — οῦδες	παππούς παπποῦδες
— ης pl. — ηδες	σκουπιδιάρης σκουπιδιάρηδες, ζηλιάρης ζηλιάρηδες

Feminine

— οὺ pl. — οῦδες	ἀλεποὺ ἀλεποῦδες, καωματοῦ καωματοῦδες
— ὲ pl. — έδες	νενὲ νενέδες, χαφιὲ (ς) χαφιέδες
— ὰ pl. — άδες	ὀκὰ ὀκάδες

The largest adjectival group is characterized by the following endings.

SINGULAR

	Masculine	Feminine	Neuter
Nom.	— ος, — ας	— η, — α	— ο(ν)
Gen.	— ου, — α	— ης, — ας	— ου
Accus.	— ο(ν) — α(ν)	— η(ν), — α(ν)	— ο(ν)

PLURAL

	Masculine	Feminine	Neuter
Nom.	— οι, — ες	— ες	— α
Gen.	— ων, — ων	— ων	— ων
Accus.	— ους, — ες	— ες	— α

Two small groups of adjectives have the following endings:

		SINGULAR	PLURAL
a)	Masculine	— ὺς βαθὺς	— εις βαθεῖς
	Feminine	— υὰ βαθυὰ	— ειὲς βαθειὲς
	Neuter	— ὺ βαθὺ	— υὰ βαθυὰ

		SINGULAR	PLURAL
b)	Masculine and Feminine	— ης ἀληθὴς	— εις ἀληθεῖς
	Neuter	— ες ἀληθὲς	— η ἀληθῆ

The endings of these adjectives are puristic, but they are used in the demotic also.

The only important irregular adjective is πολὺς pl. πολλοὶ (much, many), e.g., πολὺς κόπος (much trouble), πολὺς κόσμος (many people). The comparative degree of this adjective is also irregular: περισσότερος (more).

Generally, *the comparative degree* of adjectives is made by changing the endings into: M. —ότερος, F. —ότερη, N. —ότερο, e. g. μικρός, μικρότερος, μικρότερη, μικρότερο (smaller, younger); εὔκολος, εὐκολότερος, εὐκολότερη, εὐκολότερο (easier). Most usually, however, modern Greek adjectives form their comparative by placing the particle πιὸ (more) in front of them. They are then followed by the preposition ἀπὸ and the accusative, e.g.,

Ὁ φίλος μου εἶναι πιὸ ἔξυπνος ἀπὸ τὸν γυιό σας.
O phílοz mou eéne pyó éxeepnos apo ton yó sas.
My friend is smarter than your son.

Very few adjectives form their comparative irregularly, by changing the endings,

Masculine	—ος to	— ύτερος
Feminine	—η or —α to	— ύτερη
Neuter	—ο to	— ύτερο

e. g.,

καλὸς καλύτερος	better
μεγάλος μεγαλύτερος	bigger, older

The comparative of κακὸς (bad) is χειρότερος (worse) extremely irregular.

The superlative is formed by putting the definite article in front of the comparative. The superlative is followed by either the preposition σὲ (σ') or the genitive case (as in classical Greek), e. g.,

Ἡ Ἀθήνα εἶναι ἡ πιὸ ὡραία πόλις τῆς Ἑλλάδος.
I Aϑína eéne i pyó oréa pólis tis Elládos.
Athens is the most beautiful city in Greece.

Ὁ ἀδελφός μου εἶναι ὁ καλύτερος μαθητὴς στὴν τάξη του.
O aδelfós mou eéne o kaleéteros maϑitís stin táxi tou.
My brother is the best student in his class.

Another way of forming the superlative is by changing the endings,

Masculine	—ος to	— ότατος
Feminine	—η or —α to	— ότατη
Neuter	—ο to	— ότατο

e. g.,
Ὁ πατέρας σας εἶναι καλότατος
O patéras sas eéne kalótatos.
Your father is very good.

Τὸ κατάστημά σας εἶναι πλουσιότατο.
To katástimá sas eéne plousiótato.
Your store is very rich.

There are some adjectives which form their comparative only by means of the particle πιό. They are: unchangeable adjectives as γκρὶ (gray) and μπλὲ (blue); adjectives that are primarily used as nouns as ὁ ζηλιάρης (jealous), ὁ κατεργάρης (sly), ὁ τεμπέλης (lazy); certain of the longer adjectives as ὁ περίεργος (curious), ὁ ἀσυγύριστος (untidy); a few of the shorter adjectives as ὁ κρύος (cold); most of the adjectives denoting color as ὁ ἄσπρος (white), ὁ μαῦρος (black), ὁ πράσινος (green).

The comparison of inferiority is expressed by (less) plus the adjective plus ἀπὸ with accusative or very seldom plus παρὰ with nominative:

Ὁ Νῖκος εἶναι λιγώτερο ἔξυπνος ἀπὸ τὸν Κώστα.
O Níkos eéne lighótero éxeepnos apó ton Kósta.
Nick is not as smart as Costa.

The comparsion of equality is expressed by:

a) τόσο... ὅσο καὶ plus the definite article, plus nominative:

Ὁ πατέρας μου εἶναι τόσο πλούσιος, ὅσο καὶ ὁ πατέρας σου.
O patéraz mou eéne tóso ploùsios óso ke o patéras sou.
My father is as rich as your father.

b) σὰν (καὶ) plus the definite article plus accusative:

> 'Ο Παῦλος εἶναι (τόσο) ἔξυπνος σὰν (καὶ) τὸν Πέτρο.
> O Pávlos eéne (tóso) éxeepnos sán (ke) ton Pétro.
> Paul is as clever as Peter.

The latter is preferred in negative sentences.

36. THE AUXILIARY VERBS TO HAVE, TO BE

TO HAVE

νὰ ἔχω, na écho

PRESENT

ἔχω	écho	I have
ἔχεις	échis	you have
ἔχει	échi	he, she, it has
ἔχομε(ν)*	échome(n)	we have
ἔχετε	échete	you have
ἔχουν (ε)	échoun(e)	they have

FUTURE

θὰ ἔχω	ϑa écho	I shall have
θὰ ἔχεις	ϑa échees	you will have
θὰ ἔχει	ϑa échee	he, she, it will have
θὰ ἔχομε(ν)*	ϑa échome(n)	we shall have
θὰ ἔχετε	ϑa échete	you will have
θὰ ἔχουν	ϑa échoun	they will have

PAST

εἶχα	eécha	I had
εἶχες	eéches	you had
εἶχε	eéche	he, she, it had
εἴχαμε(ν)	eéchame(n)	we had
εἴχατε	eéchate	you had
εἶχαν(ε)	eéchan(e)	they had

*Also ἔχουμε

INTERROGATION

is indicated by the tone of the voice and the question mark.

ἔχω;	écho?	do I have?
ἔχεις;	échees?	do you have?
θὰ ἔχω;	ϑa écho?	shall I have?
εἶχα;	eécha?	did I have?

NEGATION

δὲν ἔχω	δén écho	I do not have
δὲν ἔχεις	δén échees	you do not have
δὲν θὰ ἔχω	δén ϑa écho	I shall not have
δὲν εἶχα	δén eécha	I did not have

CONDITIONAL

θὰ εἶχα	ϑa eécha	I should have
θὰ εἶχες	ϑa eéches	you would have

NEGATION

δὲν θὰ εἶχα	δén ϑa eécha	I should not have

PRESENT PARTICIPLE

(ἔχων) (échon)*	ekeénos pou échee	having
(ἔχουσα) (échousa)*	ekeénee pou échee	
(ἔχον) (échon)*	ekeéno pou échee	

TO BE

νὰ εἶμαι, na eéme

PRESENT

εἶμαι	eéme	I am
εἶσαι	eése	you are
εἶναι	eéne	he, she, it is
εἴμαστε (εἴμεθα)*	eémaste (eémeϑa)*	we are
εἶστε (εἶσθε)*	eéste (eésϑe)*	you are
εἶναι	eéne	they are

*The forms in parentheses are the ones used in the Puristic. They are given only when they differ from those of the Demotic.

FUTURE

θὰ εἶμαι	ϑa eéme	I shall be
θὰ εἶσαι	ϑa eése	you will be
θὰ εἶναι	ϑa eéne	he, she, it will be
θὰ εἴμαστε	ϑa eémaste	we shall be
θὰ εἶστε	ϑa eéste	you will be
θὰ εἶναι	ϑa eéne	they will be

PAST

ἤμουν(α)*	ímoun(a)*	I was
ἤσουν(α)*	ísoun(a)*	you were
ἦτανε (ἦταν)*	ítane (ítan)*	he, she, it was
ἤμαστε	ímaste	we were
ἤσαστε	ísaste	you were
ἦτανε (ἦσαν)*	ítane (ísan)*	they were

INTERROGATION

εἶμαι;	eéme?	am I?
εἶσαι;	eése?	are you?
θὰ εἶμαι;	ϑa eéme?	shall I be?
ἤμουν;	ímoun?	was I?

NEGATION

δὲν εἶμαι	δén eéme	I am not
δὲν εἶσαι	δén eése	you are not
δὲν θὰ εἶμαι	δén ϑa eéme	I shall not be
δὲν ἤμουνα	δén ímouna	I was not

CONDITIONAL

θὰ ἤμουνα	ϑa ímouna	I should be
θὰ ἤσουνα	ϑa ísouna	you would be

NEGATION

δὲν θὰ ἤμουνα	δén ϑa ímouna	I should not be

PRESENT PARTICIPLE

(ὤν)	(ón) óndas, ὄντας	ekeénos pou eéne ekeéni pou eéne ekeéno pou eéne	being

*The forms in parentheses are the ones used in the Puristic. They are given only when they differ from those of the Demotic.

37. THE PRONOUN

a) The *personal* pronouns used as *subjects* of verbs are:

SINGULAR		PLURAL	
I	ἐγὼ	we	ἐμεῖς (ἡμεῖς)
you	ἐσὺ (σὺ)	you	ἐσεῖς (σεῖς)
he	αὐτὸς	they (M.)	αὐτοὶ
she	αὐτὴ	they (F.)	αὐτὲς (αὐταὶ)
it	αὐτὸ	they (N.)	αὐτὰ

The second person singular σὺ is used only in addressing a friend or relative. On the contrary, the second person plural σεῖς is used in addressing an acquaintance or a person of high social position and profession, as an expression of politeness and respect.

The *personal* subject pronouns are generally omitted, except in case of ambiguity or emphasis:

'Εγὼ διαβάζω καὶ σεῖς μιλᾶτε.
Eghó δyavázo ke seés miláte.
I read and you talk.

b) The *object* pronouns are:

SIMPLE FORMS

	1st person	2nd person	3rd person		
			SINGULAR		
			Masculine	Feminine	Neuter
Gen.	μοῦ	σοῦ	τοῦ	τῆς	τοῦ
Acc.	μέ	σὲ	τὸν	τὴν	τὸ
			PLURAL		
			Masculine	Feminine	Neuter
Gen.	μᾶς	σᾶς		τοὺς or τῶν	
Acc.	μᾶς	σᾶς	τούς	τὶς (τὲς)	τὰ

EMPHATIC FORMS

SINGULAR

			Masculine	Feminine	Neuter
Gen.			αὐτου(νοῦ)	αὐτη(νῆς)	αὐτου(νοῦ)
Acc.	(ἐ)μένα	(ἐ)σένα	αὐτὸν	αὐτὴν	αὐτὸ

PLURAL

			Masculine	Feminine	Neuter
Gen.				αὐτῶν or αὐτονῶν	
Acc.	(ἐ)μᾶς	(ἐ)σᾶς	αὐτοὺς	αὐτὲς	αὐτὰ

The *object* pronouns are placed before the verb except only in the case of an imperative, when they follow the verb:

Μοῦ τὸ ἔφερε.
Mou to éphere.
He (she) brought it to me.

Δός μου τὸ βιβλίο.
δóz mou to vivlío.
Give me the book.

The negative precedes the object pronouns:

Δὲν τοῦ τὸ ἔδωσα.
δén dou to éδosa.
I did not give it to him.

c) The *possessive* pronouns are identical in form with the genitive of the object pronouns with the difference that they are not accented because they are enclitic words following the nouns they modify, e. g., ἡ μητέρα μου, ὁ ἀδελφός σου, etc.

The forms of the possessive pronouns are:

μου	my	μας	our
σου	your (familiar)	σας	your
του	his	τους or των	their
της	her		
του	its		

d) *Relative* pronouns:

SINGULAR

	Masculine	Feminine	Neuter	
Nom.	ὁ ὁποῖος	ἡ ὁποία	τὸ ὁποῖον, πού	who, which
Gen.	τοῦ ὁποίου	τῆς ὁποίας	τοῦ ὁποίου	whose, of which
Dat.	στὸν ὁποῖον	στὴν ὁποίαν	στὸ ὁποῖον	to whom, to which
Accus.	τὸν ὁποῖον	τὴν ὁποίαν	τὸ ὁποῖον	whom, which

PLURAL

	Masculine	Feminine	Neuter	
Nom.	οἱ ὁποῖοι	οἱ ὁποῖες	τὰ ὁποῖα	who, which
Gen.	τῶν ὁποίων	τῶν ὁποίων	τῶν ὁποίων	whose, of which
Dat.	στοὺς ὁποίους	στὶ(ὲ)ς ὁποῖες	στὰ ὁποῖα	to whom, to which
Accus.	τοὺς ὁποίους	τὶ(ὲ)ς ὁποῖες	τὰ ὁποῖα	whom, which

Note: The most common of the relative pronouns in Demotic is the invariable ποὺ (who, whom, which, that) which stands for all the forms that are expressed in Puristic by ὁ ὁποῖος, ἡ ὁποία, τὸ ὁποῖον and their plurals.

EXERCISES

Ὁ πατέρας μου εἶναι ἐκεῖνος, ὁ ὁποῖος (ποὺ) φορᾶ καφὲ κουστούμι.
O patéraz mou eéne ekeénos, o opeéos (pou) phorà kafè koustoumi.
My father is the one who is wearing a brown suit.

Ἡ κοπέλα, ἡ ὁποία (ποὺ) γελᾶ εἶναι (ἡ) ἀδελφή μου.
I kopéla i opeéa (pou) yelà eéne (i) aδelphí mou.
The girl who is laughing is my sister.

Ἐκεῖνος ὁ νέος, τοῦ ὁποίου (ποὺ) τὰ μαλλιὰ εἶναι ξανθὰ ἔχει πολλὰ λεφτά.
Ekeénos o néos tou opeéou (pou) tamallià eéne xanϑà échee pollà leftà.
That young man whose hair is blond has much money.

Ὁ Γιῶργος, στὸν ὁποῖον (ποὺ) ἐδάνεισα ἑκατὸ δολλάρια εἶναι ὑπέροχο παιδί.
O Yórghos ston opeéon (pou) eδáneesa ekató δollária eéne eepérocho peδí.
George, to whom I lent one hundred dollars, is an exceptional boy.

Τὸ Ἑλληνικό μου λεξικό, τὸ ὁποῖον (ποὺ) ἔχασα εἶναι πολὺ ἀκριβό.
To Elliniкó mou lexikó to opeéon (pou) échasa eéne polí akrivó.
The Greek dictionary which I lost was very expensive.

Τὰ πορτοκάλια, τὰ ὁποῖα (ποὺ) πῆρα χτὲς δὲν ἦταν γλυκά.
Ta portokália ta opeéa (pou) píra chϑès δen ítan ghliká.
The oranges which I bought yesterday were not sweet.

Ὁ κύριος, τὸν ὁποῖον (ποὺ) συνάντησες σήμερα εἶναι ἀδελφός μου.
O keérios, ton opeéon (pou) seenándises símera eéne aδelphóz mou.
The gentleman whom you met today is my brother.

Παρακαλῶ, φέρτε μου τὰ παπούτσια, τὰ ὁποῖα (ποὺ) εἶναι μέσα στὴν κρεβατοκάμαρη.
Parakaló, férte mou ta papoùtsia, ta opeéa (pou) eéne mésa stin krevatokámari.
Please, bring me the shoes which are in the bedroom.

e) *Interrogative* pronouns:

SINGULAR

	Masculine	Feminine	Neuter	
Nom.	Ποιός; (ποῖος;)	ποιά; (ποία;)	ποιό; (ποῖο)	who?
Gen.	ποιοῦ; (πιανοῦ, τίνος;)	ποιᾶς; (ποίας;)	ποιοῦ;	whose?
Dat.	σὲ ποιόν; (σὲ ποῖον;)	σὲ ποιάν;	σὲ ποιό;	to whom?
Accus.	ποιόν; (ποῖον;)	ποιάν; (ποίαν;)	ποιό; (ποῖο;)	whom? which?

PLURAL

	Masculine	Feminine	Neuter	
Nom.	ποιοί; (ποῖοι;)	ποιές; (ποῖες;)	ποιά; (ποῖα;)	who?
Gen.	ποιῶν; (ποιανῶν, τίνων;)	ποιῶν;	ποιῶν;	whose?
Dat.	σὲ ποιούς;	σὲ ποιές;	σὲ ποιά;	to whom?
Accus.	ποιούς;	ποιές;	ποιά;	whom? which?

What? Τί;

EXERCISES

Ποιὸς εἶναι αὐτός;
Pyós eéne aftós?
Who is this?

Τίνος εἶναι αὐτὴ ἡ τσάντα;
Tínos eéne aftí i tsánda?
Whose bag (briefcase) is this?

Ποιοῦ (ποιανοῦ, τίνος) εἶναι ἐκεῖνο τὸ καπέλο;
Pyoù (pyanoù, tínos) eéne ekeéno to kapélo?
Whose hat is that?

Ποιᾶς (ποιανῆς, τίνος) εἶναι αὐτὸ τὸ κοκκινάδι;
Pyás (pyanís, tínos) eéne aftó to kokkináδi?
Whose lipstick is this?

Τί κάνετε;
Tí kánete?
What are you doing?

Ποιὸ ἀπὸ αὐτὰ τὰ φορέματα σοῦ ἀρέσει πιὸ πολύ;
Pyó apó aftà ta phorémata sou arésee pyó polí?
Which of these dresses do you like most?

Σὲ ποιὸν τηλεφωνεῖτε;
Se pyón tilephoníte?
Whom are you calling?

Ποῦ ζῆτε στὴν Ἑλλάδα;
Poù zíte stin Elláδa?
Where do you live in Greece?

Ποιοὶ εἶστε;
Pyeé eéste?
Who are you?

Ποιοὺς ζητᾶτε;
Pyoùs zitáte?
For whom are you looking?

THE DEFINITE ARTICLE AND THE THREE GENDERS OF NOUNS AND ADJECTIVES

CASE	SINGULAR			PLURAL		
	M	F	N	M	F	N
Nominative	ὁ	ἡ	τὸ	οἱ	οἱ	τὰ
Subject	—ος —ας —ης	—η —α	—ο —ι	—οι —ες	—ες	—α —ια
Genitive	τοῦ	τῆς	τοῦ	τῶν	τῶν	τῶν
of=possession	—ου —α —η	—ης —ας	—ου —ιου	—ων	— ων	— ων
Dative	στὸ(ν)	στὴ(ν)	στὸ	στοὺς	στὶς	στὰ
to	—ο(ν) —α(ν) —η(ν)	—η(ν) —α(ν)	—ο —ι	—ους —ες	—ες	—α —ια
Accusative	τὸ(ν)	τὴ(ν)	τὸ	τοὺς	τὶς	τὰ
object	—ο(ν) —α(ν) —η(ν)	—η(ν) —α(ν)	—ο —ι	—ους —ες	—ες	—α —ια

38. NUMERALS

TABLE OF CARDINAL AND ORDINAL NUMBERS

	CARDINAL NUMERALS	ORDINAL NUMERALS
0	μηδὲν	
1	ἕνας, μία (μιά), ἕνα	πρῶτος
2	δύο (δυὸ)	δεύτερος
3	τρεῖς, τρία (N.)	τρίτος
4	τέσσερε(ι)ς, τέσσερα (N.)	τέταρτος
5	πέντε	πέμπτος
6	ἕξι	ἕκτος
7	ἑπτὰ (ἑφτὰ)	ἕβδομος
8	ὀκτὼ (ὀχτὼ)	ὄγδοος
9	ἐννέα (ἐννιὰ)	ἔνατος
10	δέκα	δέκατος
11	ἕνδεκα (ἕντεκα)	ἑνδέκατος (ἑντέκατος)
12	δώδεκα	δωδέκατος
13	δεκατρεῖς, δεκατρία (N.)	δέκατος τρίτος
14	δεκατέσσερε(ι)ς, δεκατέσσερα (N.)	δέκατος τέταρτος
15	δεκαπέντε	δέκατος πέμπτος
16	δεκαέξι (δεκάξι)	δέκατος ἕκτος
17	δεκαεπτὰ (-εφτὰ)	δέκατος ἕβδομος
18	δεκαοκτὼ (-οχτὼ)	δέκατος ὄγδοος
19	δεκαεννέα (-ενιὰ)	δέκατος ἔνατος
20	εἴκοσι	εἰκοστὸς
21	εἴκοσι ἕνας (μία, ἕνα)	εἰκοστὸς πρῶτος
22	εἴκοσι δύο	εἰκοστὸς δεύτερος
30	τριάντα	τριακοστὸς
40	σαράντα	τεσσαρακοστὸς
50	πενήντα	πεντηκοστὸς
60	ἑξήντα	ἑξηκοστὸς
70	ἑβδομήντα	ἑβδομηκοστὸς
80	ὀγδόντα	ὀγδοηκοστὸς
90	ἐνενήντα	ἐνενηκοστὸς
100	ἑκατὸ(ν)	ἑκατοστὸς
101	ἑκατὸν ἕνας (μία, ἕνα)	ἑκατοστὸς πρῶτος
102	ἑκατὸν δύο	ἑκατοστὸς δεύτερος
200	διακόσιοι, —ες, —α	διακοσιοστὸς
300	τριακόσιοι, —ες, —α	τριακοσιοστὸς
400	τετρακόσιοι, —ες, —α	τετρακοσιοστὸς

CARDINAL NUMERALS		ORDINAL NUMERALS
500	πεντακόσιοι, —ες, —α	πεντακοσιοστὸς
600	ἑξακόσιοι, —ες, —α	ἑξακοσιοστὸς
700	ἑπ(φ)τακόσιοι, —ες, —α	ἑπ(φ)τακοσιοστὸς
800	ὀκ(χ)τακόσιοι, —ες, —α	ὀκ(χ)τακοσιοστὸς
900	ἐννιακόσιοι, —ες, —α	ἐννιακοσιοστὸς
1000	χίλιοι, —ες, —α	χιλιοστὸς
2000	δύο χιλιάδες	δισχιλιοστὸς
10.000	δέκα χιλιάδες	δεκακισχιλιοστὸς
100.000	ἑκατὸ χιλιάδες	ἑκατοντάκισχιλιοστὸς
1.000.000	ἕνα ἑκατομμύριο	ἑκατομμυριοστὸς
1.000.000.000	ἕνα δισεκατομμύριο	δισεκατομμυριοστὸς

39. REGULAR ACTIVE VERBS

FUTURE AND SIMPLE PAST

	VERB ENDING	FUTURE	PAST
A	— ω — ζω — νω — φτω	— σω	— σα
B	— βω — υω — πω	— ψω	— ψα
C	— ζω — χνω — χω — γω	— ξω	— ξα
D	— ῶ	— ήσω	— ησα
E	— ῶ	— άσω	— ασα

EXAMPLES

A

ακούω,	I hear
κλείω,	I close
ἀρχίζω,	I begin
ἀποφασίζω	I decide
γυρίζω,	I turn, tour
γνωρίζω,	I know
γεμίζω,	I fill
ἐξετάζω,	I examine
μοιάζω,	I resemble
νομίζω,	I think
συνεχίζω,	I continue
φροντίζω,	I care for
ἀφίνω,	I leave
ἁπλώνω,	I spread
πιάνω,	I take
σηκώνω,	I lift
φτάνω,	I reach
χάνω,	I lose
πέφτω,	I fall

B

ἀνάβω,	I light
κόβω,	I cut
κρύβω,	I hide
δουλεύω,	I work
μαζεύω,	I collect
θαρεύω,	I take courage
χορεύω,	I dance
λείπω,	I am absent, away

C

κοιτάζω,	I look (at)
ἀλλάζω,	I change
δείχνω,	I show
ρίχνω,	I throw
σπρώχνω,	I push
ψάχνω,	I search
φτιάχνω,	I make, fix, repair
προσέχω,	I pay attention, take care of
ὑπάρχω,	I exist
ἀνοίγω,	I open

D

ἀπαντῶ,	I answer
ἀποχτῶ,	I obtain, acquire
ἀγαπῶ,	I love
ζῶ,	I live
ζητῶ,	I seek
κουνῶ,	I move
κρατῶ,	I hold
μιλῶ,	I talk
ξυπνῶ,	I wake
παρατῶ,	I abandon, give up
παρακολουθῶ,	I follow, watch, spy
προχωρῶ,	I proceed, advance
προσπαθῶ,	I try
ρωτῶ,	I ask
σταματῶ,	I stop
συμφωνῶ,	I agree
φιλῶ,	I kiss

E

γελῶ,	I laugh
χαμογελῶ,	I smile
χαλῶ,	I demolish, spoil

ACTIVE VOICE

Present	Indicative Imperfect	Durative Future	Subjunctive Present	Imperative Present
λύν-ω	ἔλυν-α	θὰ λύνω	νὰ λύν-ω	λύν-ε
λύν-εις	ἔλυν-ες	θὰ λύνης	νὰ λύν-ης	
λύν-ει	ἔλυν-ε	θὰ λύνη	νὰ λύν-η	
λύν-ομε	(ἐ)λύν-αμε	θὰ λύνωμε	νὰ λύν-ωμε	
λύν-ετε	(ἐ)λύν-ατε	θὰ λύνετε	νὰ λύν-ετε	λύν-ετε
λύν-ουν	ἔλυν-αν	θὰ λύνουν	νὰ λύν-ουν	

Aorist	Punctual Future	Aorist	Aorist
ἔλυσ-α	θὰ λύσω	νὰ λύσ-ω	
ἔλυσ-ες	θὰ λύσης	νὰ λύσ-ης	λύσ-ε
ἔλυσ-ε	θὰ λύση	νὰ λύσ-η	
(ἐ)λύσ-αμε	θὰ λύσωμε	νὰ λύσ-ωμε	
(ἐ)λύσ-ατε	θὰ λύσετε	νὰ λύσ-ετε	λύσ-(ε)τε
ἔλυσ-αν	θὰ λύσουν	νὰ λύσ-ουν	

Perfect	Pluperfect	Future Perfect	Perfect
ἔχω λύσει	εἶχα λύσει	θὰ ἔχω λύσει	νὰ ἔχω λύσει

PASSIVE VOICE

Present	Indicative Imperfect	Durative Future	Subjunctive Present	Imperative Present
λύν-ομαι	λυν-όμουν	θὰ λύνωμαι	νὰ λύνωμαι	
λύν-εσαι	λυν-όσουν	θὰ λύνεσαι	νὰ λύνεσαι	(uncommon form)
λύν-εται	λυν-όταν	θὰ λύνεται	νὰ λύνεται	
λυν-όμαστε	λυν-όμαστε	θὰ λυνόμαστε	νὰ λυνόμαστε	
λύν-εστε	λυν-όσαστε	θὰ λύνεστε	νὰ λύνεστε	
λύν-ονται	λύν-ονταν	θὰ λύνωνται	νὰ λύνωνται	

Aorist	Punctual Future	Aorist	Aorist
λύθηκα	θὰ λυθῶ	νὰ λυθῶ	
λύθηκες	θὰ λυθῇς	νὰ λυθῇς	λύσου
λύθηκε	θὰ λυθῇ	νὰ λυθῇ	
λυθήκαμε	θὰ λυθοῦμε	νὰ λυθοῦμε	
λυθήκατε	θὰ λυθῆτε	νὰ λυθῆτε	λυθῆτε
λύθηκαν	θὰ λυθοῦν	νὰ λυθοῦν	

Perfect	Pluperfect	Future Perfect	Perfect
ἔχω λυθῆ	εἶχα λυθῆ	θὰ ἔχω λυθῆ	νὰ ἔχω λυθῆ.

ACTIVE VOICE

Present	Indicative Imperfect	Durative Future	Subjunctive Present	Imperative Present
ἀγαπ-ῶ	ἀγαπ-οῦσα	θὰ ἀγαπῶ	νὰ ἀγαπῶ	
ἀγαπ-ᾶς	ἀγαπ-οῦσες	θὰ ἀγαπᾶς	νὰ ἀγαπᾶς	ἀγάπα
ἀγαπ-ᾶ	ἀγαπ-οῦσε	θὰ ἀγαπᾶ	νὰ ἀγαπᾶ	
ἀγαπ-οῦμε	ἀγαπ-ούσαμε	θὰ ἀγαποῦμε	νὰ ἀγαποῦμε	
ἀγαπ-ᾶτε	ἀγαπ-ούσατε	θὰ ἀγαπᾶτε	νὰ ἀγαπᾶτε	ἀγαπᾶτε
ἀγαπ-οῦν	ἀγαπ-οῦσαν	θὰ ἀγαποῦν	νὰ ἀγαποῦν	

Aorist	Punctual Future	Aorist	Aorist
ἀγάπησ-α	θὰ ἀγαπήσω	νὰ ἀγαπήσω	
ἀγάπησ-ες	θὰ ἀγαπήσης	νὰ ἀγαπήσης	ἀγάπησε
ἀγάπησ-ε	θὰ ἀγαπήση	νὰ ἀγαπήση	
ἀγαπήσ-αμε	θὰ ἀγαπήσωμε	νὰ ἀγαπήσωμε	
ἀγαπήσ-ατε	θὰ ἀγαπήσετε	νὰ ἀγαπήσετε	ἀγαπῆστε
ἀγάπησ-αν	θὰ ἀγαπήσουν	νὰ ἀγαπήσουν	

Perfect	Pluperfect	Future Perfect	Perfect
ἔχω ἀγαπήσει	εἶχα ἀγαπήσει	θὰ ἔχω ἀγαπήσει	νὰ ἔχω ἀγαπήσει

PASSIVE VOICE

Present	Indicative Imperfect	Durative Future	Subjunctive Present	Imperative Present
ἀγαπιέμαι	ἀγαπιόμουν	θὰ ἀγαπιέμαι	νὰ ἀγαπιέμαι	
ἀγαπιέσαι	ἀγαπιόσουν	θὰ ἀγαπιέσαι	νὰ ἀγαπιέσαι	
ἀγαπιέται	ἀγαπιόταν	θὰ ἀγαπιέται	νὰ ἀγαπιέται	(No form)
ἀγαπιούμαστε	ἀγαπιόμαστε	θὰ ἀγαπιούμαστε	νὰ ἀγαπιούμαστε	
ἀγαπιέστε	ἀγαπιόσαστε	θὰ ἀγαπιέστε	νὰ ἀγαπιέστε	
ἀγαπιοῦνται	ἀγαπιόνταν	θὰ ἀγαπιοῦνται	νὰ ἀγαπιοῦνται	

Aorist	Punctual Future	Aorist	Aorist
ἀγαπήθηκα	θὰ ἀγαπηθῶ	νὰ ἀγαπηθῶ	
ἀγαπήθηκες	θὰ ἀγαπηθῆς	νὰ ἀγαπηθῆς	ἀγαπήσου
ἀγαπήθηκε	θὰ ἀγαπηθῆ	νὰ ἀγαπηθῆ	
ἀγαπηθήκαμε	θὰ ἀγαπηθοῦμε	νὰ ἀγαπηθοῦμε	
ἀγαπηθήκατε	θὰ ἀγαπηθῆτε	νὰ ἀγαπηθῆτε	ἀγαπηθῆτε
ἀγαπήθηκαν	θὰ ἀγαπηθοῦν	νὰ ἀγαπηθοῦν	

Perfect	Pluperfect	Future Perfect	Perfect
ἔχω ἀγαπηθῆ	εἶχα ἀγαπηθῆ	θὰ ἔχω ἀγαπηθῆ	νὰ ἔχω ἀγαπηθῆ

REMARKS

The Past Tense:

The first person singular of the Past tense is formed from the Indefinite by:

1. Changing the final –ω to –α.
2. Moving the accent to the third syllable from the end, e. g., Pres. ἀρχίζω (I begin); Indef. ἀρχίσω; Past ἄρχισα. Pres. ἀνάβω (I light); Indef. ἀνάψω; Past ἄναψα. Pres. ἀνοίγω (I open); Indef. ἀνοίξω; Past ἄνοιξα. Pres. ἀπαντῶ (I answer); Indef. ἀπαντήσω;

Past ἀπάντησα. Pres. γελῶ (I laugh); Indef. γελάσω; Past γέλασα.

The other persons of the Past tense are formed as follows:

SINGULAR		PLURAL	
1	ἄρχισ-α	1	ἀρχίσ-αμε
2	ἄρχισ-ες	2	ἀρχίσ-ατε
3	ἄρχισ-ε	3	ἄρχισ-αν or ἀρχίσ-ανε

The two-syllabic and monosyllabic verbs take the augment ε– (a vowel prefixed to the verb) in singular, which, however, they usually drop in the first and second persons plural. These forms can dispense with the augment as they have three syllables, e. g.,

ἔχασα	I lost	ἔζησα	I lived
ἔχασες	you lost	ἔζησες	you lived
ἔχασε	he (she) lost	ἔζησε	he (she) lived
χάσαμε	we lost	ζήσαμε	we lived
χάσατε	you lost	ζήσατε	you lived
ἔχασαν or χάσανε	they lost	ἔζησαν or ζήσανε	they lived

The Future Tense:

Before all the persons of the Future forms of the verb the particle θα (θὰ) must be added.

The Imperfect Tense:

The Imperfect tense is formed in the same way as the Past tense but by using as basis the Present instead of the Indefinite (so for classes A, B, C). Verbs of classes D, E change the final –ω of the Present to –οῦσα (accented) or –αγα (unaccented) and drop the augment, e. g.

μιλῶ	μιλοῦσα	μίλαγα	I was talking
φιλῶ	φιλοῦσα	φίλαγα	I was kissing
ζῶ	ζοῦσα		I was living
γελῶ	γελοῦσα	γέλαγα	I was laughing
χαμογελῶ	χαμογελοῦσα	χαμογέλαγα	I was smiling

The suffix –αγα is used only in two - syllabled verbs. The imperfect of the irregular verb θέλω is ἤθελα. When θὰ is placed before the Imperfect form of a verb it expresses wish or condition, e.g.,

θὰ ἤθελα ἕνα ποτήρι κρασί.
θa íθela éna potíri krasí.
I would like a glass of wine.

When the θὰ and the Imperfect initiates the second sentence preceeded by the ἂν (if) and the Imperfect the condition refers to an event in the past, e. g.,

Ἂν πήγαινα στὸ σινεμὰ χθές, θὰ ἔβλεπα ἕνα καλὸ φίλμ.
An píyena sto sinemà chθés, θa évlepa éna kaló film.
If I had gone to the cinema yesterday, I would have seen a good film.

40. IRREGULAR VERBS

(This list includes the most common verbs of spoken Demotic)

PRESENT	FUTURE*	PAST	PASSIVE PAST	PAST PASSIVE PARTICIPLE **
αἰσθάνομαι (I feel)	αἰσθανθῶ	αἰσθάνθηκα		
ἀναγγέλλω (I announce)	ἀναγγείλω	ἀνάγγειλα	ἀναγγέλθηκα	
ἀνεβαίνω (I go up; climb)	ἀνεβῶ	ἀνέβηκα		ἀνεβασμένος
ἀναβάλλω (I postpone)	ἀναβάλω	ἀνέβαλα		
ἀρέσω (I like; I am liked)	ἀρέσω	ἄρεσα		
αὐξάνω (I increase)	αὐξήσω	αὔξησα	αὐξήθηκα	αὐξημένος
ἀφήνω (I leave; let)	ἀφήσω	ἄφησα	ἀφέθηκα	ἀφημένος
βάζω (βάλλω) (I put)	βάλω	ἔβαλα	βάλθηκα	βαλμένος

*The particle θά should be placed before the Future forms.
**The Past Passive Participle is used as adjective if preceded by εἶμαι.

PRESENT	FUTURE*	PAST	PASSIVE PAST	PAST PASSIVE PARTICIPLE**
βαστῶ (I hold)	βαστάξω	βάσταξα	βαστάχθηκα	βαστανμένος
βγάζω (I take out)	βγάλω	ἔβγαλα	βγάλθηκα	βγαλμένος
βγαίνω (I come out, I go out)	βγῶ	βγῆκα	βγάλθηκα	βγαλμένος
βλέπω (I see)	δῶ	εἶδα		
βρέχω (I wet)	βρέξω	ἔβρεξα	βράχηκα	βρε(γ)μένος
βρίσκομαι (I am, I find myself)	βρεθῶ	βρέθηκα		
βρίσκω (I find)	βρῶ	βρῆκα	βρέθηκα	
γδέρνω (I flay, I skin)	γδάρω	ἔγδαρα	γδάρθηκα	γδαρμένος
γίνομαι (I become)	γίνω	ἔγινα	γίνηκα	γινωμένος
γελῶ (I laugh)	γελάσω	γέλασα	γελάσθηκα	γελασμένος
γέρνω (I lean)	γείρω	ἔγειρα		γερμένος
γε(η)ρνῶ (I get old)	γε(η)ράσω	γέ(ή)ρασα		γε(η)ρασμένος
δέρνω (I beat)	δείρω	ἔδειρα	δάρθηκα	δαρμένος
διαβαίνω (I pass through)	διαβῶ	διάβηκα		
διαμαρτύρομαι (I protest)	διαμαρτυρηθῶ		διαμαρτυρήθηκα	διαμαρτυρημένος
διδάσκω (I teach)	διδάξω	δίδαξα	διδάχθηκα	διδαγμένος
δίνω (δίδω) (I give)	δώσω	ἔδωσα	δόθηκα	δοσμένος
διψῶ (I am thirsty)	διψάσω	δίψασα		διψασμένος
ἐγκατασταίνω (I establish)	ἐγκαταστήσω	ἐγκατέστησα	ἐγκαταστάθηκα	ἐγκατεστημένος
ἔρχομαι (I come)	ἔρ(λ)θω	ἦρ(λ)θα		
εὑρίσκω (I find)	εὕρω	ηὗρα (βρῆκα)	εὑρέθην	
εὔχομαι (I wish)	εὐχηθῶ	εὐχήθηκα		
θέλω (I want)	θελήσω	θέλησα		
θέτω (I set; I place)	θέσω	ἔθεσα	ἐτέθην	
κάθομαι (I sit down)	καθίσω	κάθι(η)σα		καθισμένος
καίω (I burn)	κάψω	ἔκαψα	κάηκα	καμένος
κά(μ)νω (I do; I make)	κάμω	ἔκαμα		καμωμένος
καταλαβαίνω (I understand)	καταλάβω	κατάλαβα		
κατεβαίνω (I descend)	κατεβῶ	κατέβηκα		κατεβασμένος
κεντῶ (I embroider; prick)	κεντήσω	κέντησα		κεντημένος
κλαίω (I weep; cry)	κλάψω	ἔκλαψα	κλαύθηκα	κλαμένος
κοιτῶ (I look at; search)	κοιτάξω	κοίταξα	κοιτάχθηκα	
λαβαίνω (λαμβάνω) (I take; receive)	λάβω	ἔλαβα		
λέγω (λέω) (I say)	πῶ	εἶπα		εἰπωμένος
λυπῶ (I afflict)	λυπήσω	λύπησα	λυπήθηκα	λυπημένος
μαθαίνω (μανθάνω) (I learn)	μάθω	ἔμαθα	μαθεύτηκα	μαθημένος*
μένω (I stay; live)	μείνω	ἔμεινα		

*εἶμαι μαθημένος = I am accustomed to, I used to.

*The particle θά should be placed before the Future forms.

**The Past Passive Participle is used as adjective if preceded by εἶμαι.

PRESENT	FUTURE*	PAST	PASSIVE PAST	PAST PASSIVE PARTICIPLE**
μιλῶ (I speak)	μιλήσω	μίλησα	μιλήθηκα	
μπαίνω (I enter)	μπῶ	μπῆκα		μπασμένος
μπορῶ (I can)	μπορέσω	μπόρεσα		
ντρέπομαι (I am shy; ashamed)	ντραπῶ	ντράπηκα		ντροπιασμένος
ξέρω (I know)	ξέρω (μάθω)	ἤξερα		
παθαίνω (I suffer)	πάθω	ἔπαθα		
παραγγέλνω (I order; send word to)	παραγγείλω	παράγγειλα		παραγγελμένος
πεθαίνω (I die)	πεθάνω	πέθανα		πεθαμ(μ)ένος
πείθω (I persuade)	πείσω	ἔπεισα	πείστ(θ)ηκα	πεπεισμένος
περνῶ (I pass)	περάσω	πέρασα	(ξε)περάστηκα	περασμένος
πετυχαίνω (I succeed)	πετύχω	πέτυχα		πετυχημένος
ἀποτυχαίνω (ἀποτυγχάνω) (I fail; to be a failure)	ἀποτύχω	ἀπέτυχα		ἀποτυχημένος
πέφτω (πίπτω) (I fall)	πέσω	ἔπεσα		
πηγαίνω (I go)	πάω	(ἐ)πῆγα		πεσμένος
πίνω (I drink)	πιῶ	ἤπια		πιωμένος
πλένω (πλύνω) (I wash)	πλύνω	ἔπλυνα	πλύθηκα	πλυμ(μ)ένος
προσβάλλω (I insult)	προσβάλω	πρόσβαλα	προσβάλθηκα	προσβαλμένος
προχωρῶ (I advance)	προχωρήσω	προχώρησα		προχωρημένος
σέβομαι (I respect)	σεβαστ(θ)ῶ	σεβάστηκα		σεβαστὸς
σέρνω (σύρω) (I drag)	σύρω	ἔσυρα	σύρθηκα	συρμένος
σπέρνω (σπείρω) (I sow)	σπείρω	ἔσπειρα	σπάρθηκα	σπαρμένος
στέκομαι (I stand up; stop moving)	σταθῶ	στάθηκα		σταματημένος
στέλνω (στέλλω) (I send)	στείλω	ἔστειλα	στάλθηκα	σταλμένος
στρέφω (I turn)	στρέψω	ἔστρεψα	στράφηκα	στραμμένος
ἐπιστρέφω (I return)	ἐπιστρέψω	ἐπέστρεψα		
καταστρέφω (I destroy)	καταστρέψω	κατέστρεψα	καταστράφηκα	κατεστραμμένος
σωπαίνω (σιωπῶ) (I keep silent)	σωπάσω (σιωπήσω)	σώπασα (σιώπησα)		σιωπηλὸς
τραβῶ (I drag; pull; suffer)	τραβήξω	τράβηξα	τραβήχθηκα	τραβηγμένος
τρώ(γ)ω (I eat)	φά(γ)ω	ἔφα(γ)α	φαγώθηκα	φαγωμένος
τυχαίνω (I meet by chance; to happen by chance)	τύχω	ἔτυχα		
ὑπόσχομαι (I promise)	ὑποσχεθῶ	ὑποσχέθηκα		ὑποσχεμένος
φαίνομαι (I seem; I prove myself)	φανῶ	φάνηκα		
φεύγω (I leave; flee)	φύγω	ἔφυγα		
χαίρομαι (I am glad)	χαρῶ	(ἐ)χάρηκα		χαρούμενος
χορταίνω (I am satiated; I am full)	χορτάσω	χόρτασα		χορτασμένος
ψέλνω (ψάλλω) (I chant)	ψάλω	ἔψαλα	ψάλθηκα	ψαλμένος
ὠφελῶ (I do good)	ὠφελήσω	ὠφέλησα	ὠφελήθηκα	ὠφελημένος

*The particle θά should be placed before the Future forms.
**The Past Passive Participle is used as adjective if preceded by εἶμαι.

FULL CONJUGATION OF THE ACTIVE IRREGULAR VERBS

1. I put – βάζω

FUTURE		PAST	
θὰ βάλω	I shall put	ἔβαλα	I put
θὰ βάλεις	you will put	ἔβαλες	you put
θὰ βάλει	he, she will put	ἔβαλε	he, she put
θὰ βάλωμε	we shall put	βάλαμε	we put
θὰ βάλετε	you will put	βάλατε	you put
θὰ βάλουν	they will put	ἔβαλαν	they put

2. I go out – βγαίνω

FUTURE		PAST	
θὰ βγῶ	I shall go out	βγῆκα	I went out
θὰ βγεῖς	you will go out	βγῆκες	you went out
θὰ βγεῖ	he, she will go out	βγῆκε	he, she went out
θὰ βγοῦμε	we shall go out	βγήκαμε	we went out
θὰ βγεῖτε	you will go out	βγήκατε	you went out
θὰ βγοῦν	they will go out	βγῆκαν	they went out

3. I see – βλέπω

FUTURE		PAST	
θὰ (ἰ)δῶ	I shall see	εἶδα	I saw
θὰ (ἰ)δεῖς	you will see	εἶδες	you saw
θὰ (ἰ)δεῖ	he, she will see	εἶδε	he, she saw
θὰ (ἰ)δοῦμε	we shall see	εἴδαμε	we saw
θὰ (ἰ)δεῖτε	you will see	εἴδατε	you saw
θὰ (ἰ)δοῦν	they will see	εἶδαν	they saw

4. I find – βρίσκω

FUTURE		PAST	
θὰ βρῶ	I shall find	βρῆκα	I found
θὰ βρεῖς	you will find	βρῆκες	you found
θὰ βρεῖ	he, she will find	βρῆκε	he, she found

FUTURE		PAST	
θὰ βροῦμε	we shall find	βρήκαμε	we found
θὰ βρῆτε	you will find	βρήκατε	you found
θὰ βροῦν	they will find	βρῆκαν(ε)	they found

5. I pass through – διαβαίνω

FUTURE		PAST	
θὰ διαβῶ	I shall pass through	διάβηκα	I passed through
θὰ διαβεῖς	you will pass through	διάβηκες	you passed through
θὰ διαβεῖ	he, she will pass through	διάβηκε	he passed through
θὰ διαβοῦμε	we shall pass through	διαβήκαμε	we passed through
θὰ διαβῆτε	you will pass through	διαβήκατε	you passed through
θὰ διαβοῦν	they will pass through	διάβηκαν	they passed through

6. I give – δίνω

FUTURE		PAST	
θὰ δώσω	I shall give	ἔδωσα	I gave
θὰ δώσεις	you will give	ἔδωσες	you gave
θὰ δώσει	he, she will give	ἔδωσε	he, she gave
θὰ δώσωμε	we shall give	δώσαμε(ν)	we gave
θὰ δώσετε	you will give	δώσατε	you gave
θὰ δώσουν	they will give	ἔδωσαν (δώσανε)	they gave

7. I understand – καταλαβαίνω

FUTURE		PAST	
θὰ καταλάβω	I shall understand	κατάλαβα	I understood
θὰ καταλάβεις	you will understand	κατάλαβες	you understood
θὰ καταλάβει	he, she will understand	κατάλαβε	he understood
θὰ καταλάβωμε	we shall understand	καταλάβαμε	we understood
θὰ καταλάβετε	you will understand	καταλάβατε	you understood
θὰ καταλάβουν	they shall understand	κατάλαβαν (καταλάβανε)	they understood

8. I descend — κατεβαίνω

FUTURE		PAST	
θὰ κατεβῶ	I shall descend	κατέβηκα	I descended
θὰ κατεβεῖς	you will descend	κατέβηκες	you descended
θὰ κατεβεῖ	he, she will descend	κατέβηκε	he descended
θὰ κατεβοῦμε	we shall descend	κατεβήκαμε	we descended
θὰ κατεβῆτε	you will descend	κατεβήκατε	you descended
θὰ κατεβοῦν	they will descend	κατέβηκαν	they descended

9. I say — λέ(γ)ω

FUTURE		PAST	
θὰ πῶ	I shall say	εἶπα	I said
θὰ πεῖς	you will say	εἶπες	you said
θὰ πεῖ	he, she will say	εἶπε(ν)	he, she said
θὰ ποῦμε	we shall say	εἴπαμε	we said
θὰ πεῖτε	you will say	εἴπατε	you said
θὰ ποῦν(ε)	they will say	εἶπαν(ε)	they said

10. I enter — μπαίνω

FUTURE		PAST	
θὰ μπῶ	I shall enter	μπῆκα	I entered
θὰ μπεῖς	you will enter	μπῆκες	you entered
θὰ μπεῖ	he, she will enter	μπῆκε	he entered
θὰ μποῦμε	we shall enter	μπήκαμε	we entered
θὰ μπεῖτε	you will enter	μπήκατε	you entered
θὰ μποῦν	they will enter	μπῆκαν	they entered

11. I take — παίρνω

FUTURE		PAST	
θὰ πάρω	I shall take	πῆρα	I took
θὰ πάρεις	you will take	πῆρες	you took
θὰ πάρει	he, she will take	πῆρε	he took
θὰ πάρωμε	we shall take	πήραμε	we took
θὰ πάρετε	you will take	πήρατε	you took
θὰ πάρουν	they will take	πῆραν(ε)	they took

12. I go — πηγαίνω

FUTURE		PAST	
θὰ πάω	I shall go	πῆγα	I went
θὰ πάεις (πᾶς)	you will go	πῆγες	you went
θὰ πάει	he, she will go	πῆγε	he went
θὰ πᾶμε	we shall go	πήγαμε	we went
θὰπᾶτε	you will go	πήγατε	you went
θὰ πᾶνε	they will go	πῆγαν(ε)	they went

13. I drink — πίνω

FUTURE		PAST	
θὰ πιῶ	I shall drink	ἤπια	I drank
θὰ πιεῖς	you will drink	ἤπιες	you drank
θὰ πιεῖ	he, she will drink	ἤπιε	he drank
θὰ πιοῦμε	we shall drink	ἤπιαμε	we drank
θὰ πιεῖτε	you will drink	ἤπιατε	you drank
θὰ πιοῦν(ε)	they will drink	ἤπιαν(ε)	they drank

14. I keep silent — (σιωπῶ) σωπαίνω

FUTURE		PAST	
θὰ σωπάσω	I shall keep silent	σώπασα	I kept silent
θὰ σωπάσεις	you will keep silent	σώπασες	you kept silent
θὰ σωπάσει	he will keep silent	σώπασε	he kept silent
θὰ σωπάσωμε	we shall keep silent	σωπάσαμε	we kept silent
θὰ σωπάσετε	you will keep silent	σωπάσατε	you kept silent
θὰ σωπάσουν(ε)	they will keep silent	σώπασαν (σωπάσανε)	they kept silent

15. I send — στέλνω

FUTURE		PAST	
θὰ στείλω	I shall send	ἔστειλα	I sent
θὰ στείλεις	you will send	ἔστειλες	you sent
θὰ στείλει	he, she will send	ἔστειλε	he, she sent
θὰ στείλωμε	we shall send	στείλαμε	we sent
θὰ στείλετε	you will send	στείλατε	you sent
θὰ στείλουν(ε)	they will send	ἔστειλαν	they sent

16. I eat – τρώγω

FUTURE		PAST	
θὰ φάω	I shall eat	ἔφαγα	I ate
θὰ φάεις (φᾶς)	you will eat	ἔφαγες	you ate
θὰ φάει	he, she will eat	ἔφαγε	he, she ate
θὰ φᾶμε	we shall eat	φάγαμε	we ate
θὰ φᾶτε	you will eat	φάγατε	you ate
θὰ φᾶνε	they will eat	ἔφαγαν (φάγανε)	they ate

17. I bring – φέρνω

FUTURE		PAST	
θὰ φέρω	I shall bring	ἔφερα	I brought
θὰ φέρεις	you will bring	ἔφερες	you brought
θὰ φέρει	he, she will bring	ἔφερε	he, she brought
θὰ φέρωμε(ν)	we shall bring	φέραμε	we brought
θὰ φέρετε	you will bring	φέρατε	you brought
θὰ φέρουν(ε)	they will bring	ἔφεραν (φέρανε)	they brought

18. I leave – φεύγω

FUTURE		PAST	
θὰ φύγω	I shall leave	ἔφυγα	I left
θὰ φύγεις	you will leave	ἔφυγες	you left
θὰ φύγει	he, she will leave	ἔφυγε	he, she left
θὰ φύγωμε(ν)	we shall leave	φύγαμε	we left
θὰ φύγετε	you will leave	φύγατε	you left
θὰ φύγουν(ε)	they will leave	ἔφυγαν (φύγανε)	they left

41. PASSIVE VERBS

Since there are two classes of contracted verbs, these have been designated by the following Class A and Class B (page 177).

CLASS A

1. I become – γίνομαι

PRESENT	FUTURE	PAST
γίν-ομαι	ϑὰ γίν-ω	ἔγιν-α
γίν-εσαι	ϑὰ γίν-εις	ἔγιν-ες
γίν-εται	ϑὰ γίν-ει	ἔγιν-ε(ν)
γιν-όμαστε	ϑὰ γίν-ωμε(ν)	γίν-αμε
γίν-εστε	ϑὰ γίν-ετε	γίν-ατε
γίν-ονται	ϑὰ γίν-ουν(ε)	ἔγιν-αν (γίνανε)

2. I come – ἔρχομαι

PRESENT	FUTURE	PAST
ἔρχομαι	ϑὰ ἔρ(λ)ϑω	ἦρ(λ)ϑα
ἔρχεσαι	ϑὰ ἔρ(λ)ϑεις	ἦρ(λ)ϑες
ἔρχεται	ϑὰ ἔρ(λ)ϑει	ἦρ(λ)ϑε
ἐρχόμαστε	ϑὰ ἔρ(λ)ϑωμε	ἤρ(λ)ϑαμε
ἔρχεστε	ϑὰ ἔρ(λ)ϑετε	ἤρ(λ)ϑατε
ἔρχονται	ϑὰ ἔρ(λ)ϑουν	ἦρ(λ)ϑαν(ε)

3. I wish – εὔχομαι

PRESENT	FUTURE	PAST
εὔχομαι	ϑὰ εὐχηϑῶ	εὐχήϑηκα
εὔχεσαι	ϑὰ εὐχηϑεῖς	εὐχήϑηκες
εὔχεται	ϑὰ εὐχηϑεῖ	εὐχήϑηκε
εὐχόμαστε	ϑὰ εὐχηϑοῦμε(ν)	εὐχηϑήκαμε(ν)
εὔχεστε	ϑὰ εὐχηϑῆτε	εὐχηϑήκατε
εὔχονται	ϑὰ εὐχηϑοῦν(ε)	εὐχήϑηκαν (εὐχηϑήκανε)

4. I protest – διαμαρτύρομαι

PRESENT	FUTURE	PAST
διαμαρτύρομαι	ϑὰ διαμαρτυρηϑῶ	διαμαρτυρήϑηκα
διαμαρτύρεσαι	ϑὰ διαμαρτυρηϑῆς	διαμαρτυρήϑηκες
διαμαρτύρεται	ϑὰ διαμαρτυρηϑῆ	διαμαρτυρήϑηκε
διαμαρτυρόμαστε	ϑὰ διαμαρτυρηϑοῦμε	διαμαρτυρηϑήκαμε
διαμαρτύρεστε	ϑὰ διαμαρτυρηϑῆτε	διαμαρτυρηϑήκατε
διαμαρτύρονται	ϑὰ διαμαρτυρηϑοῦν(ε)	διαμαρτυρήϑηκαν

5. I sit – κάθομαι

PRESENT	FUTURE	PAST
κάθομαι	θὰ καθήσω	κάθησα
κάθεσαι	θὰ καθήσεις	κάθησες
κάθεται	θὰ καθήσει	κάθησε
καθόμαστε	θὰ καθήσωμε(ν)	καθήσαμε
κάθεστε	θὰ καθήσετε	καθήσατε
κάθονται	θὰ καθήσουν	κάθησαν (καθήσανε)

6. I am ashamed – ντρέπομαι

PRESENT	FUTURE	PAST
ντρέπομαι	θὰ ντραπῶ	ντράπηκα
ντρέπεσαι	θὰ ντραπῆς	ντράπηκες
ντρέπεται	θὰ ντραπῆ	ντράπηκε
ντρεπόμαστε	θὰ ντραποῦμε	ντραπήκαμε
ντρέπεστε	θὰ ντραπῆτε	ντραπήκατε
ντρέπονται	θὰ ντραποῦν(ε)	ντράπηκαν (ντραπήκανε)

7. I respect – σέβομαι

PRESENT	FUTURE	PAST
σέβομαι	θὰ σεβαστῶ	σεβάστηκα
σέβεσαι	θὰ σεβαστῆς	σεβάστηκες
σέβεται	θὰ σεβαστῆ	σεβάστηκε
σεβόμαστε	θὰ σεβαστοῦμε	σεβαστήκαμε
σέβεστε	θὰ σεβαστῆτε	σεβαστήκατε
σέβονται	θὰ σεβαστοῦν	σεβάστηκαν (σεβαστήκανε)

8. I stand up – στέκομαι

PRESENT	FUTURE	PAST
στέκομαι	θὰ σταθῶ	στάθηκα
στέκεσαι	θὰ σταθῆς	στάθηκες
στέκεται	θὰ σταθῆ	στάθηκε
στεκόμαστε	θὰ σταθοῦμε	σταθήκαμε
στεκόσαστε	θὰ σταθῆτε	σταθήκατε
στέκονται	θὰ σταθοῦν(ε)	στάθηκαν (σταθήκανε)

9. I seem – φαίνομαι

PRESENT	FUTURE	PAST
φαίνομαι	θὰ φανῶ	φάνηκα
φαίνεσαι	θὰ φανῆς	φάνηκες
φαίνεται	θὰ φανῆ	φάνηκε
φαινόμαστε	θὰ φανοῦμε	φανήκαμε
φαίνεστε	θὰ φανῆτε	φανήκατε
φαίνονται	θὰ φανοῦν(ε)	φάνηκαν (φανήκανε)

10. I am glad – χαίρομαι

PRESENT	FUTURE	PAST
χαίρομαι	θὰ χαρῶ	χάρηκα
χαίρεσαι	θὰ χαρῇς	χάρηκες
χαίρεται	θὰ χαρῇ	χάρηκε
χαιρόμαστε	θὰ χαροῦμε	χαρήκαμε
χαίρεστε	θὰ χαρῆτε	χαρήκατε
χαίρονται	θὰ χαροῦν(ε)	χάρηκαν (χαρήκανε)

11. I promise – ὑπόσχομαι

PRESENT	FUTURE	PAST
ὑπόσχομαι	θὰ ὑποσχεθῶ	ὑποσχέθηκα
ὑπόσχεσαι	θὰ ὑποσχεθῇς	ὑποσχέθηκες
ὑπόσχεται	θὰ ὑποσχεθῇ	ὑποσχέθηκε
ὑποσχόμαστε	θὰ ὑποσχεθοῦμε	ὑποσχεθήκαμε
ὑπόσχεστε	θὰ ὑποσχεθῆτε	ὑποσχεθήκατε
ὑπόσχονται	θὰ ὑποσχεθοῦν(ε)	ὑποσχέθηκαν (ὑποσχεθήκανε)

IMPERFECT

The Imperfect tense of the above verbs is formed by changing the endings of the Present to:

SINGULAR	PLURAL
— όμουνα	— όμασταν
— όσουνα	— όσασταν
— ότανε	— όντανε
	— όντουσαν

EXAMPLES

γινόμουνα	ἐρχόμουνα
γινόσουνα	ἐρχόσουνα
γινότανε	ἐρχότανε
γινόμασταν	ἐρχόμασταν
γινόσασταν	ἐρχόσασταν
γινόντανε (γινόντουσαν)	ἐρχόντανε (ἐρχόντουσαν)

CLASS B

PRESENT

ἀγαπιέμαι (I am in love)	συγκινοῦμαι (I am moved)	φοβᾶμαι (I am afraid)
ἀγαπιέσαι	συγκινεῖσαι	φοβᾶσαι
ἀγαπιέται	συγκινεῖται	φοβᾶται
ἀγαπιόμαστε	συγκινούμαστε	φοβούμαστε
ἀγαπιέστε	συγκινεῖστε	φοβᾶστε
ἀγαπιοῦνται	συγκινοῦνται	φοβοῦνται

ἀναρωτιέμαι (I ask myself)	κρατοῦμαι (I support myself)	θυμᾶμαι (I remember)
ἀναμετριέμαι (I compete)	εὐχαριστοῦμαι (I enjoy myself)	λυπᾶμαι (I am sad)
εὐχαριστιέμαι (I enjoy myself)		κοιμᾶμαι (I sleep)
καταριέμαι (I curse)		

FUTURE

θὰ ἀγαπηθῶ	θὰ συγκινηθῶ	θὰ φοβηθῶ
θὰ ἀγαπηθῆς	θὰ συγκινηθῆς	θὰ φοβηθῆς
θὰ ἀγαπηθῆ	θὰ συγκινηθῆ	θὰ φοβηθῆ
θὰ ἀγαπηθοῦμε	θὰ συγκινηθοῦμε	θὰ φοβηθοῦμε
θὰ ἀγαπηθῆτε	θὰ συγκινηθῆτε	θὰ φοβηθῆτε
θὰ ἀγαπηθοῦν(ε)	θὰ συγκινηθοῦν(ε)	θὰ φοβηθοῦν(ε)

PAST

ἀγαπήθηκα	συγκινήθηκα	φοβήθηκα
ἀγαπήθηκες	συγκινήθηκες	φοβήθηκες
ἀγαπήθηκε	συγκινήθηκε	φοβήθηκε
ἀγαπηθήκαμε	συγκινηθήκαμε	φοβηθήκαμε
ἀγαπηθήκατε	συγκινηθήκατε	φοβηθήκατε
ἀγαπήθηκαν (ἀγαπηθήκανε)	συγκινήθηκαν	φοβήθηκαν

The Imperfect tense of Class B is formed in the same way as that of Class A.

42. IMPERSONAL VERBS

Πρέπει νὰ + indefinite form = I must, e. g. πρέπει νὰ φύγω.
Ἔπρεπε νὰ + indefinite form = I ought to, I should have, ἔπρεπε νὰ πάω.
Πειράζει = it bothers.
Μὲ πειράζει = it bothers me; it annoys me. Δὲν πειράζει = never mind; it does not matter.
Συμβαίνει = it happens. Τί συμβαίνει; = what is going on.
Βρέχει = it rains. Χιονίζει = it snows. Ἀστράφτει = it is lightning.
Βροντᾶ = it thunders. Νυχ(κ)τώνει = it gets dark.
Ξημερώνει = it gets light. Μὲ μέλει (νοιάζει) = I do care.
Δὲ μὲ μέλει (νοιάζει) = I don't care.
Τί σὲ μέλει (νοιάζει); = why should you care (worry).
Δὲν ἀξίζει = it is worthless.

EXAMPLES

1. Πρέπει νὰ σηκωθῆ κανεὶς (ἐ)νωρὶς τὸ πρωῒ καὶ δὲν πειράζει ἂν εἶναι κρύο ἢ ἂν χιονίζει.
2. Τί συμβαίνει; Τί σοῦ συμβαίνει (τί ἔχεις), τέλος πάντων, καὶ εἶσαι τόσο λυπημένος (κατσουφιασμένος);
3. Ἔπρεπε νὰ φύγω πρὶν μία ὥρα γιὰ νὰ πρόφθανα τὸ τραῖνο.
4. Νυχτώνει τόσο νωρὶς καὶ οἱ μέρες εἶναι τόσο μικρές.
5. Δὲ μὲ μέλει ὅταν βρέχει, μὰ ὅταν βροντᾶ μὲ πειράζει (ἐνοχλεῖ).
6. Τὸ καλοκαίρι κάποτε ἀστράφτει.
7. Τὸ χειμῶνα ἀργεῖ (it takes long) νὰ ξημερώνει.
8. Φαίνεται (it seems) πὼς (ὅτι, that) θὰ χιονίσει πάλι (ξανά).
9. Σήμερα κάνει κρύο (ζέστη, ψύχρα, ὑγρασία, παγωνιά).
10. Αὐτὸ τὸ αὐτοκίνητο δὲν ἀξίζει.

GREEK-ENGLISH VOCABULARY

The abbreviations in the vocabulary list are m = masculine; f = feminine; n = neuter; v = verb; adv = adverb.

A

ἀγαπῶ	v. I love
ἄγγελος	m. angel
'Αγγλία	f. England
ἄγκυρα	f. anchor
ἀγορὰ	f. market
ἀγοράζω	v. I buy
ἀγρίμι	n. wild person
ἀγώνας	m. struggle
ἀδελφὸς (ἀδερφὸς)	m. brother
ἀδελφὴ (ἀδερφὴ)	f. sister
ἀέρας	m. air
ἀεροδρόμιο	n. airport
ἀεροπλάνο	n. airplane
ἀεροπορικῶς	adv. airmail
'Αθήνα	f. Athens
αἷμα	n. blood
αἰσθάνομαι	v. I feel
ἀκάθαρτος, -η -ο	filthy
ἀκοινώνητος, -η, -ο	unsociable person
ἀκόμα (ἀκόμη)	still, more, yet
ἀκριβὸ	n. expensive
ἀκριβῶς	adv. exactly
ἀκούω	v. I hear, listen
ἁλάτι	n. salt
ἀλλὰ	but
ἀλλάζω	v. I change
ἀλεπού	f. fox
ἀλήθεια	f. truth; adv. truly
ἀληθής, -ὲς	sincere
ἀλήτης	m. vagabond
'Αμερικὴ	f. America
ἀμοιβὴ	f. fee
ἀμφιβολία	f. doubt
ἀνάγκη	f. need, necessity
ἀναίδεια	f. impudence, shamelessness
ἀναφέρω	v. I mention
ἀνέτως	adv. in comfort
ἀνεχτικός, -ή, -ὸ	tolerant
ἄνθρωπος	m. man
ἀνιαρός, -ή, -ό	boring

ἀνοίγω	v. I open
ἄνοιξις	f. spring
ἀντάμωση	f. meeting
ἀντιθέτως	adv. on the contrary
ἀντίληψις	f. conception
ἀντιπρόεδρος	m. vice president
ἀντίρρηση	f. objection
ἀξιοπρεπὴς	m. f., -ές dignified
ἀξίωσις	f. demand
ἀπεργία	f. strike
ἀπασχολημένος,-η,-ο	busy
ἀπόγευμα	n. afternoon
ἀποδοχὲς	f. gain
ἀποσκευὲς	f. luggage
ἀπόφαση	f. decision
ἀποφασίζω	v. I decide
ἀπόψε	tonight
ἀραβωνιαστικός,-ιὰ	fiancé, fiancée
ἀργῶ	v. I am late
ἀρετὴ	f. virtue
ἀριθμὸς	m. number
ἀριστερὰ	adv. left
ἀρκετὰ	adv. enough
ἀρνὶ	n. lamb
ἀρχὴ	f. beginning
ἀρρώστεια	f. illness
ἄρρωστος, -η, -ο	ill
ἀστακὸς	m. lobster
ἀστεῖο	n. joke
ἀστυνομία	f. police
ἀστυνόμος	m. policeman
ἀστυνομικὸν τμῆμα	n. police station
ἀστυφύλακας	m. policeman
ἀσυγύριστος, -η, -ο	untidy
ἀσφαλῶς	adv. certainly
ἄσχημα	adv. badly
ἄσχημος, -η, -ο	ugly
ἄσωτος, -η, -ο	prodigal
αὐγὴ	f. dawn
αὐγὸ	n. egg

αὐθημερὸν	adv. on the same day	αὐστηρός, -ή, -ό	strict, severe
αὐλὴ	f. yard.	αὐτοκίνητο	n. car
αὔριο	tomorrow	ἀφήνω	v. I leave, allow
		ἀχόρταγα	adv. insatiably

B

βάζω	v. I put, place	βιαστικός, -ιά,-ὁ	in a hurry
βαθιὰ	adv. deep, deeply	βιβλίο	n. book
βαθύς, -ειά, -ὺ	deep	βίος	m. life
βαλίτσα	f. suitcase	βλάκας	m. stupid
βαμβάκι	n. cotton	βλέπω	v. I see
βάσανα	n. troubles	βοηθῶ	v. I help
βασιληᾶς,	king	βουλευτὴς	m. member of Parliament
βασίλισσα	queen	βούτυρο	n. butter
βενζίνη	f. gas	βράδυ	n. evening
βῆμα	n. step, platform	βράζω	v. I boil
βήχω	v. I cough	βρίσκω	v. I find
βία	f. force	βροχὴ	f. rain
βιάζομαι	v. I am in a hurry	βρωμοδουλειὰ	f. crooked business

Γ

γάλα	n. milk	γλέντι	n. entertainment, dance
γαλάζιος, -ια, -ο	blue	γλυκὸ	n. dessert, sweet
γαλαχτομπούρικο	n. custard with filo	γλυκοαίματος,-η,-ο	lovable
γάμος	m. wedding	γνώση	f. knowledge, brains
γαρίδες	f. shrimps	γόνατο	n. knee
γαυγίζω	v. I bark	γονεῖς	m. parents
γειά (σου)	hello, goodbye	γραβάτα	f. tie
γείτονας (γειτόνισσα)	m. f. neighbor	γράμμα	n. letter
γειτονιὰ	f. neighborhood	γραμματεὺς	m. f. secretary
γελειοποιῶ	v. I ridicule	γραμματοκιβώτιο	n. letter box
γέλιο	n. laugh	γραμματόσημο	n. stamp
γελῶ	v. I laugh	γραφεῖο	n. office, desk
γενναιόδωρος, -η, -ο	generous	γράφω	v. I write
γέρος	m. old man	γρηὰ	f. old woman
γεῦμα	n. lunch	γρήγορα	adv. hurry up, quickly
γιαγιὰ	f. grandmother	γυαλιὰ	n. glasses
γιαούρτι	n. yogurt	γυαλίζω	v. I shine, polish
γιατί (;)	(why?) because	γυιὸς	m. son
γιατρός, γιάτρισσα	m. f. doctor	γυμνάσιο	n. high school
γίνομαι	I become	γυναίκα	f. woman, wife
γκαμήλα	f. camel	γυναικὰς	m. woman-lover
γκρίνια	f. complaints, grumbling, quarrel	γυναικεῖο	n. ladies' room

Δ

δανείζω	v. I lend	δασκάλα	f. teacher
δάσκαλος,	m. teacher	δάχτυλο	n. finger

δεῖπνο	n. dinner
δείχνω	v. I show
δέμα	n. package
δέντρο	n. tree
δεξιὰ	adv. right
δέρμα	n. skin
δεσποινὶς	v. I declare, report
δηλώνω	f. miss, young lady
δήμαρχος	m. mayor
δημοσιογράφος	m. f. journalist
διαβάζω	v. I read
διαβατήριο	n. passport
διάβολος	m. devil
διάθεση	f. mood
διακοπὲς	f. vacation
διάλεξη	f. lecture
διαμέρισμα	n. apartment
διαρκεῖ	v. lasts
διατύπωσις	f. procedure, formality
διαφορὰ	f. difference
διεύθυνση	f. address
δίκαιο	n. right, justice
δικαστήριο	n. court
δικαστὴς	m. judge
δικηγόρος	m. lawyer
δίνω	v. I give
διορθώνω	v. I repair, fix
δίπλα	by, next to
δίπλωμα	n. degree, diploma
δόντι	n. tooth
δουλειὰ	f. job, work
δουλευτής,	m. hard worker
δουλεύτρια	f. hard worker
δουλεύω	I work
δραστήριος	m. active
δρόμος	m. road, way
δύναμη	f. power, strength
δυνατὰ	adv. strongly, loudly
δυσκολία	f. difficulty
δυστύχημα	n. accident, misfortune
δυστυχῶς	adv. unfortunately
δωμάτιο	n. room
δῶρο	n. gift

E

ἑβδομάδα	f. week
ἔγκλημα	n crime
ἔγκυος	f. pregnant
ἐγχείρηση	f. surgery
ἐδῶ	here
εἴδησις	f. news
εἰλικρίνεια	f. sincerity
εἰσιτήριο	n. ticket
εἴσοδος	f. entrance
ἔκδοση	f. edition
ἐκεῖ	adv. there
ἐκκλησία	f. church
ἔκπτωση	f. discount
Ἑλλάδα	f. Greece
ἐλπίδα	f. hope
ἐλπίζω	v. I hope
ἐμπορικὸ	n. department store
ἔμπορος	m. merchant
ἐμπρὸς	hello (on telephone) ahead, before, in front of
ἔνοια	f. care, worry
ἐνοχλῶ	v. I bother, annoy
ἐντελῶς	adv. entirely
ἐξάδελφος (-ερφος)	m. cousin
ἐξαδέλφη (-έρφη)	f. cousin
ἐξαιρετικός, -ή, -ό	exceptional
ἐξαίσια	adv. wonderfully
ἔξοδα	expenses
ἔξυπνος, -η, -ο	smart, intelligent
ἐξωτερικὸ	n. abroad
ἔξω	outside
ἔπαινος	m. praise
ἐπανειλημμένως	adv. repeatedly
ἐπάνοδος	f. return
ἐπεῖγον	n. special delivery
ἐπειδὴ	since, because
ἐπίδεσμος	m. bandage
ἐπιδόρπιο	n. dessert
ἐπιθεωρητής,	m. inspector
ἐπιθεωρήτρια	f. inspector
ἐπικίνδυνος, -η, -ο	dangerous
ἔπιπλο	n. furniture
ἐπίσης	also, same to you
ἐπισκέπτης,	m. visitor
ἐπισκέπτρια	f. visitor
ἐπιστήθιος	m. very dear
ἐπιστροφὴ	f. return
ἐπιταγὴ	f. money order, check
ἐπιχειρηματίας	m. businessman
ἐπιχείρηση	f. business

ἐποχή	f. season
ἐργάζομαι	v. I work
ἐργατικός, -ή, -ό	industrious
ἐργοδότης,	m. employer
ἐργοδότρια	f employer
ἐργολάβος	m. f. contractor
ἔρχομαι	v. I come
ἐρωτεύομαι	v. I fall in love
ἐρωτόληπτος	m. f. amorous
ἑστιατόριον	n. restaurant
ἐσώρουχα	n underwear
ἑταιρία	f. company, society
ἕτοιμος, -η, -ο	ready
ἔτος	n. year
εὐαίσθητος, -η, -ο	sensitive
εὐγενής, -ές	polite
εὐθύνη	f. responsibility
εὐκαιρία	f. opportunity
εὔκολος, -η, -ο	easy
Εὐρώπη	f. Europe
εὐτυχής, -ές	happy
εὐχαρίστως	adv. with pleasure
εὐχαριστῶ	v. I thank
ἐφέτος	this year
ἐφημερίδα	f. newspaper

Z

ζεστός, -ή, -ό	warm
ζευγάρι	n. pair
ζηλεύω	v. I am jealous of, envy
ζήλια	f. jealousy
ζηλιάρης, -α, -ικο	jealous
ζήτημα	n. matter, question
ζητῶ	v. I look for, ask
ζόρικος, -η, -ο	difficult
ζῶ	v. I live
ζωή	f. life
ζωηρός, -ή, -ό	active, restless
ζωνάρι	n. belt
ζώνη	f. belt, zone

H

ἠθοποιός	m. f. actor, actress
ἡσυχία	f. quiet
ηὗρα	v. I found

Θ

θάλασσα	f. sea
θάνατος	m. death
θάρρος	n. courage, confidence
θαυμάσια	adv. wonderfully
θέατρο	n. theater
θεῖος, θεία	m f. uncle, aunt
θέλω	v. I want, need
θερμά	adv. warmly
θέση	f. seat, position
θυμᾶμαι	v. I remember
θυμός	m. anger
θυμώνω	v. I get angry

I

ἰδιαίτερο	n. rest room
ἰδιότροπος, -η, -ο	peculiar
ἰσόπαλος, -η, -ο	of equal strength
ἰσχυρογνώμων	m. f. stubborn
Ἰταλία	f. Italy
ἴχνος	n. trace

K

καθαρίζω	v. I clean
καθαριστήριο	n. dry cleaners
καθῆκον	n. duty
κάθισμα	n. chair, seat
καμήλα	f. camel
κανένας	m. someone, no one
καπέλο	n hat
καπετάνιος,	m. captain
κάθομαι	v. I sit, stay, live
καθυστέρηση	f. delay

καλημέρα	good morning
καληνύχτα	good night
καλησπέρα	good evening
καινούργιος, -α, -ο	new
καιρὸς	m. weather, time
καλλιτέχνης (καλλιτέχνις)	m. f. artist
καλοκαίρι	n. summer
καλός, -ή, -ό	good, kind
κάλτσες	f. socks, stockings
καλοφαγᾶς	m. good eater
καλωσύνη	f. goodness, kindness
καπετάνισα	f. captain, headstrong woman
καπνίζω	v. I smoke
κάπνισμα	n smoking
καπνὸς	m. smoke
κάποτε	sometimes
κάρβουνο	n. coal
καρδιὰ	f. heart
καρδιακός, -ιά, -ό	afflicted with heart disease
καρκῖνος	m. cancer
καταλαβαίνω	v. I understand
κατάλογος	m. menu
καταντῶ	v. I become, am reduced to
κατάστασις	f. situation, condition
καταστηματάρχης	m. manager
κατάστημα	n. store, shop
καταστροφὴ	f. destruction
κατάστρωμα	n. deck
κατεργάρης (κατεργάρισα) (κατεργάρικο)	m. f. n. rascal, sly
κατοχὴ	f. (foreign) occupation
καυγᾶς	m. fight, quarrel
καϋμὸς	m. grief, sorrow
καφὲς	m. coffee
καωματοῦ	f. shrewed and tricky woman
κέντρον	n. center, night club, operator
κερδίζω	v. I win, gain
κεφάλι	n. head
κινηματογράφος	m. movies
κλαίω	v. I cry
κλέβω	v. I steal
κλειδὶ	n. key
κλείνω	v. I close
κλεψιὰ	f. theft
κλῖμα	n. climate
κόβω	v. I cut
κοιμᾶμαι	v. I sleep
κοινωνία	f. society
κόκκαλο	n. bone
κόλακας	m. flatterer
κολύμπι	n. swimming
κομπόστο	n. stewed fruit
κομμωτήριον	n. beauty salon
κομμωτής (κομμώτρια)	m. f. hairdresser
κοντὰ	near, close
κοπέλλα	f. girl
κόπος	m. trouble
κορδόνια	n. shoestrings
κόρη	f. girl, daughter
κορίτσι	n. girl
κοροϊδεύω	v. I make fun of, deceive
κόσμος	m. people, world
κουδούνι	n. bell
κουλούρα	f. roll
κουμπὶ	n. button
κουράγιο	n. courage
κούραση	f. fatigue
κουρασμένος,-η,-ο	tired
κουρέας	m. barber
κουρεῖον	n. barber shop
κουφόβραση	f. humid
κρασὶ	n. wine
κρατῶ	v. I keep, reserve
κρέας	n. meat
κρεβάτι	n. bed
κρεβατοκάμαρα	f. bedroom
κρῖμα	pity! (interjection)
κρότος	m. noise
κρυολόγημα	n. cold
κρύος, -α, -ο	cool, antipathetic
κρυφὰ	secretly
κτίριο	n. building
κυρία	f. Mrs., wife, lady

Λ

λαγὸς	m. rabbit
λάδι	n. oil
λάθος	n. mistake, error
λαιμὸς	m. neck
λαμπρός, -ή, -ό	bright
λείπω	v. I am away, I am absent
λεμονάδα	f. lemonade

λεμόνι n. lemon
λέξη f. word
λεξικὸ n. dictionary
λεπτότητα f. politeness,
λευτεριὰ f. freedom
λεφτὰ n. money
λεωφορεῖο n. bus
λίγο a little
λιμάνι n. port
λογαριασμὸς m. bill, check
λοιπὸν well, then
λουκάνικο n. sausage
λουκούμι n. Turkish delight
λύνω v. I solve, untie
λυπᾶμαι v. I am sorry, regret

M

μὰ but
μαγαζὶ n. store, shop
μαγειρεύω v. I cook
μαζεύω v. I collect
μαζὶ together
μαθαίνω v. I learn, hear
μαθητὴς m. student
μαλακός, -ιά, -ό mild, soft
μαλλιὰ n. hair
μάλιστα yes, certainly
μάνα f. mother
μαντίλι n. handkerchief
μαρμελάδα f. marmalade, jam
μαχαίρι n. knife
μεγάλος, -η, -ο large, big, old
μελαγχολία f. melancholy
μένω v. I live, stay
μέρα f. day
μέρος n. men's room, ladies' room, rest room
μέσα inside
μεσημέρι n. noon
μετανοιώνω v. I change my mind, regret
μετριοπαθὴς m. f. modest
μήνας m. month
μητέρα f. mother
μηχανὴ f. engine, machine
μηχανικὸς m. engineer, mechanic
μικρὸς m. young, small
μιλῶ v. I speak, talk
μισθὸς m. salary
μοιάζω v. I resemble
μοναξιὰ f. loneliness
μουσεῖον n. museum
μπάνιο n. bath
μπεκρῆς m. drunkard
μπλούζα f. blouse
μπορῶ v. I can, may, am able
μπουκάλι n. bottle
μπύρα f. beer
μυαλὸ n. brain
μυρίζω v. I smell
μύτη f. nose

N

ναὶ yes
ναυτία f. seasickness
νειᾶτα n. youth
νεολαία f. youth
νέον n. new
νέος, -α, -ο young man, young woman
νερὸ n. water
νευριάζω v. I become nervous
νευρικός, ιά, -ό nervous
νησὶ n. island
νόημα n. meaning
νοικιάζω v. I rent
νοικοκύρης (νοικοκυρὰ) m. f. landlord, landlady
νόμος m. law
νοσοκομεῖον n. hospital
νοῦς m. mind
ντολμάδες m. stuffed grape leaves
ντομάτα f. tomato
ντρέπομαι v. I am bashful, shy
ντροπαλός, -ή, -ό shy, bashful
ντύνομαι v. I get dressed
νύχτα f. night

Ξ

ξανὰ	again
ξαφνικὰ	suddenly
ξενοδοχεῖο	n. hotel, restaurant
ξέρω	v. I know
ξεσκεπάζω	v. I reveal
ξεχνῶ	v. I forget
ξοδεύω	v. I spend
ξορκισμένος	m. devil
ξύδι	n. vinegar
ξύλο	n. beating, wood
ξυρίζω	v. I shave
ξύρισμα	n. shave
ξυράφι	n. razor blade

Ο

ὀδοντογιατρὸς	m. dentist
ὁδὸς	f. street
οἰκογένεια	f. family
ὀμελέτα	f. omelet
ὀμορφιὰ	f. beauty
ὄμορφος, -η, -ο	handsome, pretty
ὀμπρέλλα	f. umbrella
ὅμως	but, yet
ὄνομα	n. name
ὀνομάζομαι	v. my name is, I am called
ὁπωσδήποτε	in any case
ὀρεκτικὰ	n. appetizers
ὄρεξη	f. appetite, help yourself
ὁρίστε	good mood, come in
ὁ,τιδήποτε	anything
οὐρανὸς	m. sky, heaven
ὀφείλω	v. I owe
ὄχι	no

Π

παιδὶ	n. boy, child
παίζω	v. I play
παίρνω	v. I take, receive
πάλι	again
παλτὸ	n. coat
πανεπιστήμιο	n. university
παντελῶς	completely
παντελόνι	n. trouser
παντρειὰ	f. marriage
παπὰς	m. priest
παπποὺς	m. grandfather
παπούτσι	n. shoe
παπουτσίδικο	n. shoe store, shoe repair shop
παράθυρο	n. window
παρακαλῶ	v. please, welcome
παράξενος, -η, -ο	peculiar, strange
παράπονο	n. complaint
παράστασις	f. performance
παρέα	f. company
Πάσχα	n. Easter
πατέρας	m. father
πεθερὰ	f. mother-in-law
πεθερὸς	m. father-in-law
πεῖνα	f. hunger
πεῖσμα	n. stubbornness, obstinacy
πεπόνι	n. melon(cantaloupe)
περίεργος, -η, -ο	curious
περιμένω	v. I wait, wait for
περιοδικὸ	n. magazine
περίπου	about
πέρσυ	last year
πετσέτα	f. towel
πέφτω	v. I fall
πίκρα	f. grief
πινακὶς	f. tablet, board
πίνω	v. I drink
πιὸ	more
πιπέρι	n. pepper
πληγὴ	f. wound
πληροφορία	f. information
πληρώνω	v. I pay
πλησιάζω	v. I approach, come near
πλοῖο	n. ship
πλούσιος	m. rich, wealthy
πλύσιμο	n. wash
ποδήλατο	n. bicycle
ποιός;(ποιά;)(ποιό;)	who? which?
ποιοτὸ	n. drink
πόλη	f. city, town
πολὺ	very, much
πονόδοντος	m. toothache

πονοκέφαλος	m. headache
πόνος	m. pain
πονόψυχος, -η, -ο	kind, compassionate
πορτοκαλλάδα	f. orange juice
πορτοκάλλι	n. orange
πορτοφόλι	n. wallet
πόσο;	how much?
πόσα;	how many?
πότε	when?
ποτήρι	n. glass
πουκάμισο	n. shirt
ποῦ;	where? that, which, where
πράγματι	actually
πρακτορεῖο	n. agency
πρεσβεία	f. embassy
πρόβατο	n. sheep
πρόγραμμα	n. program, schedule
προϊστάμενος, -η	m. f. supervisor, boss
προλαβαίνω	v. I catch, reach
προξενεῖο	n. consulate
προσκαλεσμένος, -η, -ο	guest, invited
προσοχὴ	f. attention, care
πρόσωπο	n. face, person
προτιμῶ	v. I prefer
πρωϊνὸ	n. breakfast
πρωτεύουσα	f. capital
προφθάνω	v. I reach, catch
πυρετὸς	m. temperature
πυροβολῶ	v. I shoot

Ρ

ράφτης (ράφτρια)	m. f. tailor
ρίζι	n. rice
ριζόγαλο	n. rice pudding
ριψοκινδυνεύω	v. I take the risk
ρολόϊ	n. watch
ροῦχα	n. clothes

Σ

σάλτσα	f. sauce
σαπούνι	n. soap
σαρδέλλες	f. sardines
σεισμὸς	m. earthquake
σερβίρω	v. I serve
σερβιτόρος, -α	m. f. waiter, waitress
σήμερα	today
σιγὰ	slowly, low
σίγουρα	for sure
σίδερο	n. iron
σιδερώνω	v. I iron
σιδηρόδρομος	m. train
σιωπηλός, -ή, -ό	silent
σκέπτομαι	v. I think, plan
σκέψη	f. thought
σκουπιδιάρης	m. garbage collector
σκοπὸς	m. purpose, guard, intention
σκοτώνω	v. I kill
σκύλος m. (σκυλὶ)	n. dog
σοβαρός, -η, -ο	serious
σοῦπα	f. soup
σπανακόπητα	f. spinach pie
σπίτι	n. house
σπιτονοικοκυρὰ	f. landlady
συγκάτοικος, -η	m. f. roommate, living in the same house
συγχαρητήρια	congratulations
σύζυγος	m. f. wife, husband
συλλυπητήρια	sympathy
συμβουλὴ	f. advice
συμπεριφορὰ	f. behavior
συναντοῦμαι	v. I meet
συναντῶ	v. I meet
συνδέω	v. I connect
συνεπὴς	m. f. consistent
συνεπῶς	consequently
συνέταιρος	m. partner
συνήθεια(συνήθειο)	f., n. habit
συνηθισμένο	n. usual
συνοδεύω	v. I accompany
συνοδὸς	m. f. stewardess, escort
σπουδάζω	v. I study
σπουδαῖος, -αία, -ο	important
σταθμὸς	m. station
σταυροδρόμι	n. crossroad
στέλνω	v. I send
στεφάνι	n. crown

στῆθος	n. chest, bosom
στολίζομαι	v. I get dressed up
στόμα	n. mouth
συγγνώμη(ν)	excuse me, pardon me
σύντομα	quickly
συστήνω	v. I recommend
συχνὰ	often
σφῆκα	f. wasp
σχέσεις	f. relations
σχοινὶ	n. string, cord
σχολεῖον	n, school
σωστὸ	n. right, true

Τ

ταμίας	m. f. treasurer
τάξη	f. classroom, order
ταξιδεύω	v. I travel
ταξίδι	n. trip
ταχυδρομεῖον	n. post office
ταχυδρόμος	m. mailman
τελειώνω	v. I finish
τελωνεῖον	n. custom house
τεμπέλης, -ισα, ικο	lazy
τεχνίτης, -ρια	m. f. craftsman, technician
τζάμι	n. glass
τηλεγράφημα	n. telegram
τηλεφώνημα	n. telephone call, phone call
τηλέφωνο	n. telephone
τηλεφωνῶ	v. I call
τιμὴ	f. honor, price
τίμιος, -α, -ο	honest
τίποτε	nothing, welcome
τουλάχιστον	at least
τοπεῖον	n. landscape
τότε	then
τραῖνο	n. train
τράπεζα	f. bank
τραπέζι	n. table
τρελλός, -ή, -ό	crazy
τρέχω	v. I run
τρικυμία	f. sea storm
τρώγω	v. I eat
τσαγγάρικο	n. shoemaker
τσάϊ	n. tea
τσάντα	f. briefcase, handbag
τσέπη	f. pocket
τσιγάρο	n. cigarette
τσιγκούνης	m. stingy
τσιρίζω	v. I talk too much
τσουρέκι	n. buns
τυπογράφος	m. printer
τυρὶ	n. cheese
τυρόπητα	f. cheese pie
τυχαίως	adv. by chance, accidentally
τύχη	f. luck
τώρα	now

Υ

ὑγεία	f. health
ὑγρασία	f. humidity, dampness
ὑπέροχος, -η, -ο	exceptional
ὑπερταχεῖα	f. super-express
ὑπηρέτρια	f. maid
ὕπνος	m. sleep
ὑπόθεση	f. matter
ὑπομονὴ	f. patience
ὑποπτεύομαι	v. I suspect
ὑπόσχεση	f. promise
ὑπόσχομαι	v. I promise
ὑποφέρω	v. I suffer
ὑποψηφιότητα	f. candidacy
ὕστερα	afterwards

Φ

φαγὰς	m. big eater
φαγητὸ	n. food
φακὲς	f. lentils, lentil soup
φάλαγξ	f. phalanx
φαμίλια	f. family
φανάρι	n. lantern, lighthouse

φαντασία	f. imagination
φαρμακεῖο	n. drugstore, pharmacy
φαρμάκι	n. poison
φασαρία	f. trouble, noise
φασόλια	n. beans
φεγγάρι	n. moon
φέρνω	v. I bring
φεύγω	v. I leave
φθάνω	v. I arrive, reach
φθηνός, -ή, -ό	cheap
φθινόπωρο	n. autumn
φιλοξενία	f. hospitality
φιλόξενος, -η, -ο	hospitable
φιλοξενῶν (οἰκοδεσπότης)	m. host
φίλος, φιλενάδα	m. f. friend
φιλότιμος -η, -ο	proud
φλυαρία	f. chatter
φονηᾶς (φόνισσα)	f. murderer
φόρεμα	n. dress
φουρτούνα	f. sea storm
φούστα	f. skirt
φουστάνι	n. dress
φροῦτο	n. fruit
φρυγανιὰ	f. toast
φτηνὰ	adv. cheaply
φτωχός, -ή, -ό	poor
φυλακὴ	f. prison, jail
φυλακίζω	v. I imprison
φωνὴ	f. voice
φῶς	n. light
φωτεινός, -ή, -ό	bright
φωτιὰ	fire
φωτογραφεῖον	n. photo studio

X

χαίρετε	goodby
χαίρω	v. I am glad
χαλῶ	v. I destroy, cash (money)
χάνω	v. I lose
χαρὰ	f. joy, happiness
χαρακτήρας	m. character
χαρτὶ	n. paper
χαρτιὰ	n. cards
χαφιὲς	m. good-for-nothing
χειμώνας	m. winter
χέρι	n. hand
χθὲς (χτὲς)	yesterday
χορεύω	v. I dance
χορὸς	m. dance
χουβαρδᾶς	m. generous, open-handed
χρειάζομαι	v. I need
χρέος	n. debt
χρεωστῶ	v. I owe
χρήματα	n. money
Χριστούγεννα	n. Christmas
χρονιὰ	f. year
χρόνος	m. year
χρουσούζης	m., f. person who brings bad luck
χρουσουζιὰ	f. bad luck
χρῶμα	n. color
χτένα	f. comb
χύνω	v. I pour, spill
χωνεύω	v. I digest
χωρατὰ	n. jokes
χωριὸ	n. town, village

Ψ

ψαρὰς	m. fisherman
ψάρεμα	n. fishing
ψάρι	n. fish
ψέμα	n. lie, falsehood
ψεύτης, (ψεύτρα)	m. f. liar
ψηλὰ	adv. high
ψηλός, -ή, -ό	tall
ψυγεῖο	n. refrigerator
ψυχὴ	f. soul
ψωμὶ	n. bread
ψωνίζω	v. I shop, buy, purchase

Ω

ὥρα	f. hour
ὡραῖος, -αία, -ο	handsome, beautiful